LANGUAGE AND LANGUAGE LEARNING

Languages and the Young School Child

LANGUAGE AND LANGUAGE LEARNING

General Editors: RONALD MACKIN and PETER STREVENS

Languages and the Young School Child

Edited by H. H. STERN

with a *RESEARCH GUIDE* by
JOHN B. CARROLL

LONDON
OXFORD UNIVERSITY PRESS: 1969

Oxford University Press, Ely House, London W.1

GLASGOW NEW YORK TORONTO MELBOURNE WELLINGTON
CAPE TOWN SALISBURY IBADAN NAIROBI LUSAKA ADDIS ABABA
BOMBAY CALCUTTA MADRAS KARACHI LAHORE DACCA
KUALA LUMPUR HONG KONG TOKYO

© Unesco Institute for Education, Hamburg, 1969

These studies are based on the work of an expert meeting held at the Unesco Institute for Education, Hamburg 13, Feldbrunnenstrasse 70, from 9 to 14 May 1966.

The meeting was organized by the Unesco Institute for Education, Hamburg, in association with Unesco, Paris, and the Council for Cultural Cooperation of the Council of Europe, Strasbourg.

The official title of the gathering was 'The International Meeting of Representatives of Institutions and Experimental Schools concerned with Second Language Teaching in Primary Education—Research and Development'.

The Unesco Institute for Education (Hamburg) is an institute of international character financed by a trust fund into which is paid, in particular, the contribution of the Government of the Federal Republic of Germany. While the programmes of the Institute are established in consultation with the Director-General of Unesco, the publications of the Institute are issued by the Institute under its sole responsibility, and Unesco as an organization is not responsible for their content.

The points of view, selection of facts and opinions expressed in the present report are those of the authors, and do not necessarily coincide with official positions of the Unesco Institute for Education or of other sponsors of the 1966 meeting of experts.

PRINTED IN GREAT BRITAIN BY HEADLEY BROTHERS LTD
109 KINGSWAY LONDON WC2 AND ASHFORD KENT

Preface

This international collection of studies is based on the documentation, discussions and findings of an expert meeting organized in May 1966 by the Unesco Institute for Education, Hamburg, in association with Unesco, Paris,[1] and the Council for Cultural Co-operation of the Council of Europe, Strasbourg. As a companion volume to a previous report[2] deriving from a similar expert meeting (Hamburg, 9 to 14 April 1962), it reviews more recent developments, investigates certain important issues with a view to further research and makes specific proposals for national and international research in this developing field of language teaching.

As a result, the Governing Board of the Unesco Institute for Education, Hamburg, decided in early April 1968 'to initiate a Co-ordinated Research Project on the Teaching of a Foreign or Second Language in Primary Schools, taking as a procedure pattern the formula previously adopted by the International Project for the Evaluation of Educational Achievement (I.E.A.)'. To that end a Steering Committee, to meet in Hamburg from 16 to 18 April 1969, will define the procedure to be adopted and the financial and other forms of aid to be secured before launching such a co-ordinated research project, based on research undertaken in various sociolinguistic contexts by national research institutions concerned with the problems of teaching a foreign or second language in primary schools; the Steering Committee will also prepare a preliminary working paper and suggest a list of representatives of research institutions to be invited to the fuller meeting of experts (1970) whose task it will be to formulate precise recommendations for the

---

[1] The opinions expressed in this collection of studies should not be considered as representing the official views of Unesco.

[2] *Foreign Languages in Primary Education*, originally published in 1963 as one of the International Studies in Education of the Unesco Institute for Education, Hamburg. A French version of the original report was also published, in 1965, by the Unesco Institute for Education. A revised English edition was published in 1967 by Oxford University Press as No. 14 of its Language and Language Learning series. For further details see the bibliographical note on p. 8 below,

actual implementation of the co-ordinated research project. The Unesco Institute for Education, Hamburg,[1] would appreciate receiving information, comments, suggestions and proposals for possible co-operation from all competent sources.

[1] The Unesco Institute for Education, Feldbrunnenstrasse 70, 2 Hamburg 13, Federal Republic of Germany.

Contents

PART II: RESEARCH GUIDE

PART I: STUDIES

1

Introduction

The problems of language teaching in primary education have been widely discussed in many countries over the last ten years or so. Is it right to bring languages into the education of young children? Are children better language learners than adults? Can all children benefit from language instruction? Who should do the teaching? What materials should be used and what methods should be employed? What effect is the teaching of a foreign language likely to have on the child's general educational progress? These and similar questions which have been asked by educators for some time and are still asked today have not yet found a definitive answer.

In 1962, the Unesco Institute for Education in Hamburg made a first attempt to come to grips with them on an international scale by convening an expert meeting on primary school language teaching (Stern 1963, 1965, 1967).[1] This conference examined the principal arguments for an early start in a foreign language at the primary stage of education. It gathered much valuable information on experiments and experiences in this field and studied the available methods and materials. It defined a number of research topics and it concluded with recommendations for the practice of language teaching to younger children.

The meeting gave its approval to foreign languages in primary schools, but it coupled with it a demand for critical long-term research and experimentation on the many theoretical and practical questions that were raised by this new trend in language teaching. As these developments were taking place more or less simultaneously in different countries it was a matter of obvious economy to think of the research needs internationally. And it was valuable that Unesco used its influence to stimulate such an international approach to research in this area.

As a first step in following up the 1962 meeting Unesco commissioned Professor J. B. Carroll of Harvard University, USA, to

[1] For references see the bibliography on pp. 260–7.

compose a research guide.[1] The next step was to convene a second
meeting of specialists to define the research priorities and make more
specific recommendations for investigations than had been possible
at the more broadly conceived conference in 1962. This was the
object of the meeting that took place in May 1966, again at the
Unesco Institute for Education in Hamburg. This second international meeting was sponsored not only by Unesco but also by the
Council for Cultural Cooperation of the Council of Europe, together
with the Unesco Institute for Education, Hamburg. The present
study is the outcome of this last meeting.

THE MAJOR PROBLEMS

In February 1966, a few months before the conference took place, a
small steering committee was convened in Hamburg in order to
define the problems which the main conference should take up.
The various themes were compiled into a working paper. Although
not all the subjects were treated at the conference, the working paper
constitutes a record of those problems which in the view of the
steering committee demanded discussion or research. The following
topics and questions were listed:

'1 *Fundamental issues*
A critical review of the arguments for languages in primary education which formed the subject of Part I of the first Hamburg report.

How far should primary education become multicultural and
multilingual? Or in terms of a proposition the same question could
be expressed in this way: that in the past primary education was
unilingual and unicultural, but in the future multilingualism and the
recognition of other cultures must be built into an educational
system from the start.

'2 *The timetable of language learning*
This topic includes such problems as: the optimal age for formal
language instruction; the question of a preschool start in second
language learning without formal instruction; the simultaneous
learning of two languages; and the effect of an early start in a
foreign language on later learning of languages.

'3 *Social and emotional factors in language learning at the primary stage*
The assumption is that motivation is a key factor in successful

---

[1] Published as Part II of the present volume.

language learning. Motivation in children is strongly influenced by attitudes of families and the community. Of particular importance for this type of investigation would be measures of attitudes to language learning, to languages and to other nations.

'4 *Community development and second language learning in primary schools*
Studies under this heading will be concerned with the special needs of bilingual and multilingual areas, also with language-learning problems of children of immigrants and minorities. They will include particularly the problems of developing countries, even though advanced countries encounter similar ones.

'5 *Content and methods of language teaching at the primary stage*
The practice of language teaching in the primary years has produced a number of problems on content and method. Content is increasingly based on preliminary linguistic and socio-psychological studies and it is determined by certain methodological choices. Among the questions that have arisen the following need answering:

(a) Should the progression be situational or structural?

(b) The delay in reading and writing: How far is it helpful? At what stage should reading and writing be introduced?

(c) How far can the acquisition of the language be left to experience? Is there a place for drills?

(d) Should the learning of the language be mainly an unconscious process? How far can conceptualization take place?

(e) What is the role of audio-visual aids? Has the language laboratory a place in the primary school?

(f) How far should the mother tongue be used in instruction? Should the work be entirely in terms of the "direct method"?

(g) Has there been any experience with the use of the foreign language as a medium of general instruction, i.e. in physical education, art, history, etc.?

'6 *Problems of continuation and articulation*
It is important at the present stage to consider very actively the follow-up from an early start to a more advanced state of language learning. (a) This presents itself in some countries as a problem of articulation of language learning at the primary stage and language learning at the secondary stage. (b) Also the possibility arises that, with an improved knowledge of the foreign language, children at school could be led to using the foreign language as a medium of

learning at the secondary stage. (c) Furthermore, the possibility of introducing other foreign languages two years or so after the first needs examining.

'7 *Differences in ability*
The slow language learner presents a special problem in the primary school which may have to be treated in the same manner as teachers have become accustomed to treating retardation in reading and arithmetic. It is first of all a question of causation. Is linguistic ability related to intelligence or to some other factors? And assuming that there will always be differences in speed and progress, what measures can be taken, and what help can be given to overcome the difficulties of the slow learner?

'8 *Attainment testing and other objective methods of assessment*
The work of the primary schools in foreign languages has led everywhere to a clear demand for objective methods of assessment.

'9 *The function of the foreign language in the primary school*
In the early stages of primary language teaching one of the chief worries was whether the addition of a language might not have a bad effect on progress in other subjects. Would it, for example, confuse and lead to a decline in the mother tongue or detract from progress in other areas of learning? By and large it has been found that language teaching has no such bad effects, but a more objective study of these relationships between language teaching and other activities of the primary school is needed. There is, for example, common ground between mother tongue and foreign language activities, but in practice the policy is often contradictory. Language teaching could also overlap with music, art, geography, history, dramatic activities, and even games and dancing. How far does language teaching lead to such enrichment of the primary curriculum?

'10 *Teacher training*
Everywhere the shortage of language teachers and the need for training has been noted. We have

(a) the problem of the role of languages in the initial training of primary teachers, and

(b) in-service training and advisory work for practising teachers. Under these headings, methods and content of teacher courses (e.g. the place of linguistics in these) and policy and operation of advisory services should be considered. A further aspect is the follow-up re-training of the secondary school foreign language specialists.'

The meeting studied most of these questions under four main heads corresponding to its four working groups:
  (a) Fundamental socio-political issues
  (b) Questions of teaching materials and methods
  (c) Teacher training
  (d) The organization of research including testing.

THE PRESENT VOLUME

It will easily be seen that the studies published in the following chapters centre round these topics. All chapters were written by individual authors most of whom attended the Hamburg conference. Some of the chapters have resulted directly from the discussions in the conference groups, in particular chapters 2, 4, 6, 7 and 17. Although these chapters too have been composed by single authors, the work of the conference and its groups is incorporated in them and where group members are listed in a footnote, they should be regarded as contributors to the studies concerned. The overall responsibility for the chapters lies, however, with the authors and the editor. Other chapters contain studies which, in the estimation of the conference, are of particular importance and should be taken into account in current and forthcoming work on primary school language teaching. The second part of this volume deals with methodology of research; it is a revised version of the Guide which Professor J. B. Carroll had prepared at the request of Unesco.

A valuable aspect of a meeting of this kind is that it stimulates the submission of papers and communications by participants and others. It is not possible to publish all these, but they formed useful source material. Those that were specifically referred to in these studies are listed in the bibliography with the initials c.p. in brackets (c.p. = conference paper).

THE 1962 REPORT AND THE PRESENT STUDY

This second Hamburg report is not intended to supersede the first report, based on the 1962 conference and first published in 1963. The two reports complement each other and differ in their emphasis.

The object of the 1962 report was to review and to take stock, and as a survey it forms the basis of the present study.

The present report attempts to discuss in greater depth some of the crucial issues which had already been adumbrated by the first report. It does not pretend to offer final answers to the questions under discussion. It merely attempts to indicate directions of research which should provide solutions to the problems which are at present still controversial.

It will be seen in the subsequent chapters that the problems of primary school language teaching have progressively become more sharply crystallized. Given resolute international cooperation it should be possible to find answers to some of the questions under discussion. It is hoped that the present volume by its strong emphasis on competently executed research will assist in this process.

BIBLIOGRAPHICAL NOTE ON THE HAMBURG REPORTS ON FOREIGN
LANGUAGES IN PRIMARY EDUCATION

The first international meeting of experts on foreign languages in primary education was held in Hamburg at the Unesco Institute for Education from 9 to 14 April 1962. The report on this meeting which was prepared by the editor of the present volume, was first published in 1963 in the series 'International Studies in Education', issued by the Unesco Institute for Education, Hamburg. The title of the work was *Foreign Languages in Primary Education* (Stern, 1963).

A French translation of this report was prepared by Unesco, Paris, and published in 1965 by the Unesco Institute for Education, Hamburg, under the title of *Les langues étrangères dans l'enseignement primaire* (Stern, 1965).

A second revised edition of *Foreign Languages in Primary Education* was published by Oxford University Press in the series *Language and Language Learning* (Stern, 1967).

These three editions are referred to in the present volume as the First Hamburg Report or the 1962 Hamburg Report (or, for short, the 1962 Report). Page or chapter references relate to the second English (1967) edition of that report.

The present volume, *Languages and the Young School Child*, based on the international meeting held in Hamburg in 1966, constitutes therefore the Second Hamburg Report or the 1966 Hamburg Report (or, for short, the 1966 Report).

2

Languages for young children: an introductory survey of current practices and problems

H. H. STERN[1]

PRESENT STATUS OF FOREIGN LANGUAGES IN PRIMARY SCHOOLS

The present chapter is intended to provide the reader with some general orientation on foreign language teaching in primary education in the mid-sixties. It is not necessary to describe here the history and development of this movement since this had already been done in the First Hamburg Report and was brought up to date in the second edition as far as it was possible without undertaking a specific inquiry.

What the 1966 meeting has clearly shown is that there is a need for factual surveys bringing together information on recent trends. The data at our disposal at present are neither comprehensive nor detailed enough to allow us to form an adequate picture of the current situation in the world today. Therefore the following remarks which are based on information collected for the second Hamburg meeting can only be regarded as provisional. Limited though the data are they provide indications of certain trends which can be diagrammatically represented as follows (Table 1).

The educational setting A is that which is commonly found in advanced countries of the world with fully developed educational systems operating in states with defined national languages, in particular the European states. Policies under type B setting are mainly found in developing countries, but under certain conditions they also occur in European-type educational systems. We shall first describe trends in type A settings.

Box A1 ('Élite') refers to the traditional policy of most European

---

[1] This survey by the editor of this volume is based on various reports and studies produced for the 1966 Hamburg meeting. Account has been taken also of group reports and the tenor of discussions at the meeting itself.

Table 1. Trends of Policy for the Introduction of Foreign or Second Languages into Primary and Secondary Schools

EDUCATIONAL SETTING A: Foreign Language Situation

(1) 'Élite'	(2) 'Expansion'	(3) 'General'	(4) 'Early Start Experiments'	(5) 'Primary and Mandatory'
FL offered only in academic secondary schools (Gymnasium, lycée, grammar school, high school)	FL offered to a more or less restricted number of pupils beyond (1) at the secondary stage	FL made a universally taught mandatory subject for all pupils at some stage at age ten or above	FL experimentally offered in a limited number of schools to children below age ten	FL offered as a mandatory subject to all or selected groups at age below ten

EDUCATIONAL SETTING B: Second Language Situation

(1) L1 before L2[1]	(2) L1 and L2 together	(3) L2 first choice
'Mother Tongue Emphasis'	'Bilingual Approach'	'Second Language Preference'
Literacy and formal education offered in L1 (vernacular, mother tongue), followed after an interval of one, two or several years by the learning of the second language	Native tongue and second language introduced into education more or less concurrently	Literacy and formal education offered mainly in the second language

[1] In this table, and elsewhere in this book, L1 denotes first or native language, and L2 denotes a second or foreign language.

systems. Primary education is offered in the mother tongue. Foreign languages are regarded as part of secondary and academic education, available only for a limited part of the child population. In this system knowing a foreign language is an indication of superior culture and of a high level of personal education. It was until recently the accepted and unquestioned policy of European countries such as France, Germany, the Netherlands, the Scandinavian countries and the United Kingdom. It should be pointed out that it produced a reasonable efficiency in language learning in these countries for a limited number of secondary school pupils, provided studies were maintained for a sufficiently long time. Thus, for example, in Germany, the Netherlands and Scandinavia where pupils in academic schools started their first foreign language at ages ten, eleven or twelve and continued to study it up to the ages of seventeen, eighteen, nineteen or even twenty, many of them achieved an efficient working knowledge of one, two and often three languages. The good language command that they attained created the false impression that *all* Dutch, Germans, Scandinavians, etc., 'are very good at languages'.

There are countries in which this pattern still prevails and where there is little interest in any drastic modification. This applies for example to the Netherlands. In most countries, however, in which this 'élite' policy (A1) was predominant there has been over the last decades a distinct shift towards an extension of language teaching mostly in the direction of (A2) of the diagram ('expansion'), in some cases to A3 ('general') and also in some to A4 ('early start experiments'). In certain countries the effort is expended in two directions at the same time, e.g. in France (A2 and A4) and in Hungary (A3 and A4).

This trend is part of the general opening out of educational opportunities. Language learning is no longer restricted to an élite type of secondary education, but is being made accessible to a larger number of young people at the secondary stage (A2). The degree to which languages have been made available varies. For example, in the Federal Republic of Germany it was estimated in 1961 that foreign languages were on the average taught to 13 per cent of the elementary school population. But in Hamburg close on 50 per cent learnt a language, while in West Berlin it was nearly 100 per cent (Schütt, c.p.). The shift from A1 to A2 and A3 has become very marked indeed during the last few years. In several countries a foreign language is already a compulsory part of the general school system (A3). This applies, for example, to Hungary (Russian, from class V), Norway (English in the nine-year school from classes IV or V), Poland (Russian, from class V), Sweden (English from age ten). It seems that where there has been an interest in the substantial expansion of language teaching there has also been an interest in experimentation at the primary level (below the age of ten), e.g. in France, the Federal Republic of Germany, Hungary and Sweden. In certain countries, e.g. the United Kingdom, the effort towards extension has immediately shifted to primary school experimentation, but in others the concern over extension in the direction of A2 or A3 appears to have acted as a brake on early-start experiments (e.g. in Israel and Poland and to a certain extent in France).

Side by side with a broadening of language learning opportunities, then, there is a distinct trend towards bringing down the starting age into the early years of the primary stage. This, however, is still treated universally as 'experimentation' (A4). Nowhere, as far as we know, has this led to a universal introduction of a language as part of the general *early* primary curriculum (A5), except in type B situations where the language is needed for literacy and instruction. This experimentation, which was already a marked feature of educational development in several countries in 1962, has increased in the last few years in some parts of the world, e.g. in France, Germany, Hungary, UK, USA and USSR. In several of these countries it is no longer a private and sporadic effort inspired by individual reformers, it has received official sanction (e.g. France, Germany, Hungary, UK and USA). On the other hand, there are a number of countries where there appear to have been no developments in this direction. Interest is widespread, but not always so great as to mobilize the necessary energies. The following sketches illustrate some of these developments in different countries, viz. Austria, France, Hungary, Italy, the Netherlands, Norway, Poland, UK and USA.

France[1] is in the midst of an educational reform which has led to a considerable expansion of secondary education (A2). This has meant that resources for experiments in primary school language teaching have been limited. Nevertheless, in the year 1965–6 three hundred primary classes offered a foreign language, 230 English and 70 German (A4). The teachers carrying out these experiments ranged from secondary school linguists and foreign assistants to

[1] Based on Evrard (c.p.). See also chapter 12 of 1962 Report.

primary teachers with specialist qualifications. The intention is to hand over increasingly any such teaching to the primary school class teacher. The legal authorization for conducting language classes in primary schools is embodied in a circular of the Minister of Education of 30 November 1964 which enables inspectors to authorize for children from the age of eight such language classes in their area wherever suitable conditions exist. Teaching methods and materials include those prepared by teachers themselves and two audio-visual courses, one prepared by BEL,[1] (*Jingle Bells*) and the other by the Centre audio-visuel de St. Cloud.[2] Both courses are still at an experimental stage.

Altogether primary school language teaching is at present still considered in France as entirely experimental but is viewed favourably, and an expansion is envisaged. The problems to be solved include development of methods, evaluation of results, and teacher training.

An organization which has been very active in this direction is BEL, now known as BELC.[3] It has contributed to the teaching of French in British primary schools, partly by its production of a French course, *Frère Jacques*, and partly by its cooperation in the training of British primary teachers in French. BEL has also produced an English course devised on similar principles to *Frère Jacques*. Both courses are designed to be used by non-specialist teachers in primary schools. They are both based on the spoken language introduced with the help of tape-recordings and flannelgraphs and consist of dialogues, practice exercises, test questions, songs and poems.

The kind of experimentation that is taking place in France is further illustrated by pilot schemes in the areas of Vichy and Lille. The project began with an Easter vacation course in 1965 for the primary teachers concerned held at the audio-visual centre of Vichy.[4] It was followed in the summer term by four hours weekly classes in English for the teachers in their own home towns. The

[1] BEL (Bureau d'Étude et de Liaison pour l'enseignement du français dans le monde) became BELC (Bureau pour l'Enseignement de la Langue et de la Civilisation françaises à l'étranger) in early 1966. The address remains: 9, rue Lhomond, Paris–5e, France. See below for relevant aspects of the work of BEL/BELC.

[2] Centre Audio-Visuel de l'École Normale Supérieure de Saint-Cloud, 2, avenue du Palais, 92-Saint-Cloud, France.

[3] See above footnote [1]. The following account is based on BEL (c.p.).

[4] Centre Audio-Visuel de Langues Modernes (CAVILAM), Boîte Postale 164, 03-Vichy, France.

experimental classes in the primary schools began in October 1965 at three levels for pupils aged eight, nine and ten. The teaching was based on *Jingle Bells*, the course developed by BEL. The first impressions after a few months of teaching English were very favourable.

Hungary.[1] There is a great deal of official interest in language teaching at the primary stage. School entry into the eight-year primary school is at the age of six. For all children Russian is compulsory from grade five (i.e. for children aged ten upwards) (A3). In addition, as a result of a ministerial circular issued in 1963, English, French, German and Russian classes for 8- and 9-year-olds (grades three and four) were authorized on an experimental basis (A4). The growing number of children learning these languages (Table 2) provides evidence for the rise of interest in language teaching for young children. The language lessons last 45 minutes each, and are held in some schools twice and in others three times a week. New textbooks have been produced for the younger age groups and the teaching methods which are recommended are in keeping with those suggested in the 1962 Hamburg Report. General impressions of results are favourable. It is estimated that the majority of children acquire between 200 and 300 words and patterns within a year.

Table 2. Number of children in experimental language classes for 8- and 9-year-olds in Hungary 1963–6

	Grade 3		Grade 4	
	1963–4	1965–6	1963–4	1965–6
English	81	488	136	507
French	20	157	—	135
German	1,919	3,464	3,005	4,357
Russian	341	1,049	1,317	2,137

Netherlands.[2] As was already pointed out in the 1962 Report the Netherlands has a history of 'illegal' teaching of foreign languages,

[1] Based on Cser (c.p.). See also chapter 10 of 1962 Report.
[2] Based on van Willigen (c.p.) and Kiestra (c.p.).

principally French, at the primary school stage.[1] Such teaching is condemned by responsible educators in the Netherlands, and has been declining in recent years. The reasons for opposing it are threefold: (a) poor quality of the teachers; (b) lack of suitable materials; and (c) the use of inappropriate methods. Had it not been for new approaches to language teaching such as those provided by language laboratories and the international movement of primary school language teaching, one might well have predicted that informed opinion in the Netherlands would have resolutely opposed language teaching at the primary stage. But as an outcome of these developments teachers and parents have been led to reconsider this question. However, apart from sporadic attempts in individual schools the chief development has been a change in the climate of opinion. In 1963 the Educational Study Centre (the Algemeen Pedagogisch Centrum) of one of the teachers' associations published a report in which the possibility of experimentation in primary school language teaching (A4) was discussed and the lines along which these experiments might be conducted were laid down. But owing to lack of funds no such experimentation has in fact taken place.

In *Poland*[2] Russian is compulsory as the first foreign language for all pupils in their fifth year of schooling (A3). On a private and purely voluntary basis English and French are taught outside school hours to classes of young children from an early age upwards in the larger city schools. These classes are organized by teachers' co-operatives.

Norway[3] is at present in a process of reorganization of the educational system in the direction of a unified nine-year school. This reorganization has already taken place in about 170 of the country's 466 local education authorities. In this system all pupils from the fifth (and in many cases from the fourth) to the eighth year learn English, after that a number will add German.[4] Under the older system, children received instruction in English in the sixth and seventh classes. This means that under the new system the starting age has been lowered by one or two years and the number of years for the teaching of languages extended.

[1] See chapter 1 of the 1962 Report, pp. 1–2.
[2] Based on Woźnicki (c.p.).
[3] Based on Sirevåg (c.p.).
[4] This means that there is a trend to move from A2 to A3.

Austria.[1] Compulsory school attendance in Austria begins at the age of six. After four years in a primary school (*Volksschule*) the children in Vienna attend either the *Hauptschule* or one of the *höhere Schulen*. Foreign languages are offered in both types of schools in the first year, i.e. foreign language teaching begins in the fifth year of schooling, after the pupils have left the primary school (A2). The foreign language is compulsory in the *höhere Schule* and for stream I of the *Hauptschule*. In stream II it is optional, but 90 per cent of the children take English.

For many children, especially the weaker ones, the transition from the primary to the secondary school is difficult. In order to enable children to adapt themselves more easily, preparatory English teaching was instituted in the Vienna primary schools in 1962 (A4). Since that time each year a number of fourth classes (with children aged nine to ten) have received preparatory English instruction. In the session 1965–6 thirteen primary schools participated in the experiment with a total of 29 classes, i.e. about 1,000 pupils and ten teachers. Each class has one English lesson of 50 minutes per week which is taught by specialist foreign language teachers.

Italy.[2] Since 1961 Italy has seen a wide and rapid spreading of languages at the primary stage of education. Several cities have tried programmes aiming at teaching pre-school and primary school children some foreign languages, e.g. English, French and German (A4). The government school authorities so far have not shown any interest in these classes which take place in after-school hours and are conducted by private teachers who are either native speakers of such languages or have been in foreign countries. On a purely impressionistic basis results seem to be positive.

More significant is a systematic experiment which has been in progress since 1963 in the city and district of Padova (Northern Italy). This experiment is sponsored by the Italian Centre for Applied Linguistics (CILA)[3] of which Professor Renzo Titone is the director. Over one hundred teachers have been trained in special refresher courses for this purpose. More than one thousand primary school children are being taught in after-school hours, but in state school buildings and the government authorities have

---

[1] Based on a report on Vienna by Hirschbold (c.p.).
[2] Based on Titone (c.p.).
[3] Centro Italiano de Linguistica Applicata, Via Dalmazia 20, Rome, Italy.

agreed to cooperate. An analysis of textbook materials according to centres of interest is being made. A code of methodological principles has been drawn up and it is intended to prepare new special course materials. While impressions of the results of this work are favourable a more objective evaluation is planned.

USA.[1] The situation in the USA, in the view of American critics, is puzzling. One would expect that a country with large immigrant and multilingual population elements would have no difficulty in solving its language learning problem. Yet, the USA seems to have found this problem at least as intractable as any other country in the world, if not more so. It is not easy to explain why this should have been so. Probably, the desire to create conditions of assimilation to the English language and the American way of life, also periods of isolationist policy and geographical factors have contributed their part to a lack of emphasis on foreign languages. In the schools foreign languages are usually offered in rather short one- or two-year sequences at high school level. As a result, in the view of American critics, languages are inadequately learned and universities have to teach foreign languages at a standard which in European countries is commonly reached at school.

In giving languages a more important place in the schools the movement commonly known by the abbreviation FLES (Foreign Languages in Elementary Schools) has been influential. An outline of these developments in the USA may be found in the 1962 Report (Chapter 11). In a recent comprehensive study of this question Andersson (1966) has shown that a powerful tradition of early language learning at the primary stage goes back to the polyglot origins of the United States in the sixteenth and seventeenth centuries. According to Andersson's view the modern FLES movement continues this long-standing tradition. In more recent times FLES programmes began to spring up after the 1914 war, the first one in Cleveland. Early programmes were in French, but gradually Spanish assumed an equal place. Towards the end of the forties FLES programmes began slowly to multiply, increasing more rapidly in the fifties. Earl J. McGrath, the US Commissioner of Education, urged in 1952 that 'as many American children as possible be given the opportunity' to learn a foreign language. His appeal led to a national conference in 1953 on the role of foreign

[1] See also chapter 11 of 1962 Report.

languages in American schools which gave added impetus to this movement.

In spite of considerable developments over the last ten or fifteen years, FLES in the sixties, according to Andersson, is in a precarious situation 'bedevilled by a lack of quality and discipline . . .'.

Most recently renewed attempts have been made to mobilize the multilingual resources of the United States for language learning, partly by cultivating in bilingual children their native tongue as well as English, and partly by recruiting and training bilinguals as teachers[1] (B2).

United Kingdom. In Britain there has been an enormous increase in foreign language teaching at the primary stage (A4). The beginnings were described in the 1962 Report against the background of language teaching in Britain generally.[2] In 1961–2 a teaching experiment in a Leeds primary school stimulated a great deal of interest in language teaching at this stage (Kellermann, 1964). Since then primary school language teaching has spread to about 5,000 schools all over the country including Scotland and Wales. Some of this teaching occurs at the individual initiative of teachers or of heads of schools. In most cases it forms part of a wider scheme sponsored by a local authority. But the most important development has been the launching of a national experiment in 1963, the so-called Pilot Scheme. As this is a unique project of considerable scope and of wider than purely national interest, this British project will be treated in detail in several of the subsequent chapters (chapters 8, 13, 14 and 16).

COMPARATIVE STUDIES

As was pointed out at the beginning of this chapter it is not possible to obtain a complete picture of developments without much more comprehensive and detailed inquiries. Such *status studies* are indeed important. They should be undertaken periodically in order to make it possible to recognize trends of development.

National language teaching policies are greatly influenced by the interpretation placed upon one's own country's policy in relation to what is happening elsewhere in the world. There is a good deal of misinterpretation and distortion in the views on the language situation in other countries. Writers on language teaching in their

[1] See on this point pp. 124–5 of the 1962 Report, and also below, chapter 9.
[2] See chapter 14 of the 1962 Report.

desire to influence public opinion may tend to exaggerate the proficiency in foreign languages achieved in other countries.

A certain degree of international cooperation in the planning of language teaching would be a great advantage. Indeed it may be assumed that the interest of the Council for Cultural Cooperation of the Council of Europe in the second Hamburg meeting was prompted by the desire in European countries to achieve a measure of regional coordination in language learning at school. International research attempting to find out common elements and differences in language teaching policy and their effect on achievement would be a useful start in such cooperation.

Experience has already been gained in international inquiries along these lines through various studies in comparative education, in particular the IEA Project.[1] This is a large-scale comparative study of curriculum and its effect upon learning in different educational systems. The IEA Project has completed its first set of investigations on the teaching of mathematics in a number of countries, but at present the field of inquiry is being extended to other curriculum subjects including the teaching of foreign languages. One of the characteristic features of the project has been that achievement as measured by specially designed tests is correlated with the teaching of the subject and other factors (e.g. teacher training, school organization) in different educational settings. In collecting the background data use is made of standardized inquiries established on comparative principles. Such experience should be drawn upon in making inquiries on foreign languages in the primary systems of different countries, and it may well be possible to associate any status inquiries on primary school language teaching with similar investigations on language teaching carried out by the IEA Project.

The framing of questionnaires and the setting up of investigations which are supposed to have validity across various educational systems demand a critical awareness of similarities and differences in linguistic, educational, political and social settings. The analysis of relevant factors offered in the final chapter of this volume[2] should be particularly useful to such status studies.

[1] International Project for the Evaluation of Educational Achievement. For an account of the work of this project see Postlethwaite (1966). The address of this project is: IEA Project, Unesco Institute for Education, 2000 Hamburg 13, Feldbrunnenstrasse 70, Federal Republic of Germany. See Part II, p. 204, below,
[2] See in particular pp. 210-13.

THE SECOND LANGUAGE SITUATION

If we now turn to the other language situation, B in the diagram in Table 1 above (p. 10), this applies particularly to the developing countries in Africa and Asia. Very briefly, in the days of colonial empires, education from the beginning of schooling was provided in the language of the 'superior' colonial power (B3). As a result of more liberal thinking and national demands it was thought that 'colonial' countries should provide education in line with that of advanced countries, which meant primary education in the vernacular (B1). This became also the accepted policy of many countries after they had attained political independence. However, the complex linguistic situation of many of these countries demanded an early start in a regional or a world language so that policy B2 (bilingual), i.e. a simultaneous start in a second language and B3 (preference for a second language) came to be recognized as having educational and socio-political advantages. The various possibilities and extremely complex problems of the language situation in the developing countries of Africa and Asia are fully discussed in chapter 3.

These policy choices do not present themselves only in developing countries. They arise also in advanced countries under certain conditions, for example, (1) in bilingual and multilingual situations, and (2) in many countries in the case of national minorities, such as groups of immigrants.

Over the last four years the outlook on bilingualism in primary education has become much more positive. There is a spreading belief—strengthened by some research evidence—that bilingualism is not likely to be harmful to intellectual and emotional development, and as a result, attitudes to bilingualism in childhood are radically changing. In the past the child from a foreign language home was often treated as if he was handicapped. While such a child is obviously at a disadvantage in his knowledge of the language of the community, his knowledge of his own language is beginning to be treated as a personal and national asset. Resulting from this shift of outlook, children in a bilingual situation are no longer treated as if the sole educational objective was to help them to acquire the major language of national literacy; there is the additional demand made today to assist such children to maintain and cultivate the minority language, in other words a deliberate bilingual policy (B2).

This strengthening of bilingualism in primary education has

been a very notable new development in the USA to which attention was already drawn in the 1967 edition of the First Hamburg
Report.[1] It was confirmed by reports from Wales (see below) and
several reports from the USA. One of these is a strongly worded
resolution by a Conference of the Southwest Council of Foreign
Language Teachers of 15 November 1965 which stresses the
educational needs of bilingual children and concludes with the
paragraph:

'. . . that, recognizing the importance of the mother tongue as a symbol of
an inherited culture and as an enrichment of our total culture, all bilingual
citizens be encouraged to cultivate their ancestral language as well as the
official language, English.' (Andersson, c.p.)

The other is the report on a new bilingual primary school which is
published in chapter 9.

Wales.[2] As was stated in the 1962 Report English has been the only
official language in Wales since the Act of Union of England and
Wales 1536. In 1965 the British Government adopted the principle
of equal validity for Welsh and English in Wales and legislation
to that effect is expected shortly. Such government action is likely
to increase the economic and prestige value of English-Welsh
bilingualism in Wales.

Two national television services for Wales, one presented by the British
Broadcasting Corporation and the other by a commercial company, have
been established since 1962. Both services present network programmes
produced to appeal to Britain as a whole by the British Broadcasting
Corporation and the major commercial companies in England, but they
also present about five hours per week of programmes in the Welsh language.
The Welsh language is brought into English-speaking homes in Wales in
this manner and this appears to have led to an increase in desire to become
bilingual, which in effect means a wish to acquire command of the minority
national language in addition to command of English, the dominant
language with which social, cultural and educational advance has been
associated for some hundreds of years. Such developments have strengthened
the motivation to learn Welsh as a second language.

Welsh-medium nursery schools which were already mentioned in the
1962 Report continue to turn monoglots into Welsh-English bilinguals and
a policy of teaching Welsh as a second language in English-medium schools

[1] See p. 125 of the First Hamburg Report, especially the reference to Gaarder,
1965, in footnote 1.
[2] This section is based on Williams (c.p.). See also chapter 9 of the 1962 Report.

to pupils from the earliest stages of school attendance has been formally adopted by three local education authorities (A5).

In addition Wales shares with the rest of the United Kingdom the interest in the teaching of foreign languages in primary schools and as a result there have been three experiments in recent years (A4):

1 Teaching French as a second language in a group of primary schools in a largely English speaking part of Wales;

2 an experiment in the teaching of French as a third language to pupils of a Welsh-medium primary school at Bangor; and

3 an experiment in the teaching of German as a third language in a Welsh-medium primary school at Aberystwyth (Dodson, 1966).

INTERNATIONAL, BILINGUAL AND MULTILINGUAL SCHOOLS[1]

In the 1962 Report one chapter was devoted to a small but important group of schools in various parts of the world, particularly in the Soviet Union and Western Europe, in which children receive their education in two or more languages.[2] Such schools exploit for educational purposes an existing international and multilingual situation in which the children happen to be, or they deliberately create a foreign-language milieu. It has become clear that they constitute important pilot experiments in multilingual education and that they are of interest not only in themselves, but as prototypes of educational developments generally.

The 1966 meeting had at its disposal progress reports from the École Active Bilingue in Paris (Manuel, c.p.), the École Européenne de Bruxelles (Donnen, c.p.), the École Européenne de Mol (Junker, c.p.), the John F. Kennedy School of Berlin (Müller, c.p.), the Toronto French School (Giles, c.p.) and the bilingual primary school in Miami, Florida, described in chapter 9 below.

These reports indicate that these schools have continued to grow in size and strength; they appear to solve their complex organizational problems and enable their pupils to reach standards of education which compare favourably with the attainments of pupils in monoglot schools and, in addition, give their pupils a very extended experience in learning and effectively using a new language.

There are at present six European schools: Luxembourg (founded in 1953), Brussels (1958), Mol-Geel (Belgium, 1960), Varese (Italy,

---

[1] Within the area in which they function the language teaching policy of these schools may be looked upon as falling into cells A(5) or B(2) of Table 1, p. 10.
[2] See chapter 17 of the 1962 Report.

1960), Karlsruhe (Federal Republic of Germany, 1962), and Bergen (Netherlands, 1963).

These schools educate a considerable number of children of various nations. For example, the school population of the École Européenne de Bruxelles is approximately 1,900 (1966). The primary section of this school has 890 boys and girls divided into 36 classes which according to nationality distribute themselves as follows:

   12 classes of French-Belgian origin
   10 classes of German origin
    8 classes of Dutch-Flemish origin
    6 classes of Italian origin

The size of classes ranges from 18 to 35.

At the École Active Bilingue in Paris numbers have risen from 700 in 1964 to 800 in 1965 and the estimated intake for 1966 is 1,100. Approximately 75 per cent of the children are of French-speaking origin, 20 per cent of English-speaking background, while the remaining 5 per cent come from various other nationalities.

The John F. Kennedy School in Berlin had, in 1966, 668 boys and girls, of whom 322 were German, 283 American and 63 from other countries.

The five-year primary school of the École Européenne de Bruxelles teaches French and German. All German, Italian, Dutch and Dutch-speaking Belgian children learn French, and all French and French-speaking Belgian children learn German. Second language teaching begins in the first year of the primary stage and is continued throughout this stage for five years at the rate of a daily 45-minute lesson. In addition, from year 3 upwards $4\frac{1}{2}$ hours per week are set aside as 'European Classes'. These are classes in handicraft and art, music and physical education, all of which are always offered in the second language.

In order to cope adequately with varying standards of English, the École Active Bilingue, Paris, has divided its school population according to attainments in English into three streams: I 'beginners', II 'intermediate and advanced', III 'bilinguals or native speakers', and offers a progressive syllabus in accordance with these different standards. Children who have attained a level appropriate for stream II in English are given the opportunity to learn a second foreign language (German, Russian or Spanish) from the first primary year upwards. For early stages of English-teaching the École Active has revised its policy. It no longer relies on native speakers, but gives preference to carefully programmed audio-visual material, handled by a trained French primary teacher who knows some English, but is no expert. It has been found that this approach gives very satisfactory results. Likewise, the École Européenne de Mol uses the CREDIF audio-visual course *Bonjour Line*[1] with very satisfactory results for initial teaching of French.

A new school on which information was received is the Toronto French School[2] which was established in 1962 with a view to bringing into existence a medium by which children could achieve English-French bilingualism. It was concerned with the development of a programme and of appropriate methods.

The school is located in the cosmopolitan but English-speaking city of Toronto, Canada, with a metropolitan population of over 1½ million inhabitants. The school draws its teachers from France, Switzerland, Belgium, the United States, the United Kingdom, Canada and other countries. Most of its pupils are English-speaking Canadians. It started by developing preschool classes and as these classes advanced, the school added a grade per year. It now has a population of 421 children between ages three to eight.

Children in the kindergarten classes for ages 3 to 5 are taught entirely in French. This is continued in grade 1 and English is first introduced in grade 2 and then only for an average of one hour per day. In planning the programme it was argued that competence in French would be more difficult to achieve than competence in English for these children who live in an English milieu, and therefore it was decided to teach reading in French first and only after competence was achieved in that language would the children be taught to read English. All reading taught in grade 1 is in French and French is the language of the class. In grade 2 English is first introduced when history, English reading and grammar, and mathematics are taught for a total of 60 minutes per day. First impressions suggest that the cultivation of bilingualism by schooling is very beneficial for the development of these children.

The reports that the Hamburg meeting received from international schools, of which the above summaries can give only a brief impression, suggest that their experience can be valuable for the solution of problems of language learning in primary education. These special schools are pioneering in an intensive way certain developments which on a more reduced scale are being tried in national systems of education. Their experience should therefore be made more widely available. It would be useful to have systematic

[1] See chapter 12 for details.
[2] Based on Giles (c.p.).

and disinterested investigations on their work, its successes as well as its problems, difficulties and failures, and it is hoped that some research on these schools will be initiated.

It should, however, be pointed out at once that there are essential differences between these schools and ordinary primary schools in national educational systems and therefore their experience cannot be automatically applied to other situations. The children going to the international schools are frequently children of international civil servants, diplomats and the like. Or, their parents have chosen the school because of their belief in international education or in the value of foreign languages. Consequently the school operates in an international or multilingual setting or climate. It is not its originator, it cultivates and reinforces an already existing multilingual influence. This is often quite different in a national educational system where the bilingualism may be the only agent of an international or foreign language element in the immediate environment of the school. Such differences will have to be allowed for by a research worker. Nevertheless, there are many aspects, e.g. planning and organization, on which these schools could offer a great deal of useful experience to the foreign language work of primary schools in national systems.[1]

FUNDAMENTAL ISSUES

In the foregoing pages we have reviewed a number of developments in language teaching in primary schools in different parts of the world that had been reported to the 1966 Hamburg meeting. On the strength of this information and other reports on recent developments it can be stated that the trends which were observed in 1962 have continued and have gained in strength. This does suggest that in the coming five to ten years national systems will, with increasing urgency, be faced with the question of when and how to introduce foreign and second languages into education, what scope to give to such teaching and what results to aim at. This is why the Hamburg meeting regarded it as very important at this stage to re-examine the fundamental, social, political, psychological

[1] A demand for research on language teaching in international schools was made by Spangenberg and Müller (1966) at the 1966 Conference of the International Schools Association held at the International School of Geneva. Such research, so Spangenberg and Müller believed, would be of value to the international schools themselves and at the same time would be a service to national school systems.

2

and educational issues of this language teaching policy.[1] The major
sociological and psychological issues involved are treated in chapters
4 and 5 and the problem of community development is dealt with
in relation to countries in Africa and Asia in chapter 3.

These discussions clearly show that it is important not to view
these problems in terms of single factors, such as young children's
power of imitation. In the last resort it is a matter of interpretation
of many facts and trends, and demands policy decisions of a socio-
linguistic kind which will affect the whole educational system and
the distribution of language learning in it.

For primary education the issue is becoming more and more
clearly defined in two opposing 'theories' on the nature of primary
education. (a) One view is that primary education is vernacular
education. According to this point of view children must first settle
down in one cultural and linguistic milieu, namely their own, and
only when they feel reasonably at home in it are they allowed to
advance to foreign languages and foreign cultures. This is the
rationale of the traditional conception of primary education and its
relationship to secondary education, according to which primary
education is identical with mother-tongue education and foreign
languages are resolutely deferred until a secondary stage after four
or five years of schooling has been reached.

(b) Against this theory stands the newer point of view, which has
been gaining ground over the last ten or fifteen years, i.e. that
primary education should not be purely in terms of the native
tongue, but that it could well be bilingual education. Or, as it was
expressed in the 1962 Report, the acquisition of a foreign language
must become part of the basic literacy of the child on a par with
reading and writing. It is argued that the traditional point of view
of primary education as vernacular education is unrealistic, because
even by a narrow definition of bilingualism at least half of the
world's population is bilingual (Fishman, 1966); and in any case
everyone lives in a world in which many different languages are
spoken and therefore it is not defensible to create through education
a rigidly monolinguistic setting. If education is to reflect the realities
with which we have to live, other languages and other cultures
should impinge on children from the earliest stage of formal
education.

[1] Especially Sections 1 (Fundamental issues) and 4 (Community development) of
the problems listed in the working paper, quoted in the Introduction, pp. 4 and 5
above.

A further argument arising out of the previous one against the older policy is that it is psychologically unsound, because it over-trains children in unilingual and unicultural ways of thinking and therefore makes the transition to other languages and cultures unnecessarily difficult and artificial when it does come. And as a result older children and adolescents tend to resist when they are faced with foreign languages.

This second point of view which was already formulated in the 1962 Report[1] has gained increasing support in the last few years. The consequences of a marked shift in this direction are far-reaching for the whole educational process. This is why it is important at present to think about this issue carefully and to initiate research. It is quite clear from the experience of the last few years that fundamental changes in language teaching policy are costly and time consuming and have repercussions over a whole system of education; and, therefore, once an educational system is committed to one policy of language education, it cannot lightly change and adopt another.

METHODS AND MATERIALS

Methodological questions and the problems of producing the right kinds of materials for young children are fully discussed in various parts of this report. Chapter 6 deals with the question of methods and materials in general, and chapters 12 and 13 describe and discuss two approaches to the production of materials.

In order to see these discussions in perspective it is necessary to draw attention to three characteristic trends of recent years.

1 *The feasibility of language teaching to younger children*
Although many questions have been raised on methods and materials of teaching languages at the primary level, one conclusion has been reached beyond doubt as the result of the numerous experiments and experiences of the last few years: effective teaching of languages to young children is a feasible achievement.[2] This conviction based on widespread observations has added strength to the arguments of those who favour an early start. This important and positive answer to earlier questions on language learning in childhood has to some extent in past discussions been obscured by the exaggerated

[1] See chapter 3 of 1962 Report.
[2] See on this point also chapter 5, p. 60.

desire to prove that young children are better language learners than adolescents and adults. Chapter 5 shows how difficult it would be to produce evidence to this effect. It is in our view not necessary to justify language learning at the primary stage on such excessive expectations. The more restrained claim that can be made is *that children have been proved to make an effective start in language learning under school conditions and this early start appears to lay a good foundation for continued language study throughout the total period of full-time schooling.* Needless to say that not all experiences in this area have been favourable. But the problems, difficulties and failures have not been of a kind as to throw doubt on the value of the entire operation. They are generally viewed as caused by deficiencies in teaching and preparation which can be identified and remedied.[1] They have given rise to the discussion on methodological choices and materials which was pursued at the Hamburg meeting and which is reflected in chapter 6.

2 *The new technology of language teaching*

Since the early sixties there has been a marked increase in the application of technological aids to foreign language teaching. In Britain, for example, the first language laboratory in an educational institution was installed in 1961. Since then, £1,000,000 has been spent on language laboratories in schools, colleges and universities (Riddy, 1965). In the USA, since the late 1950s language laboratories in universities and colleges have increased from 250 to well over 1,000, and in secondary schools from a few dozen to almost 10,000 (Hutchinson, 1966). Films, film strips, ciné loop projections and television have also increasingly been employed in foreign language instruction. Furthermore there is a rising interest in making use of programmed instruction in language teaching. These developments have impinged on the methodology of foreign language teaching at the primary stage. Technical aids can mitigate the chronic shortage of teachers. Moreover language teachers in their own training nowadays have become accustomed to technical aids and this increased facility and familiarity with new media has led to an acceptance of these aids in the primary school.

This trend was already indicated in 1962.[2] Perhaps the most substantial advance since then is the greater availability of primary

---

[1] For a more detailed discussion of failures and difficulties, see Stern (1966).

[2] See in particular references to the *Parlons français* Project in chapters 11, 18 and also on p. 126 of the 1962 Report. See also Garry and Mauriello (1961).

school courses and materials making use of a variety of aids including discs, tapes, teachers' guides, films, film strips and flannelgraph
figurines. One of the best known of recent primary school French
courses, *Bonjour Line* (see chapter 12), is based on film strip projections and magnetic tape recordings. Likewise the Nuffield courses
(see chapter 13) use a variety of modern aids, including tape
recorders, films and film strips. The comparison of these two sets of
materials alone will show that the role of technical aids and the
timing within a course is subject to many variations.

One thing is certain: young children adjust themselves comfortably to the application of all kinds of modern aids and handle even
the intricacies of a language laboratory without great difficulties.
Experience has shown that modern aids, including programmed
instruction and language laboratories, have their place in primary
schools as much as in the teaching of older language learners. The
older view that young children are *a priori* too young to benefit
from the educational use of technical equipment in language
teaching is no longer tenable. But what role such equipment should
play in this situation is again a matter for further research.

3 *The application of linguistics to language teaching*
Among developments which are influencing language teaching
today, one of the most remarkable is probably the widespread
interest aroused by linguistics and the possibility of its application
to language teaching. At the time of the first Hamburg Report
linguistics in language teaching was already well in the forefront,
but its relevance to primary school language teaching was still
regarded as marginal. Admittedly, Carroll (1963) in his list of
background studies included contrastive studies of languages.
But apart from that linguistics was hardly mentioned in the discussions which were mainly concerned with the pedagogical and
psychological aspects of the problem. Since then, it has been more
widely recognized that language teaching materials and methods
imply a theory of language as much as theories of learning (Mackey,
1965) and that what is taught and how it is taught should be based
on adequate linguistic foundations.

Present-day linguistic thought is in a state of scientific ferment.
Different models of language have been elaborated to account for
the complex phonological, grammatical and semantic data of
natural languages (Revzin, 1966). Three such theoretical formula-
tions have in recent years become particularly influential:

(a) the descriptive approach of American structuralism which originated in the work of Sapir, Bloomfield, Fries, and others. Much of the work in American language teaching in the last fifteen years has been based on this model, for example the language teaching inspired by Bloomfield, Fries, Hill and Lado.

(b) Another approach which has developed out of certain theoretical weaknesses of structuralism is the generative model of transformational grammar, developed by Chomsky.

(c) A third position, favoured particularly in Britain, is the so-called scale-and-category theory, formulated by Halliday and founded on the linguistic tradition established by Sweet and Jones in phonetics and Firth in general linguistics. It is an attempt at an ordered and systematically coherent presentation of all linguistic phenomena. A number of research studies undertaken in Britain, for example the Nuffield Child Language Survey (see chapter 14) are based on this model.

Language teachers have difficulties in orientating themselves among the different viewpoints in linguistics, and linguists themselves are sometimes inclined to be sceptical about the immediate applicability of their scientific studies to the practice of language teaching. Undoubtedly, the interaction between language teaching and linguistics must be handled with sensitivity and caution. But the point of no return has been reached. Linguistics has given new perspectives and critical standards and therefore cannot be ignored. It is right therefore to examine materials and methods in the light of linguistics and to obtain data for language teaching from linguistic studies. What this amounts to in practice can be seen from several chapters, i.e. those on the new materials such as the Nuffield Course (see chapter 13) and *Bonjour Line* (see chapter 12) and in particular the chapters on the child language surveys (see chapters 14 and 15), which describe a linguistic project providing data for language teaching materials at the primary stage. It is also important to give teacher training a linguistic orientation—as was suggested by the group in Hamburg discussing the content of teachers' courses (see chapter 7). Language teaching in the primary schools of Africa and Asia also urgently demands basic linguistic studies in order to give such teaching a sound basis (see chapter 3).

EXPERIMENTATION AND RESEARCH

The magic words 'experiment' and 'research' are used in educational circles in a variety of ways. Often a teacher who tries a slight modification in his teaching technique is 'making an experiment'; a school which introduces a mild revision into its teaching programme becomes an 'experimental school'; a primary school which starts teaching French in one of its classes is 'doing research into language teaching'. To the professional educational research worker the application of the terms 'research' and 'experiment' in this way is anathema. Seeing in it nothing but *naïveté*, wishful thinking and a misguided reforming zeal he condemns the absence of rigour, of a proper research design and the lack of adequate controls.

There is no doubt that much of the 'experimental' work in language teaching at the primary level is open to such criticisms. However, it is important not to dampen the enthusiasm for reform and innovation because of certain confusions in intention and terminology. The needs of educational reform are various. New problems cannot immediately be studied in a neat and carefully planned research project. The well structured, fully-fledged experiment is often the outcome of groping and exploratory work without which the more sophisticated study would not be possible. Reform often begins with an untested hunch, a new notion, even a craze. Thus the impulse to introduce language learning at the primary level did not come from well attested research but from a mixture of criticisms, discontents and certain hunches about language learning in childhood. A number of questions were raised and proposals put forward, and a trial-and-error phase began. After a while the new notions were followed up by 'educational experiments' in the broad sense. Children were taught and experience was gathered on how it worked. The experimenter—individual teacher, school or educational system—may or may not have made observations with a certain degree of precision. In many instances the 'investigator' may have been content with getting the feel of a new situation and gathering experience. On the other hand, he may well have collected his impressions and organized them in a 'research report' or indeed, he may even have gone to the length of assessing his results by tests or other means. Most of the experimental work on primary school language teaching carried out so far falls into this very wide class of experiences and experiments in a broad sense.

It would be quite unjustifiable to condemn this necessary, exploratory experimentation because it has not always obeyed all the canons of rigorous educational research. If education is to advance such explorations are vital and it would be wrong to inhibit the adventurous teacher and educational reformer by imposing upon him the rigid demands of educational research requirements. Indeed the educational world is greatly indebted to these experimenters for their initiative, ingenuity, energy and thought.

However, after a period of trial-and-error a stage is reached when certain major issues have become defined and little can be gained by merely continuing on a global exploratory type of investigation. At this point a more rigorous approach is essential. It was the conviction of the 1966 meeting that in the teaching of languages at the primary stage this point had been reached and that is why in the present report particular emphasis is being laid upon research: asking the right questions, planning and designing studies in an expert manner and seeing to it that the execution and the reporting of results correspond to the best standards of educational research. The reader who, at the present time, is interested in undertaking or evaluating research in foreign languages at the primary stage should therefore study chapter 17 and Part II in which research procedures are discussed in detail.

Nevertheless, as there is a whole gradation of studies all of which have contributed to the present thinking on the problem of language teaching at the primary level—ranging from the exploratory teaching experiment to the full-scale, ambitious research project— this volume includes samples of the various types of study: the recorded observations of an individual teacher such as those of Miss E. Sipmann on the experimental teaching of German in an English primary school (see chapter 11), the systematic experimental teaching project of Dr P. Doyé in 15 Berlin primary schools (chapter 10) or the large-scale feasibility study that is at present being conducted under the Schools Council in Great Britain (chapter 8) in conjunction with a clearly defined research project of the National Foundation for Educational Research (chapter 16).

These reports should serve to illustrate the range of studies that have already been undertaken. Other investigations on which reports were received can only be briefly referred to. Some of these had results which deserve further investigation because they did not support commonly held beliefs.

For example, in Sweden, Eriksson and Ekstrand tested 40 primary classes in different regions of Sweden on (a) comprehension and (b) pronunciation after they had been taught English by the audio-visual course *Engelsk utan bok*,[1] in order to find out at which

[1] See chapter 10 (pp. 43–4) of the 1962 Report.

age children were most receptive to language learning. Ekstrand found the older the pupils the lower the error scores in pronunciation and comprehension. This result, if confirmed, could constitute an argument against an early start (Ekstrand, 1964).

Findings by Dodson (1966) in Wales in a teaching experiment on German in a primary school, linked with a methodological research project, questioned other commonly held beliefs (Williams, c.p.). The evidence from this experiment suggested: (a) Best results were obtained when sentence meaning is presented through a language already known (the so-called Bilingual Method) especially in conjunction with pictures. (b) The availability of the printed word helps the learner. (c) Practice in switching rapidly from one language to another is desirable. (d) The language laboratory can be used effectively at primary school level. (e) The young language learner has an advantage over older learners in mastering pronunciation and accent, but capacity to imitate and produce sentences increases with age up to about the age of eighteen.

Another study by Schütt and Kahl (Schütt, c.p.)[1] has reached conclusions which are more in keeping with recently formulated views on language teaching in primary schools. This three-year English-teaching experiment in 35 Hamburg classes was designed to explore methods and materials suitable for pupils who in the past had been excluded from the opportunity of learning English because of their poor general school attainments. The investigators found that, with appropriate methods and materials, it is possible to reach a satisfactory standard and they reach the conclusion that there is no justification for excluding these pupils from language instruction.

Research recommendations.[2] As research is the subject of several of the chapters of this volume there is no need to consider details in this part, but some of the most important recommendations of the 1966 Hamburg meeting should be emphasized. Two types of research

[1] A report on this study by the two investigators, *Englisch für alle Volksschüler*, will be published in 1969.
[2] These recommendations on research which were formulated by the Research and Assessment Group during the 1966 Hamburg meeting were endorsed by all the participants in plenary session. The Group consisted of Professor J. B. Carroll (USA, Chairman), Mrs C. Burstall (UK, Rapporteur), Miss A. Chari (India), Mr P. Doyé (Federal Republic of Germany), Mr L. Kiestra (Netherlands), Mrs A. Manuel (France), Mr G. Müller (Federal Republic of Germany), Mr G. Perren (UK), Mr N. Postlethwaite (IEA, Unesco Institute for Education).

are particularly needed: (a) controlled experiments at the national level, and (b) national and international survey research.

(a) It is difficult to organize controlled experiments on an international level. It was therefore suggested that these experiments should be set up by national research organizations or institutes and that the research teams should include three categories of persons: (1) educational research workers with training in psychology, (2) modern language specialists, and (3) practising teachers. All efforts should be made to disseminate the results of such research internationally in research journals and modern language journals.

Furthermore, the 1966 meeting considered it desirable that an international register of ongoing research in this area should be published annually and circulated to all interested. It seemed to the participants that the Unesco Institute for Education, Hamburg, might be the most appropriate agency to undertake this task.

(b) Survey research, on the other hand, can be carried out internationally, and as was already pointed out in an earlier section (see p. 18, *seq.*), national and international surveys on language teaching at the primary stage were recommended.

It was further suggested, as we have mentioned earlier, that—for the sake of economy of effort and finance—such international survey studies might be associated with the planned international studies of French-as-a-foreign-language and English-as-a-foreign-language of the IEA Project.[1]

Systematic research on language learning inevitably involves some form of objective testing of results. The almost complete lack of objective tests of modern language achievement at the primary level has been a very great handicap. It has forced students of this problem to make up tests which, according to principles of educational research, are often of little value and may indeed be misleading. The participants therefore urged that suitable tests of the linguistic skills: listening comprehension, oral expression, reading comprehension and written expression, should be developed by teams, which include professional test constructors, modern language specialists and practising primary school teachers.

It cannot be sufficiently emphasized that the construction of efficient language tests requires not only psychometric skill and linguistic expertise, but also appropriate technical procedures and

[1] See page 19 above for details of this project.

sufficient time for the development and refinement of test materials. A good test cannot be made at short notice, nor, as it is designed for one situation, can it always be simply adopted for use in another. In selecting any existing tests or test material, a teacher or educational administrator must satisfy himself that they have an adequate basis of research.

Details of a number of questions which demand investigation by research methods can be found in subsequent chapters throughout this book in addition to those questions already discussed in this introductory survey.

3

Second language teaching to younger children in Africa and Asia

G. E. PERREN and A. CHARI[1]

Unlike most European countries, many of the developing countries of Asia and Africa must necessarily use second languages as media of instruction in their educational systems. At some stage—primary, secondary or tertiary—the whole progress of the pupil or student either in general education or in specialized studies may thus depend on having an adequate command of a language, other than his mother tongue, which he has to learn in school. Efficient language teaching is therefore vital in a sense unknown in European countries.

AFRICA

In Africa, south of the Sahara, English or French are often the only media used for secondary education: in many areas they are also the media of primary teaching. The origins of this situation are not only historical—the influence of former colonial powers, but also demographic and linguistic—the enormous number and variety of languages spoken in Africa, often by comparatively small groups.[2] Moreover, such African languages of wider communication which exist—as for example, Hausa or Swahili—possess at present very limited written resources. They are widely used often only in their spoken form.

The dominant European second languages have in fact become languages of national unity in many states. In Africa, unlike Asia, only rarely has an indigenous language been designated as a national

[1] Miss Ahalya Chari is Principal of the Regional College of Education, Mysore, India, and Mr G. E. Perren is Director of the Centre for Information on Language Teaching, State House, 63 High Holborn, London WC1, UK.—Ed.
[2] It has been estimated, for example, that there are 16 indigenous languages in Sierra Leone, 50 in Ghana, 100 in Tanganyika and 150 in Nigeria. (Spencer, 1963). See also Perren and Holloway, 1965, pp. 8–9, 17–21.

(or even more rarely as an official) language.[1] In one African state, Cameroon, both English and French are official languages, and there is now a policy (with its attendant problems) of providing bilingual education in two second languages.

In Anglophone countries, the introduction of English, either as a subject or as a medium in the curriculum of primary schools has, both in colonial times and more recently, been conditioned by numerous, sometimes conflicting, factors: the desire of administrators and educators to use African languages (preferably the children's mother tongues) as the most suitable media of widespread primary education, the desire of Africans to learn English, the availability of teachers of English, the linguistic heterogeneity of many schools, the needs of secondary education. The problem of *whether* to teach English as a second language was hardly debatable;[2] the question of when to begin depended on a balance of administrative, as well as educational considerations. The need for educational progress (as an essential prerequisite for economic, social and political development) gives the whole question of how best to teach English an urgency which is greater now than ever. Not only is the second language at present necessary for full primary and secondary education, but its later use in occupations arising from government, law, commerce and science is unavoidable.

Motivation is economic, social and political. Countries such as Ghana, Kenya, Uganda and Zambia are developing the use of English as a medium in the earliest stages of primary education.

In Francophone areas, the use of French as the sole medium of both primary and subsequent education has been general for many years. More recently the claims of African languages as media for primary education have been considered but, as in Anglophone areas, the great variety and numbers of African languages and the need for rapid development make the more widespread and efficient teaching of the European second language imperative. In both Anglophone and Francophone areas the chief problems are the efficient training of large numbers of teachers and the production of effective teaching materials to teach second languages.

[1] Swahili has been made the national language of Tanzania. In Mauritania, Arabic has been declared the *national* language, while French remains the *official* language. In Madagascar, Malagasy is an official language together with French.
[2] Although it was, of course, extensively discussed by administrators before much education had been established.

An aspect of the growing national consciousness of many African states is a rising demand for French to be taught in Anglophone and English to be taught in Francophone areas so as to provide for inter-communication between them. A growing number of Africans wish to be able to use two European languages, entirely to facilitate communication with other Africans.

Materials and methods

No one has ever claimed that the teaching of English (or indeed of French) has been particularly scientific or carefully planned in Africa. The surprising fact is that both languages have been comparatively well learned. In the past this has been a result of the high degree of selection of pupils for schooling, and the large proportion of expatriate teachers (especially of French), who were at least good language informants — all within a limited number of schools.

More recently, however, rapid expansion of education has led to many poorly qualified teachers teaching more and more unselected pupils. Methods and materials found effective in limited and favourable circumstances are seen to be less applicable to more widespread education. At present, however, Africa's commitment to second language teaching cannot be reduced; somehow teaching resources must be increased and made more efficient.

The Anglophone countries have normally begun teaching English as a subject (while using African languages as general media), later switching to its exclusive use as a medium in late primary or secondary classes. Learning English was, to a large extent, regarded as an essential preliminary for secondary education. This meant that in primary schools too much weight was often attached to the secondary schools' own interpretation of language teaching. Primary teachers and pupils tended to be over-influenced by secondary school aims and materials. Since, in their turn, the secondary schools had their eyes firmly fixed on the demands of school-leaving examinations (such as the Cambridge Overseas School Certificate and its derivatives) which were closely modelled on those of the metropolitan country, this encouraged an academic separation of English teaching from its real function—of servicing all education by establishing skill in a vehicular language. The comparative lack of primary method experts with conscious skill in language teaching (who might have redressed the balance) led to English becoming a content subject in primary classes rather than a skill. In fact English has been, and still is, largely learned through exposure to its use as a medium, and because of the intense motivation of the pupils, rather than because of the materials and methods employed in its early teaching.

Francophone countries, with a more thorough commitment to the use of French as a medium from the earliest stages, supported by larger numbers of expatriate teachers, have to some extent avoided the ambivalence of the Anglophone countries, which, while teaching English inefficiently as a *subject*, compensated for this by its later use as a *medium*.

Today the extension of English teaching to lower and younger classes, often on the grounds that the sooner they begin, the more they will learn, has shown very clearly the need for new approaches. In the past, primary pupils learned English because it was obviously necessary to them to qualify for secondary schooling; but there seems to be a lower age limit where this incentive to learn a language for its *future* rather than its present use is inoperative, or certainly not strong enough to offset unsuitable materials and techniques. Such seems to be the situation where English is attempted as a foreign language, or only as a subject, but not used as a medium, during the first three years of primary schooling. Better teaching methods, better training of teachers, and better materials may overcome this problem, but it has yet to be proved.

New primary approaches in teaching English
Recognition of the comparative ineffectiveness and wastefulness of vernacular medium teaching in the early classes, the accepted need to learn English, and the sterility of much instruction in language when taught as a 'subject' have led to the adoption of planned and controlled English medium teaching at the earliest stages in some countries. Ghana and Kenya pioneered this approach, although the Kenya experiments have been the more thoroughgoing. In Kenya, the original concept of using a new approach to English teaching as a means to reform and vitalize *all* primary teaching generated what is now called there the New Primary Approach. As this involves the sole use of English as the medium from the beginning, it raises very great problems of training and retraining teachers and of materials production.[1]

[1] These problems have been analysed in depth by Hutasoit and Prator (1965) in a study of the 'New Primary Approach' in the schools of Kenya. See also 'Training to Teach in English', in Perren (1968) ch. 7.

Dangers may lie in the very success of such projects. While there seems no doubt whatsoever that programmes like these are highly successful when properly supported and controlled, their rapid extension *without* adequate control and guidance can easily lead to dilution, inefficiency and an intolerable strain on teacher-training resources. Moreover, it should perhaps be remembered that both materials and methods at this level cannot effectively be trans-planted from one country to another, even in Africa. The younger the children, the more closely teaching must be linked with family, social and cultural environment; the more necessary it is for materials to be based on local research and development and on try-out and validation in the hands of local teachers. It has been all too easy for Europeans to regard Africa as an area having simple common needs rather than as a continent comprising many states with vastly different social, political and linguistic factors.

The need for research
Africa has attracted a good deal of linguistic research, but on the whole this has been linked to anthropology or sociology rather than to education. Studies of African languages have seldom been made with a view to teaching them as educational media, and have often been applied to the linguistically more 'interesting' languages, spoken only by small groups. Educational research, rare enough in Africa, has as yet done little for language teaching there. The problems of mass teaching of second languages by teachers who themselves are products of African schools and training colleges have yet to be fully recognized. The maintenance of standards of intelligibility where a second language is learnt at second- or third-hand is a special problem of Anglophone areas. But what are such standards? They have yet to be defined. The use of mass media like radio or television has yet to be assessed fully in Africa: aids such as language laboratories are at present certainly not feasible on a wide scale because of their expense, but how far can they be used in training colleges to improve the teachers' command of English or French? This question would repay careful study.

Both English and French must be taught in Africa as African languages, rather than as extensions of European cultural be-haviour. On this depends not merely their acceptance by the pupils, but also their usefulness to Africa. The implications are that studies of the current use of English and French by Africans should underlie the construction of teaching materials based on

African interests and needs, as well as on the requirements of younger children.[1]

Partly because there has hitherto been comparatively little educational research in Africa, new findings based on only limited investigation run the danger of being accepted uncritically before they can be carefully validated. This can only be guarded against by increasing research facilities within Africa itself.

ASIA

If in Asia the status of English or French in primary education is unlike that in Africa, the problems of second language teaching are more complex. Countries such as India, Pakistan, Ceylon, Burma, Malaysia, Singapore, Thailand and the Philippines all have declared national language policies and have accepted the task of establishing an Asian language as a national language for educational use as well as a means to develop national unity. At the same time, all of them wish to extend or maintain the teaching of a world language (usually English) as an essential auxiliary for technical and economic development. Although in the primary schools the major need is for the better teaching of languages such as Hindi, Urdu, Sinhalese, Malay and Indonesian to those who do not already speak them, the teaching of English is compulsory in primary schools in many parts of India, in Ceylon, Burma, Malaysia, Singapore, Thailand and the Philippines.

But whatever the relative size and importance of the problems of teaching national languages, it seems that in Asia so far more effort has been expended on research and development directed towards improving the teaching of English. Moreover, there has been all too little work in which problems of teaching both national and world languages have been considered as complementary, closely related or fit subjects for coordination. This may have been in part the result of political factors which have tended to set national language policies in opposition to past colonialist or imperialist connotations of English or French, and partly because overseas aid has been more available to develop English. A number of Asian countries have, however, drastically to increase the efficiency with which *two* second languages are taught in primary schools and it would be best for both if there were much more coordination of experience and

[1] A large-scale survey of the use of various languages in East Africa is, however, now (1968) under way. It will be some time before its findings will affect teaching.

research. The full complexity of Asian problems can only be illustrated by examples from selected countries.

India

Probably the greatest and most complex problems of language teaching in Asia (if not in the world) have to be faced by India. With a primary school enrolment of nearly five million in 1967 India has the problem not only of developing the national language, but also of establishing 15 regional languages as media of instruction at all stages of school and college. Thus, by and large, the Indian pupil has at present to learn *three* languages under the current 'three language formula':

- (a) the language of his state (which in most cases, but not all, is his mother tongue);
- (b) Hindi (or, in the case of those whose mother tongue is Hindi, another Indian language);
- (c) English.

This raises immense problems of teacher training and of the development of varying teaching materials. Different states introduce different languages at different levels: standardization of materials and techniques is not always possible for administrative, let alone linguistic, reasons.

Academic debate as to *when* it would be most profitable to start which language is regarded as a luxury India can ill afford. The compelling facts are that for inter-state communication and to meet the needs of trade, industry, science, commerce, and technology of a rapidly developing nation at least two second languages must be acquired. Evidence at present suggests that the longer they are learned the higher is the pupil's proficiency. So both, or at least one of them, according to local factors, must be started in primary schools.

Needed Research. Because many Indian languages have classical, indeed venerable, sources with established literature, developing modern methods of teaching them for day-to-day communication gives rise to special problems arising from academic conservatism. In spite of the need very little work has yet been possible in developing materials or training teachers to teach modern Indian languages as second languages. A few investigations are, however, reported in the compilation of spoken and understood vocabulary of pre-school and primary school children in Hindi, Tamil, Gujarati, and a few other Indian languages. Work in the development of Hindi includes the preparation of texts for use by non-Hindi speakers, translation of literature to and from Hindi, radio lessons in Hindi and the preparation of new technical vocabularies.

The teaching of English is being aided by the production of graded and suitably orientated texts in several states, and through the wider use of audio-visual aids and mass media such as radio (and in Delhi, television). Special institutes to retrain teachers and teacher-trainers have been established in many states, since the older traditions of teaching English (based often on its former use as a medium) do not accord well with present needs.

Malaya

There was a long tradition of English-medium teaching in Malayan primary schools, in which many children of Malay, Chinese and Tamil origin learned English through intensive exposure to the language, but recent policy has encouraged the establishment of many more Malay-medium primary schools. However, in 1965 approximately two-thirds of secondary education was still given in English. In 1967, Malay became the national and sole official language: there is need for development of materials to teach Malay as a second language in primary schools, as well as to teach English by economical methods where it is no longer used as a medium. This, as has been recognized by Malay authorities, involves far-reaching development in the Malay language itself as a vehicle to convey educational concepts (especially in written form) not hitherto associated with the language. Malaya thus has at the same time the problems of developing (and 'modernizing') a language and of teaching it more extensively both as a mother tongue and as a second language, quite apart from the needs of efficient English teaching.

The Philippines

In the Philippines, although the major vernaculars are the media of early primary instruction, they are replaced by English in the third grade—intensive teaching of English to facilitate the change being begun in grade 1. However, the national language, Pilipino, is taught as a *subject* throughout primary and secondary classes. Unlike India or Malaya, the Philippines thus are encouraging the use of a *world* language as the general medium of instruction, while teaching a *national* language for more limited purposes. Coordinated programmes of training and research relating to both languages have been of considerable help in improving efficiency in teaching both.

There is no space to examine the special problems of Ceylon, Indonesia or Burma, but all seek a balance between the need to establish national languages (sometimes having to provide for linguistic minorities) and the need for teaching a world language (usually English) to assist national economic development. All are faced by shortages of teachers with the necessary command of languages to teach them or even with basic training in pedagogics.

A REVIEW OF SOME MAJOR PROBLEMS

Enough has been said to show that the problems of language teaching in the primary schools of Africa and Asia are not only vastly greater and more complex than in those of Europe, but also very much more urgent. Many developing countries, on achieving independence, inherited from their colonial past educational systems which catered only for a fraction of their rapidly expanding populations. Moreover, these systems had sometimes been designed to produce a comparatively limited number of highly educated people rather than to serve as a basis for universal schooling. Their curricula were accordingly suitable for the selected few rather than for the majority of the population or indeed for the capabilities of the potential supply of locally-trained teachers. The need to readjust curricula to widespread education, to a relative drop in the numbers of highly trained teachers, and to the needs of new national language policies, imposed an additional strain on educational systems already being tightly stretched by expansion to meet popular demands for more schools.

Under any conditions, the development of language skills is assumed to be fundamental to primary education—whether these are simply reading and writing in a common mother tongue, or establishing a common language for oral communication. But, in Asia, particularly, the establishment of common literacy itself is no simple matter. Asian languages use a multiplicity of different scripts. The Indian primary pupil may successively have to learn to read in three kinds of characters, as well as to control the phonological, syntactical and lexical structures of three unrelated languages.

Languages of wider communication (such as English, Malay, or

Swahili) all have certain problems of instability. The more widely a language is spoken as a second language, the greater is the likelihood of accepted local variations arising in its pronunciation, syntax and lexis. Teachers of such languages have the problem of deciding a realistic *model* of pronunciation and usage, which can be achieved by their pupils. Such a model must satisfy criteria of both international and local intelligibility as well as of teachability. Aiming at classical or precise forms of the 'best' English, Malay, Swahili or Hindi may not only be unrealistic, but unprofitable if the aims are ever achieved. Certainly in Africa and Asia the learner of a language such as English must acquire a wide degree of tolerance in understanding varieties of English if the language is to be of maximum use to him.

Where the former use of a language as a medium of teaching is displaced by its teaching as a subject only (as with English in Ceylon, India or Malaya), a great change in teaching techniques is required. New, tightly organized and more intensive teaching must replace older 'exposure' techniques. There is no room for irrelevance and aims must exclude all but essentials; probably all unnecessary cultural conflicts should be avoided. It is interesting to note that in the existing state of knowledge about younger children's language learning, in both India and Africa it is assumed that the improvement of English requires teaching it sooner—giving it more time. But how much time can be spared? Is there not a danger that unless the aims and techniques of language teaching are made very much more economical and efficient, the primary (and secondary school) pupil in many countries may spend nearly all his time learning the different scripts, syntactical patterns and vocabularies of language codes which have little correlation? In this confusion, how will the need to develop clear social, mathematical and scientific concepts fare? Exactly *how far* 'language structures thought' is open to discussion; that a child's thinking is largely dependent on his control of his mother tongue is a fundamental assumption of primary education. A language may, by its particular 'code', constrain thinking. Where second languages are learnt for use (and they must be learnt for use if learnt at all) different 'codes' may conflict in constraining or affecting behaviour.[1]

Where, in this great field of effort, lie the priorities for research? And how far can research be coordinated? There are obvious problems of teacher-training, both initial and in-service, which

[1] Cf. in relation to the mother tongue, Bernstein (1965).

require study on new lines. Not only are many more teachers of languages urgently needed, but they must be trained in methods unlike those of the past. The development of new teaching materials to suit the capabilities of teachers must go hand in hand with their training. Linguistic research of many kinds is necessary, but especially to determine the range of ability in a language which is necessary for its use as a medium for learning at various levels, so that the skills to be taught shall be of the greatest relevance and use to the pupils. The psychology of language learning—especially of learning two or more new languages simultaneously—in relation to particular mother tongues, is a vast and comparatively unexplored area. It seems likely, for example, that there is a greater difference in language learning attitudes (arising from maturation) in the age range 7–12 than in any other comparable span of schooling. Thus lowering by a year the age of beginning a language in the primary school may call for a much greater change in materials and methods than a similar shift would in the secondary school. The appropriateness of various techniques to particular ages within the primary school needs defining by careful experiment. While it is clear enough that for young children, the early use of a new language as a medium provides great stimulus for learning it, this approach puts a very heavy responsibility on the teacher and, moreover, can hardly be used for more than one new language at a time.

For administrators a special problem lies in recognizing the 'surrender value' of language proficiency acquired at various levels: the needs of the early school-leaver must not be sacrificed to the demands of a higher education which he will never receive.

4

Social factors and second language policies

E. F. O'DOHERTY[1]

There is a sense in which everything one does, with the possible exceptions of idiosyncrasies and simple sensory responses, will be affected by the social setting. It is inevitable that a social institution of such importance as language will be dependent on the social setting perhaps even more than on individual personality factors. Language can be thought of primarily as a device for interpersonal communication. It is thus the social institution *par excellence*. For although organisms other than man can certainly communicate with one another, they do not do so by patterned sets of conventional signs. The language of a group is an integral component of its culture. In terms of the concept of culture-patterns, which are thought of as forming living wholes of interrelated parts, a change in the language of the group will entail far-reaching consequences for the people whose culture it is. This is fairly obvious in the case of a change from one language to another (e.g. the replacement of Irish by English in Ireland over several centuries) but is not so obvious when the replacement is not complete, but where the two languages coexist within the same culture. This is the case in perhaps a majority of nation-states in the world today, and is a consequence of the phenomenon noted in the report of the first Hamburg meeting: 'Bilingualism . . . may be almost as essential as literacy' (Stern, 1967, p. 7).

THE CHOICE OF A SECOND LANGUAGE

The rapid increase of contacts between politically separate entities

[1] The author of this chapter, Professor Rev. E. F. O'Doherty (Ireland), was chairman of group 3 of the second Hamburg meeting, and the group report formed the basis of the study. The other members of the group were: Mr J. O. J. Vanden Bossche (Unesco Institute for Education, Hamburg; rapporteur), Professor S. Baridon (Italy), Professor A. Lahlou (Morocco), and Mr A. Legrand (Unesco, Paris).—Ed.

since the Second World War, together with a reduction in the potency of the concept of sovereignty of the individual nation, has resulted in the unprecedented growth of second language teaching and learning, and of interest in the problems it produces. It is clear that the choice of the second or third language which a social group may make will be determined by a variety of social criteria which will vary with the particular group concerned. Some of the social criteria moreover will affect the individual motivations involved in second language learning. One might therefore attempt a schematic presentation of the motivations involved in the problem of second language teaching and learning as follows (see Fig. 1).

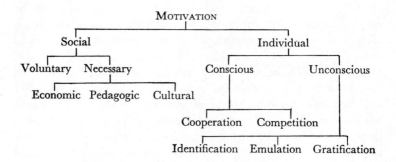

Figure 1. Motivations in second language teaching and learning

In the past, one can easily find examples of voluntary social motivations determining the choice of second language learning. French in Russia, Poland and Prussia, in the eighteenth and nineteenth centuries, is a good example. Choice of this kind is perhaps usually bound up with cultural-prestige factors, rather than with socio-economic factors. Thus, a low-prestige culture may adopt the language of a high-prestige culture as a deliberate act of choice. In this case the adopted language will be seen to fulfil a function other than that of communication: it becomes a symbol in its own right—a symbol of civilization, culture, social class, perhaps of privilege. In such circumstances, another phenomenon may rapidly appear: the *first* language of the group may acquire a new symbolic significance. It may come to symbolize the traditional values, perhaps even the cultural identity and political unity of the group. This has happened in Europe many times, and may be reasonably expected to happen in Africa fairly soon.

But in general, one may say that the choice of a second language is now much less a matter of cultural prestige than of economic necessity.

Economic factors

This is probably the most obvious of the necessary social motivations leading to the adoption of a second language. The point is made in several conference papers.[1]

Technological factors

The necessity of a second language for purposes of higher education has been recognized in some countries for a comparatively long time. Apart from considerations of higher education, however, the need for a second language of wide diffusion and high technological achievement has become apparent in many countries at much lower levels on the educational scale. In some of the new nations of Africa and Asia, which are undergoing rapid technological change, this very change itself demands a thorough grounding in a second language (English or French as the case may be) even at primary school level.

It is clear that many other factors, cultural, religious and political, may enter into the determination of the precise second language chosen in a given society (Lewis, 1965, pp. 87–137). Some of the socio-cultural aspects of second language learning—attitudes of one group to another, and the changes in such attitudes consequent upon the learning of the language of the second group (Lambert, 1965, pp. 44–55), social and cultural consequences for the individual child (Lewis, 1965, pp. 150–5)—have been dealt with in former reports. A valuable brief overview of work in this area will be found in Titone (1964, pp. 21, seq.). According to Titone, these 'external factors' of a socio-cultural kind 'are easily reducible to the motivational category'. Thus, a favourable attitude to the group whose language one is learning will ceteris paribus facilitate the learning process; and again, those who have already learned a second language will show more favourable attitudes to the group whose language it is than those who do not know the second language in question. Similar results have been found, e.g. by Riestra and Johnson (1962). The social value, prestige or status of the second language is, as one might expect, found to be related to the ease or otherwise of learning it. Culture conflict can arise if the

[1] E.g. Gineste (c.p.) and Lahlou (c.p.).

learner of a second language feels that his own native culture is threatened by the spread of the second language. Haugen (1956) underlines the importance of such culture conflicts. Problems of personality adjustment among bilinguals are due to their 'bicultural position' in the first instance, and only secondarily to internal personality factors. On the other hand, it is recognized that a second language can the more readily be learned in its own distinct cultural context. It would seem then that culture conflict of some kind is a price one has to pay for the inestimable benefits of genuine bilingualism.

SOCIAL CONSEQUENCES OF THE INTRODUCTION OF A SECOND LANGUAGE

The economic, technological and cultural values resulting from the introduction of a second language into a society must be carefully weighed against the possible adverse social consequences. The evidence from history, linguistics, and cultural anthropology must be taken into account.

History

It has perhaps been too easily taken for granted that the spread of a single *lingua franca*, or the adoption of a single national language throughout a nation-state, would operate as a unifying factor for the community. But if this is done to the detriment of a local minority language, or even if it is experienced as a threat to the local language, such a policy may be divisive and lead to serious conflict. The experience of France in relation to Breton, Spain in relation to Catalan, Italy in relation to the German-speaking regions of the north must be taken into account. A minority linguistic group, experiencing its minority language under threat of extermination, will understandably stiffen its resistance to the spread of the majority language. Care must therefore be taken to see to it that such minority languages are preserved, and their cultural and human values respected, while the need for a language of wider diffusion is sympathetically brought home to the minority language group. Parallel considerations must be borne in mind where the second language, however necessary as a temporary measure for economic, technological or educational reasons, is that of a foreign power or of a different ideology. In these circumstances, a point may be reached where the receiving culture becomes strong enough to be conscious of itself as a distinct national entity, with its native language as a symbol of its distinct identity. It is relatively easy for a language to become a symbol in its own right, as a bearer of traditional values, allegiances, and aspirations. Just as each word of a language is a symbol, or conventional sign, so the language system as a whole may become a higher-order symbol. It is commonly believed that the thought-forms and attitudes of a people are moulded by their language, so that it is easy to understand how a language change can be felt as a threat to identity. While there is in fact no evidence for the beliefs just mentioned, the fact that they are believed gives them functional significance for those who believe them, in accordance with a well-known sociological principle.

There is a further point to note here, which may have far-ranging consequences. It is the fact that a language may in a relatively short period of time attain high cultural and scientific status. The position of German would seem to be a case in point in the past. It is conceivable that other languages, not now of high international, scientific, or literary status, may rise rapidly in this way.

The conclusion to be drawn from these considerations is that those who are in charge of a second language policy in their communities must be ready at all times to keep the positions of both the first and second language under constant review, and perhaps even learn to anticipate the points at which significant changes may be expected to occur.

Languages in contact

In terms of the known history of languages in proximity, borrowings, cross-fertilization and interpenetration of each by the other is probably to be anticipated. The history of the English language after the Norman Conquest illustrates the point. The version of the Irish language as spoken by non-native speakers whose vernacular is English would repay study in this connexion. France has taken measures to preserve the purity of French, but the growth of *franglais* again illustrates the phenomenon in a small way. It is possible that languages of wide diffusion and high cultural status can survive such cross-fertilization and interpenetration, but the effects on lower-status minority languages should be reckoned with. Such languages, while standing in greater need of borrowings, neologisms, etc., may not be able to survive massive cross-fertilization. Research must be carried out by linguists and cultural anthropologists in this area.

Cultural anthropology

The closely related disciplines of cultural and social anthropology, sociology, and social psychology have their contribution to make. The function of language as a factor in a culture pattern has already been alluded to. The second Hamburg meeting drew particular attention to some of these problems. It noted in particular the phenomenon of social mobility in relation to the learning of second languages. Such mobility is of two kinds, horizontal and vertical. Horizontal mobility refers to the geographical displacement within a community, or between states, as when a minority language speaker or a dialect speaker moves for seasonal employment. Vertical mobility refers to the shift up or down the social scale within the community. It would seem that social mobility in this latter sense may be closely related to proficiency in a high-prestige second language. Within a given language, in a highly stratified society, there are 'sub-languages' characteristic of a particular class. In a rapidly developing nation, a similar phenomenon may occur with regard to the second, or foreign, language. There have been examples in the fairly recent history of Europe.

Personality factors

There is a reciprocal relationship between culture and personality. The culture is itself a creation of human persons, which in its turn through all the modes of education at its disposal, formal and informal, moulds the personalities of its members. Thus the radical changes in a culture which may result from the widespread diffusion of a second language may be expected to affect the personality of the members of the group. One cannot expect to introduce a process of change and at the same time avoid the consequences of the change one has introduced.

These principles have certain obvious consequences for the learning of second languages. The child learns very largely through the process of identification. It follows that the closer the identification with the culture of the second language, the easier will be the learning process. The second language must be given functional significance in the child's world before it can truly function as a language. Without this, it may remain at the level of a mere coding and decoding instrument. In order to give it functional significance, a 'reward' mechanism directly related to language must be built in. Entertainment, reading, television programmes and other forms of play activity must be viable in the child's world if a language is to function for the child *as a language*. The effect of language as a control mechanism in relation to behaviour, as a source of voluntary action, and as a reward mechanism in its own right, is well known to psychologists, especially as a result of the work of Luria and his colleagues in Moscow. In addition to availing of these insights in pedagogy, an adequate programme of second language teaching must avail of them as sociological phenomena.

Language learning and the family

The consequences of second language learning for the family present a rich source of research for the sociologist and the psychologist. Do families in rapid social transition (mobility up the social scale) acquire proficiency in a second language, or even change their vernacular more readily than families in a relatively more static position on the social scale? Does the acquisition of a second language by the children, when this is not known to the parents, or when the parents are not fluent in it, affect the cohesion, unity and stability of the family? Does the attempt by parents to use a second language, not their own vernacular, and not the language of ordinary social intercourse in their environment, have adverse effects on the children's linguistic competence or does it have an impoverishing effect on their conceptual capacity? There is some impressionistic evidence that all these questions should get an affirmative answer. Probably the monoglot family is the statistical norm throughout the world. But the number of families wherein the parents are of widely differing linguistic origin and background would seem to be increasing. In the monoglot family, the child probably finds a certain security in the single-language communication system. What are the effects if any when the parents communicate with him in different systems?

RESEARCH PROPOSALS

Although language is such an obvious and important social phenomenon, relatively little is known about the social psychology of second language learning. It is a matter of common experience that a child who does not speak the language of his peer group at play, will very rapidly acquire some competence in the peer group's language. If this is so, the following questions can be asked:

1 What is the minimum, maximum, and optimum size of a group for purposes of the linguistic integration of a new incoming member? (If the number is too small, the group may not be able to integrate

the new member, or may adopt his language to some extent, while
if it is too large, the new member may remain a linguistic isolate.)

2 Within the peer group, what is the order of language acquisition by
the new member, in terms of phonemes, words, formal structures, etc. ?

It would appear that some children acquire a relatively high proficiency in a second language by means of a relatively brief stay in
the second language environment. For example, a few months stay
in France might bring the average British child to a level of active
and passive mastery of French equivalent to several years of primary
school teaching. In Ireland there is some evidence that a short
sojourn of even one month or less in an exclusively Irish-speaking
environment benefits the primary school learner of Irish as a second
language more than the school itself can do in perhaps several
years. We need to ask:

3 What are the relative merits of prolonged school instruction in
the second language in the environment of the first language (e.g.
three years), compared to short experience of the linguistically
saturated environment of L2 (e.g. three months) ?

4 What are the economics of the two situations indicated in
research No. 3? In other words, if the aim of a second language
programme is the facilitation of trade, or cultural studies, etc.,
across linguistic frontiers, as distinct from a second language programme geared to the very survival of a community (e.g. Common
Market countries' second language needs, as compared to the
second language needs of the newly emergent African states), and
if investigation should show that the percentage of school children
exposed to a second language in the primary school who actually
reach the stage of using the second language as a normal means of
communication is relatively small, and if moreover it should emerge
that a similar or greater proportion could reach a comparable level
of mastery through a brief sojourn in the environment of the second
language, the economics of this could have profound effects on
second language policy.

The Report on the International Seminar held at Aberystwyth
in 1960 (Lewis, 1965, p. 109) discusses the difference between individual and social bilingualism. Some countries seem to have as
their express aim, a linguistic situation describable perhaps as
social bilingualism, i.e. where the very society itself would live and
function in two linguistic environments simultaneously, as distinct
from, e.g. the Swiss situation, where each individual may be

bilingual and the state be a multilingual state, but each social unit or linguistic community is socially monoglot. We need to know:

5 To what extent is social bilingualism possible? In other words, what happens when a society as such has at its disposal two distinct intrasocial communication systems? Has such a society ever existed? Is the result a *mélange* (Anglo-Norman-French), or the driving out of one language by the other (on the analogy of currency), or the division of the community into two linguistic groups, with possible detriment to the society as a whole? It seems clearly to be important that policy makers should understand the possible long-range effects of a language policy aimed on the one hand at producing many bilingual individuals, and on the other hand one aimed at producing a bilingual *society*.

In order to survive, a social institution must have functional significance for those for whom it is an institution. The functional significance of second language learning is fairly easily seen at university and secondary school levels (introduction to a new literature, a new culture, commerce, travel, etc.). It is not so clear that second language learning at primary school level has a functional significance *for the child*. We need to know:

6 What are the typical and significant attitudes of children at different age levels to their exposure to a second language? This raises the question of motivation, reward, reality relationships, time and space orientation in the second language, play activities, and the causes of antipathy or negativism in respect of the second language.

While there is no doubt about the value of a second language as a cultural and technological instrument in the developing countries, the whole problem of the relationship of first and second languages in a community is complicated by very powerful emotional factors. The second language may carry emotional overtones of colonialism or occupation, while the first language may become a symbol in its own right (of liberation, or cultural identity, etc.). We need to know:

7 What factors lead up to the critical flashpoint when the second language is likely to be rejected in favour of the first language? Historical, social, anthropological studies are necessary here.

8 It is strongly recommended that a full-scale conference be convened composed of experts in the social sciences (sociology, anthropology, psychology, history, and many others) who have shown an interest and a competence in language problems, in order to focus their expertise on some of the above problems.

5

Psychological and educational research into second language teaching to young children

JOHN B. CARROLL[1]

INTRODUCTION

Without doubt, one of the most fascinating domains of controversy in the realm of education centres around the question of whether it is desirable and feasible to teach foreign or second languages to young children. This is a matter of interest to parents, whether they belong, on the one hand, to that increasing number who feel that teaching their children a second language at an early age will give those children a host of educational advantages, or belong, on the other hand, to the group who feel that second language teaching for children at an early age is unnecessary or even harmful. It is a matter of interest to the thoughtful layman, whether he be a parent or not, if only because he will often notice the apparently remarkable results that occur when a child has the opportunity to learn a second language at an early age. And certainly it is a matter of interest to the educator, who has to weigh all the educational, social, political and economic factors that must be considered in the formulation of educational policy as to the role of second language teaching in the curriculum, and particularly as to whether second language teaching should be brought into the curriculum of the primary school, and if so, when and how.

There are, of course, certain situations in which practical necessity forces educational decisions on these matters. In developing

[1] This chapter by Professor J. B. Carroll (formerly at Harvard University) is a slightly adapted version of a paper read at Amerika-Haus, Hamburg, 11 May 1966, entitled 'Trends and Developments in Second Language Teaching to Young Children'. Professor Carroll is now a Senior Research Psychologist at Educational Testing Service, Princeton, N.J., USA.—Ed.

countries like Ghana, Senegal, or the Philippine Republic, it has been found imperative as a matter of national policy to introduce children to a second language in the early grades of the primary school.

In certain bilingual countries or regions, social and political factors are also predominant. At the other extreme, there are countries, like Australia and New Zealand, where the practical necessity for children to learn a second language is ordinarily at a minimum.

In the great majority of countries, however, it is simply a matter of conscience, so to speak, whether efforts should be expended to give young children the opportunity to learn a second language. I say it is a matter of conscience because fundamentally it is a question of how much importance is attached to foreign language competence from the standpoint of the values of a liberal education and the well-being of the individual and of the nation involved. Take the case of the United States, which belongs in this group. If the American parent or educator believes strongly in the importance of having large numbers of citizens competent in foreign languages, for whatever reason, he will certainly give attentive consideration to any arguments that may be advanced in favour of foreign language teaching for young children. Of course, he may still decide that it is better to delay the introduction of foreign languages to beyond the primary school, but if he makes this decision, it will be on the basis of psychological or economic factors. At the same time it could be true, and is true, that a fairly large segment of the American population does not attach much importance to second language competence, whether rightly or wrongly, on the grounds that the ordinary citizen has little need or use for foreign language competence.

POPULAR IDEAS ON LANGUAGE LEARNING

Whatever the situation may be, there is in every country a great deal of speculation about the values and effects of early language learning. One of the most popular ideas is that young children learn a foreign language more readily and easily than older children or adults. This idea stems from observations of the fact that under certain conditions young children do indeed become very fluent in a second language. What is often ignored is that the conditions are rather specialized and not always easily arranged or duplicated in schools, and that even under these specialized conditions not every child learns the second language as well as his mother tongue. A closely related idea is that a child who once learns a second language at an early age and then forgets it through disuse can more easily relearn it at a later age, and can do so with a much better control of pronunciation and grammar than older learners. Although one can find instances in which this has appeared to be the case, it is by no means clear that this would be true in *every* case of relearning, for it is obviously wrong to generalize from only the 'positive' instances that one happens to notice.

Another area of popular speculation is the question of whether the populations of different countries differ in their national aptitude or propensity for foreign language learning, and if so, whether those differences would show themselves in the young children of those countries. I remember that it used to be frequently said, in the United States, that Americans have less aptitude for languages than, say, continental Europeans. I am glad to say that this national inferiority complex has for the most part withered away in the face of contrary evidence, but the question still has some pertinence in view of the now well-known fact that *individuals*, at least, differ in aptitude for second language learning.

Still another area of concern is that of the methods by which young children are to be taught a foreign language, once one has decided that children *are* to be taught a foreign language. Opinion is divided as to whether second language learning is fundamentally similar to first language learning, or whether it is fundamentally different. My own view is that if it is truly a *second* language acquired after the first language is mastered to ordinary fluency and control, the acquisition of such a second language is indeed fundamentally different from learning a first language, because the learner has already acquired most of the ordinary concepts and ideational processes in which any language trades. But even if it is fundamentally different in this sense, there is still wide latitude for variation in the techniques by which a second language is taught. Should it be taught by the presentation and practice of explicit grammatical rules, or taught mainly by the use of live demonstration and imitation? To what extent should production of language use in real communication situations be emphasized? You will recognize that such questions arise in all second language teaching, but they have a special force, or special implications, when we are dealing with the teaching of young children, if only because, as the developmental psychologists tell us, young minds are in many ways different from older ones.

RESEARCH ON LANGUAGE LEARNING

Thus far I have been merely outlining the problems one faces in considering the teaching of foreign languages to children, and the popular ideas that surround this whole question. It is small wonder that many people who are concerned about problems of FLES[1] have appealed to psychologists and other researchers in education to shed light on these problems.

But now, in the eyes of many educators, the psychologist or the educational researcher is an exasperatingly frustrating person to deal with. The main trouble, it seems, is that the psychologist never seems to give any really convincing or satisfying answers. In fact, the psychologist doesn't seem even to have convinced himself of any of the answers he gives, and if he has, he is nothing but a dogmatic *poseur*. The educational researcher seems always to go to a great deal of trouble and expense, taking a great deal of time on the part of everybody concerned and causing much disturbance to normal school conditions, only to come up with an inconclusive report that ends with the statement that 'further research is needed'.

I do not wish to apologize for the educational researcher but rather to spread, if I can, greater understanding of his problems, attitudes and methods. The educational researcher is not a wilful obstructionist. Instead, his position is rather like that of a judge in a court of law, in that his business is to doubt, to be sceptical, and collect carefully all the evidence before he renders a judgement. He is at the opposite pole from the fanatic enthusiast or proponent of a particular doctrine who often in fact consciously or unconsciously ignores evidence contrary to his point of view. If he seems to be over-eager to disturb normal arrangements in schools in order to do his research, it is because it is only through special techniques of manipulating events and measuring the effects of these manipulations that he can gather the evidence he requires. If his conclusions seem not to be conclusions at all, it is only because he retains his scepticism and cautiousness even to the end of his researches.

As a matter of fact it is quite fashionable among psychologists and other behavioural scientists to say that 'next to nothing is known' about a problem. For example, some psychologists have said or

[1] FLES is the commonly used abbreviation in the USA for Foreign Languages in Elementary Schools. See chapter 2, pp. 17-18.

written that 'almost nothing' is known about child language learning, let alone second language learning. I can agree that certain aspects of these processes are not well understood, but at the same time I submit that we do indeed know a great deal about this area of investigation. Above all, we can state and describe the conditions under which children will, with high probability, learn some given skill like speaking a foreign language. Making such statements more detailed and precise is one of the very useful tasks of research, and this includes research in second language learning in young children.

For let us note here that a great many courageous educators, in many different countries, have undertaken to teach second languages to children, and on the whole their efforts have been successful. It is one of the tasks of research to document these successes. Children can and do learn second languages just as they learn other things at school. Surprisingly enough this is a fact that is often over-looked in connection with research projects. That is to say, in the researcher's zeal to find which one of several teaching methods is superior, he may fail to note adequately that his experimental sub-jects achieve remarkable gains under any or all of the methods being compared. The failure to find any one of the methods superior to the others sometimes means that the research report is never pub-lished, with the result that the information that may be more important—the amount of learning that went on—is lost to view.

CHILD AND ADULT AS LANGUAGE LEARNERS

I must now turn to the attempt to report some substantive findings on some large questions that I pointed out earlier.

What about the question of whether young children are better learners than adolescents and adults? I have stated already the obvious fact that children can and do learn second languages. The report of the 1962 Hamburg meeting contains adequate documenta-tion of this fact. But the question asks whether children learn languages better or faster than older persons. Unfortunately a satisfactory answer to this question has not yet been obtained. The reason for this is simply that nobody has yet bothered to take the kinds of precise measurements that an answer to the question requires. That is to say, before we can really determine the compara-tive rates of learning, we would have to have comparable data for child and adult learning—data on how much time is required by each group to attain definable or even quantifiable stages of learning. For example, we might find that it takes the average 8-year-old child X number of hours of instruction to attain a certain level of mastery, while it takes the average adult Y number of hours to attain that level of mastery. We then compare X and Y and decide which group is the faster in its learning. As you may see, there are some difficulties here. For one thing, the pace of instruction is ordinarily different for children and adults. In the FLES courses with which I am familiar, the child studies the foreign language only a few minutes a day, so that it takes him several years to accumulate the number of instructional hours that an adult might accumulate in a few weeks in an intensive course. My studies of intensive courses with adults suggest that it takes between 250 and 500 hours of instruction to attain a comfortable, ordinary level of control and fluency in a foreign language, and it takes much longer to attain any really high level of competence. I base these figures on certain test results. So the question of whether the child is a faster learner than an adult is one of whether he can attain the levels of mastery in less time than an adult.

But another problem presents itself: there are qualitative differences in the kind of language mastery attained by children and adults. The kinds of things children are interested in talking about are not the kinds of things adults are interested in talking about and these differences are reflected in the courses of instruction that are ordinarily provided for the two age levels. I doubt if we could persuade an adult to learn a foreign language using the materials that a child would use. Therefore any experiment comparing child and adult learning rates would probably be operationally unfeasible.

On the whole, therefore, I am pessimistic as to whether a good answer to this question of learning rates will ever be forthcoming through research. Perhaps the question is a meaningless one unless we rephrase it in terms of quite specific aspects of language learning, like the acquisition of pronunciation, or of grammar, or of vocabulary.

On the question of pronunciation, there is reasonably good evidence that children generally make faster progress than adults. Suppose we start one group of children learning a foreign language in the first grade, another in the second grade, another in the third grade, and so on up to say the tenth grade, and give them all roughly the same amount of exposure to a foreign language using good native-speaking models. No experiment of this precise form has ever been done to my knowledge, but the evidence that I do know (Kirch, 1956) suggests that the earlier the child is started, the faster he will attain a good pronunciation of the foreign language. All this makes good psychological sense, because the younger child does not have to overcome the force of previously established habits to the extent that the older child does. The situation is quite analogous to that in the development of skill in such activities as violin playing or tennis playing. It is well known that few adults ever attain high skill in such activities if they start learning them *as adults*.

I have been led to speculate, in fact, that the popular idea that children are faster learners than adults stems largely from the observation that they acquire better pronunciation. After all, a good accent is the most easily observable aspect of language competence.

On the question of the rate of acquiring grammar and vocabulary, the evidence is less clear. Presumably we could make experiments on this—starting children learning foreign languages at different ages and measuring their progress in vocabulary and grammar. On the whole, I believe the evidence suggests that children learn control of grammatical structure at about the same rate as adults, and that adults—at least young adults—can learn second language vocabulary faster than children. Most of this evidence is impressionistic, however, rather than being based on careful measurements. I simply do not know whether it would be possible to do comparative experiments that would give us clear answers on these matters. With regard to vocabulary learning, my evidence is based on the rate at which people of different ages can learn foreign language vocabulary in a laboratory setting.

PROBABLE ADVANTAGES OF AN EARLY START

Although, as you can see, I am somewhat pessimistic as to the possibility of getting clear research answers about whether children are faster language learners than adults, there are certain practical considerations that argue for early language learning. If learning a foreign language takes time, the earlier it is started the better. Children can be given more time to practise the use of a language, and they can do it over longer periods. A recent result in my own research illustrates this. I have been studying the foreign language attainments of students graduating from American colleges and universities with 'majors' in foreign languages. In the spring of 1964, I arranged for a large sample of such students to be tested with the MLA Proficiency Tests for Teachers or Advanced Students, in

French, German, Italian, Spanish or Russian, depending on the language in which the students specialized. In all, nearly 3,000 students were tested, comprising about 25 per cent of all foreign language majors graduating from college in that year. In analysing the scores on these tests, we found that in all four skills, students who reported starting their foreign language in the elementary school did strikingly better, on the average, than those who started in the secondary school; likewise, those who started their foreign language study in the secondary school did clearly better than those who started it at the college or university level. Obviously, the longer the period of study, the better the achievement, so this result is not surprising. It argues for an early start in language learning in the sense that those who do start early have more opportunity to perfect their knowledge if indeed they continue their study. Nevertheless, I must point out that not only in this research which I am now reporting, but in many other studies, there are many cases of persons who started foreign language learning at a relatively late age—in adolescence or adulthood—and still achieved very high competence, even in pronunciation. My opinion is that the amount of competence one achieves is largely a matter of the amount of time spent in learning, rather than the actual age of starting. Thus the argument for early language learning depends mostly on the fact that such an early start is likely to allow more time to be spent.

Now let us look at the problems in answering the question of whether early learning of a foreign language makes it easier to relearn that foreign language at a later age, or the related question of whether such early learning gives the student an advantage in learning still another foreign language. On the first of these questions I know of no solid research evidence. For some reason, nobody has ever bothered to conduct a relearning experiment, to my knowledge. Yet all we know about the general psychology of learning would suggest that there would in fact be a substantial advantage for an adult relearning a foreign language if he had learned it in childhood and 'forgotten' it. There is, of course, considerable anecdotal evidence in support of this idea. If this idea is true, we can conclude the early learning of a foreign language would not be a waste of time for the child who may need to relearn that language at a later age.

But what about learning *another* language? There has been some research on this question, but it is inconclusive, and in any case does not concern the effects of foreign language learning in the

primary school, but rather the effects of learning *one* language in
the secondary school on the rate of learning *another* language in the
secondary school or at the college level. Yet, it is said common
experience and anecdotal evidence support the idea that learning
one language assists in learning another language. There is great
danger in accepting this evidence, however, because, first, it does
not take account of the fact that the amount of transfer may depend
simply on linguistic factors. For example, learning Spanish will
probably assist in learning Italian because of the general similarity
of structure and vocabulary, whereas it would not assist in learning,
say, Finnish, an entirely unrelated language. Secondly, there is a
selective bias in this kind of anecdotal evidence. Persons who claim
that learning one language assists in learning other languages are
probably good language learners in any case—that is, they have
good aptitude for language learning; and thus we fail to take note
of the cases of people who have difficulty in learning their first
foreign language and probably fail even to try to learn another
language. On the other hand, my own research has suggested that
prior language learning does help in predicting success in learning
a new language independently of measured language aptitude.
Psychological learning theory, also, gives some basis for predicting
that early learning of one language may give some assistance in
learning a new language at a later age in so far as the skills and
processes of such learning are transferred.

INDIVIDUAL DIFFERENCES

Next we must address ourselves to the question of individual differences in second language learning at an early age. How much I
can say about this depends on the age at which such learning is
started. We know very little about differences in language aptitude
before the age of about 9 or 10. It is possible, although I do not
know this, that children from, say 4 to 8, would show little variation
in their readiness to learn a second language, just as in the very
early years, from 2 to 4 years of age, they show relatively little
variation in the speed with which they acquire their mother
tongue, apart from gross differences in intelligence or mental
ability. By the age of 9 or 10, and later, there is clear evidence that
children do vary in their aptitude for learning a foreign language,
that is to say, in the speed and facility with which they can acquire
a foreign language. The evidence is of two sorts. First, experience in

teaching the children at this age suggests considerable variation in language aptitude. For example, Dunkel and Pillet (1962), in their published report on teaching French in an elementary school in Chicago, say that some 10 to 20 per cent of the children who show normal or superior progress in most school subjects appear to have a distinct lack of ability in foreign languages, and these authors do not claim to know how to teach such children. A second kind of evidence comes from testing. I have found it possible to develop tests of language aptitude that can be given as early as age 9 or 10 and that predict the amount of success the child will have with the learning of a second language, at least in the normal classroom learning experience.[1] In the light of these considerations, there is some question as to whether all children can be expected to learn a second language with ease and facility. If teaching resources are limited, it may be advisable to select children for foreign language learning by means of an aptitude test.

RESEARCH ON METHODS AND MATERIALS[2]

A third major area in which there has been research interest is that of the methods and materials by which children are to be taught foreign languages. Most of the American research has in fact been concerned with various problems of this kind—particularly with reference to the competence of the teacher and the extent to which untrained teachers can be supplemented, or replaced by audio-visual aids and programmed instruction.

A major project in the United States was the Denver-Stanford project (Hayman and Johnson, 1963) whereby Spanish was taught by television in a two-year programme for the 5th and 6th grades. This project discovered, in essence, that although television teaching produced substantial results, it is much better to supplement it with teaching by live teachers with requisite preparation and experience, or even help from parents where possible.

Similar results have been obtained in other projects—for example that of Garry and Mauriello (1961), who studied the use of the

[1] This test, called 'Modern Language Aptitude Test, Elementary Form', is published by The Psychological Corporation, New York. A German version prepared by W. Correll and K. Ingenkamp was published in 1967 by J. Beltz, Weinheim, Federal Republic of Germany, under the title *Fremdsprachen-Eignungstest für die Unterstufe.*—Ed.

[2] See also chapter 6.

film series *Parlons français*. The main conclusion was that FLES by
TV was successful only to the extent that the TV lessons were
supplemented by the teacher, especially when the teacher was
fluent in French and her lessons had been well prepared.

I could go on with other research reports of this genre, but I
would prefer to turn your attention to an example of a kind of
laboratory experiment in foreign language teaching that I think
may give us insight into what is critical in successful teaching. This
was an unpublished experiment by a student of mine, Kenneth
McKinnon (1965).

McKinnon worked with grade 3 children in an American
suburban elementary school. The language taught was Police Motu,
a somewhat simplified pidgin language of New Guinea, selected
because it was of course totally unfamiliar to the children, and also
because the pronunciation of the language is not sufficiently
standardized to justify requiring the children to pronounce it
accurately.

The major experimental variable was the method of *practice*.
Before any practice sessions were given, the children were brought
to a high level of competence in the sample of Police Motu vocabulary used in the study. Also, before each practice session, there was
a short period in which three Police Motu sentences illustrating a
certain grammatical point were shown to the child with pictures
explaining their meaning; the experimenter also used gestures to
convey the meaning of each word. Now, the practice sessions
themselves exhibited variations in three different experimental
variables, only one of which was the actual method of practice.
Let me, however, describe the three variants of the practice variable
because this was found to be the most crucially important. Method I
was designed to be analogous to the 'pattern practice' method of the
language laboratory, whereby a sentence is presented and the
learner must repeat it. During the practice he was simply to play
Police Motu sentences on a Language Master machine (thus hearing
them spoken) and imitate them as often as he wished until he
thought he could say them very well. He was also told, 'Try to think
what is happening as you hear and say each sentence.' Method II
was similar to Method I except that each Language Master card
contained a pictorial representation of the sentence that was heard,
giving the child an opportunity to practise the sentence with a
concrete presentation of its meaning. In Method III, the child was
required to look at the picture on the card and try to compose the

corresponding Police Motu sentence before playing the card on the Language Master; he could replay the card as often as he wished in order to learn the correct response. It will be seen that the variation among methods was designed to introduce in Method II *situational meaning* of the sentence, and in Method III the feature of *active* rather than passive practice.

The other variables were, first, an 'inductive' vs. a 'deductive' presentation, and second, a regular programme of contrasting sentences vs. an irregular programme of contrasts. In the 'inductive' presentation, the children were not given any special instruction, being allowed to figure out the grammar for themselves. In the 'deductive' presentation, the teacher pointed out the structural features such as 'The word that tells what the person is doing comes at the end of the sentence.' The 'regular' programme presented a sequence of sentences in which only one word changed from one sentence to the next, in order to make the semantic and syntactical correspondences very clear; in the 'varied' programme, the words in each succeeding sentence changed completely.

A variety of criterion tests were employed to measure both passive and active control of the syntactical patterns presented. The results in nearly every instance showed Method III superior to Method II, and Method II in turn superior to Method I. Thus, a kind of practice involving active construction of sentences to match pictured situations was superior to passive practice of such sentences, and the latter method was in turn better than practice of sentences without referential support. These results suggest that mere repetition of sentences is not a desirable method of learning grammatical structure.

The results also showed that the 'deductive' procedure whereby structural features were pointed out and explained to the children produced superior learning. There were in general no important differences in learning produced by the difference between 'regular' and 'varied' materials. In this instance, at least, 'discovery' procedures were less efficient than procedures in which explanations were furnished to guide the children in their language learning. It is true, of course, that these explanations had been given only after a certain amount of experience with the sentences. Thus the situation was analogous to current practices whereby grammar explanations are given only after there has been some experience with the materials about which the explanations are given.

The most important recommendations that seem to come from

this experiment, in so far as it can be generalized, is that the learning of grammar is best done with what I like to call 'referential support', i.e. with the aid of semantic information concerning the content and relations involved in grammatical structures. It also points out the value of active as opposed to passive practice.

CONCLUSION

Let me conclude by giving a general appraisal of the prospects for useful research on second language learning in children. I have pointed out that certain questions in this area are fraught with tremendous methodological and even logical problems. Nevertheless, I do not believe this fact should hold us back. We have the techniques to solve or at least circumvent some of the methodological problems that are involved. What is needed now, above all, is enough public interest, and encouragement on the part of governments and philanthropic organizations (such as foundations) to enable some major research projects to be undertaken. There is also, of course, the question of adequately trained personnel to perform this research, for these are always in short supply, but in my experience even this problem can eventually be surmounted.

What is perhaps most important is that in this matter of language teaching for young children, psychologists and educational researchers have an opportunity to have a far-reaching, important, and uplifting influence on educational policy.

6

Trends and research in methods and materials
W. F. MACKEY[1]

In most parts of the world today there is a trend to begin the teaching of the foreign language earlier and to continue it for a longer period. This has created a need for new methods and materials suitable for lower age groups, and for new courses for learners who have completed the elementary language training in primary schools.

The questions posed here have to do with the relative language learning aptitudes of these groups, from learning of the basic language skills, research on what to teach, documentation on language teaching methods to the use of the foreign language as a teaching medium.

APTITUDES AND LANGUAGE ACQUISITION

With the priority of oral skills, the tendency is to reduce the number of grammatical and vocabulary items of the language requirements for the first year. First-year language teaching programmes with active vocabularies in the thousands seem to be a thing of the past. Reasons for reduction in the learning load have been stated as follows:

(a) The use of the language is more difficult than its comprehension;

(b) Oral mastery has to be more fluent than written mastery of the language;

[1] This chapter was contributed by the chairman of group 2 (Methods and Materials). Professor W. F. Mackey is Professor of Language Didactics in the Department of Linguistics of Laval University, Quebec, Canada, and executive director of the International Centre for Research on Bilingualism. The members of the group, on whose deliberations this chapter is based, were: Mrs M. Cser (Hungary), Mr H. Evrard (France), Miss C. Goldet (France; rapporteur), Mr L. Grandía Mateu (Spain), Mr K. Hirschbold (Austria), Mr L. Kiestra (Netherlands), Mrs A. Manuel (France), Mrs E. Pavluchenko (Ukrainian SSR), Miss E. Sipmann (West Berlin; rapporteur), Mr T. Sirevåg (Norway), Mr A. Spicer (UK), Mrs E. Steel (France), Mrs I. Vereshchagina (USSR), Dr T. Woźnicki (Poland).—Ed.

(c) A high percentage of the items in a first-year oral course is necessarily grammatical (structure words, word endings, word order, and such grammatical relations as concord and government);

(d) The learner's still uncertain grammatical system is likely to break down under a heavy load of vocabulary. The range of first-year vocabularies of represented countries was reported as an average of from 1·5 to 5 words per teaching hour (See Table 1).

Table 1. Estimated First-Year Active Vocabularies[1]

Country	Words	Hours	Length of Lesson (in mins.)	Age	Average per Hour
FRANCE	200	100			2
École Active Bilingue	300	60	20		5
GERMANY	600	200	45	10	3
Berlin experiment	150	80	20	8	2
POLAND	350	100	45	11	3·5
SPAIN	250	164	60	10–11	1·5–2·5
	400*				
UKRAINE	300	80	45		3
USSR	350	100	45		3·5
UNITED KINGDOM					
Nuffield experiment	250	95	30	10–14	2·5

* Depending on language.

It is not clear whether the vocabulary figures in Table 1 represent expected acquisition or minimum examination requirements, whether they are merely arbitrary or based on studies of average attainment. More studies are needed of the sort reported from Vienna in the 1950s on the active foreign vocabulary acquired by children after four years of language learning (Hirschbold, 1956).

In order to make such studies comparable it would be necessary to elaborate the standard units of measurement so that each term (like *word* and *active*) might have the same meaning for everyone.

If countries teaching foreign languages in primary schools are to build their syllabus, methods and materials on the actual language learning capacities of their children, much more information than

[1] The figures in this table are spot estimates supplied by participants at the 1966 Hamburg meeting and can therefore be considered to give only a rough indication of current trends.

we have at present is needed on the rate of foreign language acquisition. The answers may not be simple, since foreign language aptitude is likely to be a complex of many language learning capacities—varying in different languages in pronunciation, grammar, vocabulary, style, and so forth—each of which may in turn vary according to auditory capacity, intelligence, sex, age and environment. It has been suggested, for example, that the capacity to acquire pronunciation decreases with age, while capacity to imitate increases up to the age of 18 (Williams, c.p.). Semantic acquisition based on experience may also increase with age.

For each of these capacity factors, research is needed into the learning ability of children of the same age learning different languages and children of different ages learning the same language.

Since 1962, research on the relationship between ethnic attitudes and foreign language acquisition, already started at the McGill University Department of Psychology in Montreal, under W. E. Lambert, has been extended. Numerous US-financed projects on language learning have been reported in ERIC.[1] During the same period a centre for research in language and language behaviour was founded at the University of Michigan under the direction of Harlan Lane. The centre has already started research into language acquisition particularly in the field of pronunciation.

The question of the optimum age to introduce a second language to the child is still a debatable one. It was discussed at international conferences, at Hamburg in 1962, at Stockholm in 1963 and again in Geneva in 1965. Up to a certain age the child may be unaware of the fact that he is learning another language and at kindergarten level this absence of language awareness has been used educationally through simply exposing groups of children to activities in the foreign language (the 'language bath'). But the fact that they are learning another language seems to be difficult to disguise from children of school age. Being unconscious of the mechanism of the language must be a matter of degree. It has for example been said that between the ages of 5 and 9 consciousness in the child of how he is to speak prevents him from expressing himself freely. On the other hand, the lack of system may prevent retention, as was the case in the Berlin experiment with 8-year-olds,[2] which seems to indicate that the more the children learn the language through

[1] ERIC: Educational Resources Information Center, c/o Superintendent of Documents, US Government Printing Office, Washington, D.C. 20402, USA.
[2] For details on the Berlin experiment see chapter 10.

natural and playful devices, the more easily they forget it. This may have been due to the fact that in an exclusively oral course no printed material could be used for practice outside the class hours. Moreover, it is entirely possible for a course to be systematic and at the same time to be presented and practised through games and play activities.

Since the younger the child, the more unconscious his learning, it is argued that the language learning in the primary school should be mostly an unconscious process. This supposes the exclusion of the mother tongue, the presence of which tends to make language learning a conscious process. The tendency in primary school language teaching today is therefore to keep the use of the mother tongue down to a minimum. The experience of the CREDIF[1] seems to indicate that the use of the mother tongue renders the child passive towards the foreign language. On the other hand, experiments in Wales suggest that the best results are obtained when sentence meaning is presented through a language already known, and that practice in switching from one language to another *is* desirable (Dodson, 1966).[2]

In order that the results of such experiments be comparable, it is necessary to know the following:

1 the percentage of time devoted by the children to passive as opposed to active use of their first language;

2 the percentage of time devoted to the use of the first language in presentation as opposed to its use in language learning exercises;

3 the amount of first language used to explain, as distinct from the amount of translation;

4 the percentage of first language used to teach the form (grammar and pronunciation) as against the percentage used to teach the meanings;

5 the alternative procedures with which teaching through the mother tongue is compared. Are they so designed as to permit comparison? Is the gradation such that it is always possible to use the known elements of the foreign language to present the unknown elements one at a time? Is the course so designed as to permit the use of the concrete and tangible as a basis for the more abstract and mental aspects of meaning?

[1] Centre de Recherche et d'Étude pour la Diffusion du Français, 11, avenue Pozzo di Borgo, 92-Saint Cloud, France. See chapter 12 below.
[2] On this point see also chapter 2, pp. 21–2 above.

THE STAGING OF LANGUAGE SKILLS

Order

The order in which the basic skills of listening (L), speaking (S), reading (R) and writing (W) may be introduced can vary considerably. For some time it was general in schools to teach the skills of the written language (RW) before those of the spoken language (LS). Today the contrary is the case; the tendency is to introduce at least one of the skills of the spoken language (L or LS) before the skills of the written language (R or RW) are introduced. As far as order is concerned the following types of staging seem to be the most current today:

LSRW

LRSW

LSWR

Spacing

As far as spacing of skills is concerned there is a great range of variation in practice in the amount of time devoted to one skill before another is introduced. The time varies today from less than a minute to more than 100 hours; for example, the Nuffield materials in Britain are designed for a spacing of about 100 hours between the teaching of the spoken language (LS) and the introduction of reading (R).

There is also a difference between which skills are spaced and which are not. The spacing patterns most currently used for children today seem to be:[1]

1   LSRW

2   L – S – R – W

3   LS – R – W

4   L – SW – R

5   L – R – S – W

There is also some difference in practice of the amount of time which elapses before the introduction of a new skill. In one system the time in months for children aged 10 years is:

$$L - (4) - R - (2) - S - (3) - W$$

Or, in other words, in this system the instruction in the first four

---

[1] In the following tabulations the dash (–) indicates time lapse. Where the symbols are put together (e.g. LS) this indicates that the two skills are not separated by a time lag.

months is confined to listening, after which reading is started. But the children spend six months purely on the receptive skills; speaking is introduced after six months and writing is added in the last quarter of this first year of language learning.

The percentage of time devoted to maintaining one skill while another is being introduced also varies a great deal. It may be zero:

$$(L) - (S + L) - (R + L + S) - (W + L + S + R)$$
$$\% (100) - (100 + 0) - (100 + 0 + 0) - (100 + 0 + 0 + 0)$$

Under this arrangement each skill is introduced separately and practised for a time exclusively. Or the proportions may be varied. At present we have no information on the actual proportions in use, but we would require figures which would permit comparison such as the following:

ORDER LSRW

Order LSRW	$(L)-(L + S)-(L + S + R)-(L + S + R + W)$			
Country A	% 100	(50+50)	(25+25+50)	(10+15+25+50)
Country B	% 100	(75+25)	(50+25+25)	(25+50+15+10)

Theories of spacing and maintenance reveal a great deal of individual variation within each country.[1] Some teachers argue that since reading and writing are word-based, they should be introduced long after the spoken skills, based on such things as rhythm and intonation patterns, have been established. Others argue that two related skills like listening and reading should follow closely since they both give practice in language comprehension.

Experiments on staging reported to the seminar concerned only the spacing of basic skills. The Hungarian experiments with ten-year-olds learning Russian as a second language made a comparison of two courses covering the same material in a similar order but with different spacing. One course (Hlavacs-Rhédeyné) grouped the four skills to give LSRW and introduced them within the same lesson or in consecutive lessons. Another course (Moritz-Kovácsné) spaced the skills in months—following the formula:

$$LS - (4) - R - (1) - W - (3)$$

[1] For example, in the Soviet Union there are two types of schools where a foreign language is taught in primary school. There is a difference between these two types of schools in some elements of the first year of second-language instruction, as may be seen from Table 2 in continuation of this footnote on facing page.

The texts consisted only of pictures which were put into the hands of the learners. Each new skill was based on material mastered in the previous skill. In both groups, each class included between 40 and 45 pupils, using the course for three periods a week, each of 45 minutes duration. After two years, it was concluded that under the conditions described, the learner cannot follow a purely oral course with attention and interest for more than a three-month period; the optimum spacing between LS and R at this stage of the experiments seemed to be in the region of two months.[1]

The experiences of teachers involved in the English pilot scheme for the teaching of French in primary schools[2] seem to favour the opinion that 8-year-olds should have at least 12 months of oral work before they are introduced to reading the language, but that after three years of language learning they should have made some progress in reading the language and should have the ability to write some of what they can say. The difference in age between the English and Hungarian groups may perhaps explain the difference in the spacing recommended; it seems that the optimum spacing decreases with age.

Footnote [1] continued from p. 74

Table 2. First Year of Second-Language Instruction

Types of School	Age	Words	Hours		Length of Lesson	Spacing of Skills
			Week	Year		
1 Ordinary school	7–8	250	4	136	20	L S
2 School where a number of subjects is taught in a foreign language	8–9	350	4	136	45	L S/2–4 months/ R W

Type 1 schools do not include reading and writing of the second language. Type 2 schools teach reading and writing after an audiolingual start lasting from two to four months.

[1] Descriptions of the experiments may be found in the Hungarian language teachers' review, *Idegen Nyelvek Tanítása* vol. 8, no. 6.
[2] See chapter 8 below.

If age is a possible factor in spacing, so perhaps is the character of the language. The spacing between speaking and reading in the CREDIF's French course is three times as long as in its Spanish counterpart (*Vida y diálogos de España*) since the danger of spelling pronunciation in French is greater than in Spanish.

Much more research is needed into the order, spacing and maintenance of skills; but before any large-scale projects are undertaken a great deal of work will be required in research design. To begin with, the components of each of the basic skills need to be analysed and interrelated (for example, recognition as distinct from comprehension). From a learning point of view there are not only four skills, but more like a dozen. Some of them may be conflicting as is often the case in English spelling and English pronunciation; others may be complementary as in the case of oral and written comprehension. Along with these complementary and conflicting factors it is important to measure how much of one skill is included in the other.

In this way it would be possible to stage not the skills themselves, but their components: sound discrimination (D), phonemic identification (i.e. the grouping of the discriminated sounds into functional units) (P), comprehension (C), alphabet identification (A), word identification (I), reading comprehension (M), phonetic utterance (articulation) (U), sentence pronunciation (N), letter configuration (F), orthography (O), and so forth.

In this way, for example, L = DPC is a shorthand expression for saying that, in developing listening, the factors of sound discrimination (D), phonemic identification (P) and comprehension (C) are included. Or S = UN means that at a certain stage in language teaching speaking is restricted to the pronunciation of the sounds of the language (U) and the pronunciation of sentences (N).

This would enable us to study more detailed descriptions of staging with spacing of each single component indicated in hours. A sequence of stages can then be expressed as follows:

$$D - 3 - DU - 5 - CDU - 15 - P - 5 - CPN - 15 - AI - 2 - IO - 3 - CNO$$

In other words in this (purely imaginary) illustration of a planned experiment it has been decided that in stage 1 (3 hours) the emphasis should be on sound discrimination; in stage 2 (5 hours) pronunciation practice (phonetic utterance) is added, at stage 3 (15 hours) comprehension is added to the other two, and so forth. The point of this is that instead of simply saying that the first 23 hours of teaching are spent 'purely on listening', the factors comprising the listening skills are more clearly defined. The other skills are similarly quantified as a complex of factors.

This would make the experiments in staging more comparable, since it would enable us to know to which sort of activity the learner had devoted his time. At present a statement to the effect that the learners had spent so many hours practising the spoken language might mean either that they had devoted their time to pronunciation of words or to the practice of oral expression, or to both. In any experiment it is important to specify exactly how much time is devoted to each different activity; the above model is designed to make this possible for experiments in staging. The number of skill components identified and the time needed for the mastery of each depends on research into language acquisition and on descriptions of the language learning process (Wo'nicki, 1965).

RESEARCH ON WHAT TO TEACH

The language content of what a course includes is still being improved by the results of research. The vocabulary, grammar, collocations and idioms in the course are the result of a selection based on external and internal criteria.

Although no general lists based on external and internal criteria (relevance, interest and availability) exist, there is a growing collection of general selections—mostly vocabulary selections—based on internal criteria (frequency, range, availability and coverage).

The criteria of frequency, range, availability and coverage have already been quantified. There now exists for English, French, German, Russian, Spanish and other languages a choice of word lists based on frequency and range. Most of these, with the notable exception of the *Français Fondamental* and Schonell's *English Oral Vocabulary*, have been based on counts of words in printed documents.

Recent research in selection includes the following:

1 More accurate studies of frequency and range of items in the written language are based on computer computation, cumulation and critical evaluation. Computers were used in the million-word count of American English by Kučera, and also in Juilland's frequency dictionaries, now becoming available for Spanish, French, and other languages as they come off the press at the Hague (Mouton). These can be combined with existing counts based on frequency

and range (e.g. Thorndike) to give a better statistical coverage. Existing lists are now undergoing some valuable criticism (Woźnicki, 1965a).

2 There has been a great increase in the number of range and frequency counts based on samples of spoken language. Refining the field techniques of the *Français Fondamental* survey, the Spanish Ministry of Education and Science has undertaken a recording of the speech of 15 areas in Spain under the direction of Rojo-Sastre. The investigation was described by Mr Rojo-Sastre (1964) in a working paper presented to the International Course held in Madrid in April–May 1965 under the auspices of the Council of Europe.[1] Another Spanish frequency study in progress is the one under Criado del Val undertaken in 15 cities of Spain and Latin America by OFINES under the auspices of the Instituto de Cultura Hispánica in Madrid.[2]

3 Research is in progress on child language in France and England under the auspices of CREDIF and the Nuffield Language Project.[3] The purpose is to determine the type and frequency of vocabulary, grammar and centres of interest of children for probable inclusion in language courses of primary schools.[4]

4 Research into vocabulary availability (*disponibilité*) has been devoted to the refining of the concept of availability[5] and to the extension of research to other languages and into new semantic fields. There is an availability study (18 semantic fields) in progress in connection with the *Fundamental Spanish* project of Rojo-Sastre. A study of availability of English has recently been completed in Ireland by Colmán Ó Huallacháin.[6]

There has also been some comparative study in availability in order to determine the extent of regional variation which may have

---

[1] Mr Antonio Rojo-Sastre is Director, Spanish Language Research Programme, at the Ministerio de Educación Nacional, Madrid 14, Spain.

[2] OFINES is the abbreviation for Oficina Internacional de Información y Observación del Español, c/o Instituto de Cultura Hispánica, Ciudad Universitaria, Avenida de los Reyes Católicos, Madrid 3, Spain. It publishes a bulletin, entitled *El Español Actual*.

[3] See chapter 13 on the work of the Nuffield Language Project.

[4] For details, see chapters 14 and 15 below.

[5] See, for example, Fraisse *et al.* (1963).

[6] Father Colmán Ó Huallacháin, Institúid Teanga Éireann, Baile Mhic, Ghormáin, Co. Na Mí, Eire.

to be taken into account by writers of textbooks for children. Mackey has completed a study in 27 semantic fields of the available vocabulary of 1,745 Acadian children aged 8 to 18 and compared the results with similar studies by Michéa in France (Mackey, forthcoming).

5 As for studies in vocabulary coverage, this criterion has recently been quantified in its four basic factors (inclusion, extension, definition and combination). The results have been published (Mackey and Savard, 1967) and validated on a corpus of French. Figures for English are being prepared for publication.

In addition to the need for coverage and availability for the other main languages, there is also need for research to establish indices for the external criteria of selection.

TRENDS IN GRADATION AND PRESENTATION

1 *Gradation*

There is a growing opinion that the method or the teacher has to choose between a structural gradation and a situational one. There is here, however, no opposition whatsoever, since both concepts are mutually compatible; for while a gradation may appear as a situation to the learner, it may have been designed along purely structural lines. What may have suggested the opposition is the difficulty of preparing beginning materials which are graded both structurally and situationally.

The supposed opposition between situational and cultural context is equally unfounded. Just as structures appear in situations, situations appear in contexts both semantic and cultural. We can picture the relationship as a series of four concentric circles. In the centre is the structure (subject + verb + direct object + indirect object—*he is getting his ticket from the man*) embedded in a situation (a man buying a ticket to take a train), this situation belonging to a semantic field or centre of interest (travel), this in turn being part of a cultural context (the Paris Métro). All of these—structure, situation, semantic field, cultural context—can be integrated and graded.

There have been some recent studies on the gradation of cultural aspects of language teaching. Firstly there are the conclusions of the International Course on the Study of Civilization of the Country whose Language is being taught. This was held under the auspices of the Council of Europe and organized by the Spanish Government (April–May 1965).[1] There is also a French study on cultural contexts and the gradation of cultural aspects in language teaching.[2]

The role of cultural context in language teaching is a lively question today. In some language courses it is taken for granted. In cases where the language is foreign to the country, cultural context is normally that of the foreign country. It may be a factor of motivation and an important part of the course, to the point of being explained in the mother tongue before each lesson (as in the Nuffield materials) and transmitted through the use of realia, pictures, film strips and films. In the case where the language is the second national tongue, however, the cultural context may be that, not of a foreign country, but of the learners' own. There are cases, however, where cultural context may arouse feelings of antagonism or be interpreted as propaganda for the foreign country, thus functioning as a barrier to language learning. Cultural context may also have to be avoided in international courses where the type of learners is undetermined or in mixed groups in areas where the language is a national tongue. The École Active Bilingue in Paris uses stereotype figures with which the children (aged 5 to 8) can identify themselves—thus neutralizing emotional resistance to language learning. The figures are presented through various visual means including film strips.

2 Presentation

In the presentation of foreign language meanings to primary school children the tendency today is to use objects and pictures in the form of flannelgraphs, flash pictures and film strips. In any oral course for children some sort of visual material may be necessary if for no other reasons than to focus the pupil's eye on something interesting.

The advantage of flannelgraphs is that they permit physical activity on the part of the child since he can handle the objects pictured and arrange them in different relationships. Evidence that

[1] Report to be published in French, English and Spanish by the publications division of the Spanish Ministry of National Education in Madrid.

[2] These studies, initiated at the Centre de Recherches pour l'Étude de la Civilisation (CREC), are carried out at (a) Centre d'Étude de Civilisation, established by Professor Michaux, Faculté des Lettres et des Sciences Humaines, 92-Nanterre, France; (b) at the Section 'Civilisation' of BELC, 1, rue Léon-Journault, 92-Sèvres, France. Consult also the Review *Tendances* (23, rue Lapérouse, Paris, 16e, France).

the flannelgraphs may be preferable to the film strip for children under eight seems to be accumulating; but both flannelgraphs and film strips are not mutually exclusive and should continue to be used until research indicates that one is superfluous.

In examining pictorial and audio-visual courses it is important to make a distinction between visual aids and visual media, that is, between pictures which help the teacher and pictures which actually teach the language. It is also important to distinguish between the motivational and semantic functions of visual material. Research is needed in both fields, but especially in the latter (pictorial semantics) since on it may depend a learner's knowledge of what he thinks the language actually means. Research into pictorial semantics may first have to be conceptual before it can become experimental. There is a strong tendency today to put the meaning of the language on film and the form on tape. Some of the tapes are drills for the language laboratory, which is now beginning to be used in the primary school. There is a growing opinion, however, that the language laboratory has no place in the primary school. More experience is necessary before the function of the language laboratory in the primary school can be evaluated.

DOCUMENTATION AND METHOD ANALYSIS

A recent development is the creation of centres of documentation on methods and materials of foreign language teaching. Examples of such centres are those that have been created in Brazil, Canada, France, Germany, Italy, Spain, UK, USA, and USSR.[1] Some of these centres have published catalogues of their holdings, sometimes with a few lines of description for each item.

[1] Brazil: Centro de lingüística aplicada, Rua Aurora, 713–5.0 Andar, Sáo Paulo 2–SP.

Canada: Division of Language Didactics, Laval University, Quebec. Modern Language Centre, Ontario Institute for Studies in Education, 102 Bloor Street West, Toronto 5, Ontario.

Federal Republic of Germany: Sprachkybernetisches Forschungszentrum e.V., Friedrich-Ebert-Anlage 64, 69 Heidelberg.

France: Bureau pour l'Enseignement de la Langue et de la Civilisation françaises à l'étranger (BELC), 9 rue Lhomond, Paris-5e.

Italy: Centro italiano de linguistica applicata, Piazza Dell'Ateneo Salesiano 1, 00139 Roma.

Spain: Centro de Orientación Didáctica, Sagasta 27, Madrid.

(footnote continued at foot of page 82)

Since teachers require more detailed descriptions of methods and materials, there have been attempts to elaborate systems of method analysis. Methods and material analyses have been developed by Spicer in England, Walz in Germany and Mackey in Canada. In Canada an attempt has been made to elaborate a complete and detailed automatic procedure of method analysis by means of computer, with all factors integrated into a single method profile (Mackey, 1965, 1965a, 1966).

THE FOREIGN LANGUAGE AS A TEACHING MEDIUM

The foreign language is now being regarded not only as merely another school subject but also as a means for learning other school subjects. It has long been the case in parts of Africa and Asia[1] and, in the past, in Europe, where the foreign language as a medium of instruction has become common in countries like the USSR, Hungary and Bulgaria. In the USSR some 700 schools now make use of such foreign languages as English, French, German and Chinese as languages of instruction in various school subjects. Reports on these developments in the USSR may be found in several articles in the review *Innostrannyje Jazyki v Škóle*, Moscow.[2]

The transfer from one language to another for instructional purposes has generally been abrupt. When enough of the foreign

---

(Continued from foot of page 81)

United Kingdom: Centre for Information on Language Teaching, State House, 63 High Holborn, London WC1. Language Teaching Information Centre, 31 Harrogate Road, Leeds 7.

USA: Center for Applied Linguistics, 1717 Massachusetts Avenue, N.W., Washington, D.C. 20036.

USSR: Scientific Methodological Centre for Teaching of Russian Abroad, Moscow University, Krzhizhanovskogo str. 24/35, Moscow.

[1] See chapters 2 and 3 above on this point.
[2] The titles of some of these articles in English translation are as follows:
J. A. Chistyakova, 'Methods of teaching French in nursery schools', 1965; J. A. Chistyakova, E. M. Chernushko, G. I. Solina, 'Teaching foreign languages in nursery schools', 1964; U. E. Kovalenko, 'Teaching German to the pupils of the first grade in a school where a number of subjects are taught in German', 1964; E. L. Bim, 'Methods of teaching oral speech on the basis of patterns in the second grade of a school where a number of subjects are taught in German', 1964; I. N. Vereshchagina, 'Teaching oral speech (in English) of second-grade pupils in schools where a number of subjects are taught in English', 1965. See also chapters 16 and 17 of the 1962 Report.

language seemed to have been assimilated there was a complete switch of the language of instruction without any control on the comprehension of the learners. Attempts, however, have been made to determine how gradual and how early such a transfer can be and at what age and vocabulary level (Mackey and Noonan, 1952).

7

Initial and in-service training for second language teaching in the primary school

RAPHAEL GEFEN[1]

WHO SHOULD TEACH?

Ensuring the supply of professionally-trained teachers of foreign languages in the primary school involves two interrelated questions: what type of teacher is best suited for this specific task? and what kind of training will best fit him for it? Since the early stages of language learning are crucial for the pupils' motivation and progress, it is vital that the teacher should know the target language well and should be at the same time pedagogically qualified, well-versed in educational psychology and principles and so able to understand the problems of learning in general and of second language acquisition in particular. In other words, the second language teacher in a primary school must be a primary school teacher in every sense of the term; therefore the ideal person to teach the target language in the primary school is the pupils' regular classroom teacher. He knows his pupils intimately and will be able to teach the second language in full accord with the whole tenor of primary education, so minimizing the strangeness of the second language. Clearly, the second language cannot be taught at this stage and at this age in the form of regularly spaced 45–50-minute lessons; instead, frequent short spells of teaching, daily or even twice

[1] Mr Raphael Gefen, the writer of this chapter, who was a trainer of English teachers in Israel and a lecturer on descriptive and applied linguistics is now Senior Inspector of English in Elementary Schools in the Israel Ministry of Education. His paper is based on the report of the working group on Teacher Training at the 1966 Hamburg meeting. Members of the group were: Dr D. C. Riddy (United Kingdom; Chairman), Miss I. Axelsen (Denmark), Miss A. Chari (India), Mr R. Gefen (Israel), Mr T. Sirevåg (Norway), Dr W. Koelle (Federal Republic of Germany; Rapporteur).—Ed.

daily, should be given and, moreover, in a form integrated with the whole learning programme. The native speaker of the second language resident abroad or the language-teaching specialist, going from class to class, unversed in the needs and spirit of primary education, unaware of the general learning situation of the pupils, although highly skilled linguistically but often untrained pedagogically and sometimes not fully fluent in the pupils' mother tongue, is therefore hardly the most suitable teacher in this context.

However, the regular class teacher must know the second language very well indeed. In fact, a teacher with certain specialist qualifications, despite the strictures of the preceding paragraph, is to be preferred to a general teacher who is learning the second language together with his pupils and so often teaches them mistakes, unawares. There is no point, in other words, in being too rigid in determining the best type of teacher. *The class teacher is the most suitable, on condition that he knows the second language well and is trained to teach it.* Many class teachers in the primary school have not had this training and it may not prove possible to give every teacher the necessary initial or even in-service training required, while some generally gifted teachers may fall within that small group who have no aptitude for a second language. It would not be fair to them or to their pupils to oblige them to be language teachers as well.

THE SEMI-SPECIALIST

But the issue need not be in terms of a choice between the language specialist and the general teacher; instead, a class teacher who has shown the necessary aptitude for the second language and has received some special training for teaching it, may teach the second language in his own class and in one or two (but not too many) other classes. He would thereby become a 'semi-specialist'. Because he is the general teacher for his own class, he will appreciate the specific problems involved in teaching a second language in the primary school, while his aptitude and training will ensure that the pupils in the other classes receive adequate instruction, although they will not of course have the second language so well integrated in the general learning programme as would be the case were their own class teacher also to teach the second language.

It must be understood that the above comments are in terms of broad preferences and decisions on principles only. Each country must decide, naturally enough, in terms of its own situation and within the framework of its general educational policy. However, most authorities are agreed that in the specific task of primary school teaching, other things being equal, the class teacher is ideally the best second language teacher, and in certain circumstances the 'semi-specialist' trained primary school teacher is well suited. But in general the specialist does not fit into the framework of primary school teaching.

DIFFERENT FORMS OF TEACHER-TRAINING

Since second language teaching is to be integrated into the general educational framework, the training of second language teachers should form part of the initial teacher-training course. At the same time, very many practising classroom teachers will attend in-service training and retraining courses, in the light of the considerations and recommendations mentioned above.

The training programme therefore has to operate on two axes—initial training, as part of the general preparation of the intending teacher, and in-service training for the practising teacher. Furthermore, this in-service training must be aimed at two different types of practising teacher—the trained and the untrained. In many countries, far too many teachers are untrained pedagogically and this objective situation must be taken into account when providing the in-service courses for language teachers. All these varied courses have to ensure as the very minimum that the teacher has a good command of the second language, with the emphasis on speech rather than on writing, and that he is well acquainted with modern methods of language teaching.

The student-teacher undergoing initial training in a college will have more time at his disposal and so be able to extend his studies into a number of related fields, whereas the in-service trainee will not be available for such extensive study; this course will therefore have to be more intensive and more limited in scope.

INITIAL (PRE-SERVICE) TRAINING

The curriculum of the college, training teachers who will teach a second language as class teachers or as semi-specialists, may include the following subjects:

1 *Language improvement*
Although the student-teacher will not be a language-teaching

specialist, he must attain a very high standard in grammatical usage, vocabulary and pronunciation. Accordingly, the language improvement course should give him speech training to improve his pronunciation (using the term in the widest sense to include stress, rhythm and intonation); intensive drill in the syntactic structures of the target language until they become completely internalized and automatic; and effective practice in the vocabulary in general and idioms in particular. All of this course should be strictly synchronic. The student is not concerned with etymology or the history of the language—he must be exposed to contemporary usage only. 'Language Improvement' also involves an acquaintance with the written language of today, but the course as a whole is aimed at inculcating the audiolingual skills rather than reading and writing.

In this intensive learning, the language laboratory should play a central role. Every institution should possess an adequately equipped and staffed language laboratory in which every student can spend time in individual practice in pronunciation, grammar and vocabulary. Other aids, such as the film, radio, television, film strips, gramophone, etc., are also valuable in helping the student reach the necessary high level of achievement. Every institution should also contain a library stocked with modern literature and journals.

Wherever it is at all possible, the student should spend some time in the country where the second language is the mother tongue. Where circumstances permit, this period of residence abroad should be considered an integral and obligatory part of the course.

It is assumed that every student-teacher will have studied the second language for some years as a secondary school pupil and will have attained a satisfactory standard there. He will also have studied some great literary works of the past. The teacher-training course will not include any study of literature as such, except in so far as it aids command of the spoken language of today. Although the student is following a full-time course of study, he is not training to be a specialist language teacher. He will have a number of non-linguistic subjects to study and time devoted to a course in the literature of the past will take time away from his other studies, both in second language teaching and in general and pedagogical subjects.

2 Linguistics
Every language teacher should be conscious of language as a human

phenomenon; he must see it not merely as a tool for communication but as part of society, culture and human behaviour in general. Linguistics will give him a deeper insight into his subject and so contribute to successful teaching. The term 'linguistics' as used here means studying language scientifically but synchronically: it is not a study of 'philology' in the older sense with its emphasis on etymology, the history of a particular language and its general bias towards diachronic study.

However, linguistics is a very wide subject and the limited time available in the college course could lead merely to a superficial familiarity with the technical terminology of the science and some acquaintance with its often conflicting theories. Not only may the student not reap much practical benefit from his studies but he may even become hostile to linguistics as such, if he fails to see its relevance to language-teaching problems.

The linguistics course should therefore take the form of an introduction to descriptive linguistics, with an eclectic and pragmatic choice of topics all of which are concerned with the applications of linguistics to language teaching and are closely related to the classroom situation.

Part of the linguistics syllabus should be an introduction to phonetics, since a knowledge of the principles of phonetics will enable the intending teacher to identify the pupils' pronunciation mistakes and to help improve their pronunciation.

The course in linguistics can well be open to all language teachers and be orientated towards mother tongue as well as second language teaching. A joint course will point out the common concerns and essential identities. In any case, the primary school teacher of the second language will, it is assumed, be a semi-specialist or a general class teacher, so that he will also be the mother-tongue teacher of his pupils. He can only benefit from a course about human language as such, dealing with pupils whose first language acquisition was in the relatively recent past and who therefore have the prospect of attaining a considerable measure of coordinate bilingualism.

3 *The structure of the second language*

The second language teacher in the primary school will not teach 'grammar', in the sense that he will not present his pupils with syntactic or morphological rules—any such cognitive approach to grammatical structures will be done at a much higher level. The pupil learns his grammar inductively, through imitation, example and generalization.

Nevertheless, the student-teacher should study the structure of the second language, for his own background knowledge rather than for classroom presentation. This is a cognitive study distinct from the grammatical side of the language improvement course mentioned above. It will deepen his own insight into the second language and as such is valuable in itself, but it will be of direct relevance to his classroom practice in enabling him to put his inductive teaching on a sound linguistic basis and to grade the patterns he teaches according to their frequency, difficulty and other criteria.

Studying the structure of the second language should not be done according to one grammatical model exclusively. Instead, the views of different grammatical theories should be presented and this comparative approach will enable the future teacher to vary his own teaching method and to utilize all theories and models for his practical pedagogical purpose.

4 Background studies

Some knowledge of the social background of the peoples for whom the second language is the mother tongue will help the teacher in his work, since the history, behaviour and culture of these peoples will frequently be reflected in the language, to a greater or a lesser extent. The student-teacher ought, therefore, to be informed of the history, traditions and general way of life of the speech communities involved, but the actual content and scope of the information will vary from country to country. Where the target language is a 'foreign language', studied for mainly cultural reasons, more attention will be paid to this background information, but where it is a 'second language', studied for essentially practical purposes, such as a *lingua franca* or as a future medium of instruction at the secondary school level, this aspect is of less relevance and may even be dispensed with.

5 The psychology of language learning

A knowledge of psycholinguistics will be very advantageous to the intending language teacher, whether he teaches the mother tongue or a second language. This course should also be a joint one and should indicate the various theories relating to language acquisition and at the same time bring out both the similarities **and the**

4

differences in the learning of the first and the second language by young children. Psycholinguistics will therefore be very relevant in determining the strategy of second language teaching.

6 *Methodology of teaching a second language*

This course must not only be concerned with explaining the various methodological theories and principles, but must also be highly practical. The student-teacher must acquire the skills necessary for efficient teaching, including the use of all forms of teaching aids, especially audio-visual ones, and the means of dealing with large classes.

A representative selection of teaching materials should be made available to the student for study and comparison, in order to guide him to make the most effective choice and use of such material.

In order to arouse the students' intellectual curiosity, quicken their interest and enable them to contribute to their own education, much of the college course may be given in the form of discussions and seminars in which experiences and ideas will be exchanged, rather than through formal lectures.

An adequate period of *supervised teaching practice* will be an integral part of the college course.

7 *General subjects*

Like all primary school teachers-in-training, the second language student-teacher will study the same pedagogical and general subjects as his fellows at college.

IN-SERVICE TRAINING

This type of course is necessarily shorter in duration and therefore narrower in scope than the full initial training course; on the other hand, the students will be more experienced and mature. These in-service courses will accordingly be modified versions of the full college curriculum, but because of their limited duration and scope students should be encouraged to take the full course while at college rather than take an in-service course after they have graduated. However, in the immediate future there will certainly be need for many such intensive in-service courses for retraining practising primary school teachers as second language teachers.

In-service training should take the form of a part-time course of not less than 100 hours, together with a full-time intensive course of three months duration (in one unit or in two sessions of six weeks each). The full-time course would most profitably be spent in a country where the second language is the mother tongue. The part-time course might also include some lessons by correspondence, in countries where teachers are too scattered for regular meeting.

The curriculum for in-service courses may consist of:

1 *Language improvement*

This will be the major area of study, especially in the full-time section of the course. Studies in the structure of the second language and its contrasting patterns and forms with the mother tongue (subject 3 of the Initial College Training curriculum) will be part of the language improvement course, for these practising teachers.

2 *Linguistics*

This subject will have to be curtailed for these short courses. Instead, a brief introductory course dealing with the application of linguistics to language teaching will be given, together with guidance for private study by the teachers. Many references to linguistic criteria may also be made in the 'Language Improvement' course.

3 *Background studies*

This subject will likewise have to be curtailed. Some background talks and guidance for private study will be given where necessary and within the limits suggested in subject 4 of the Initial Training course.

4 *The psychology of language learning*

Here again, time will not permit more than an introduction to the subject, perhaps in the form of lectures followed by discussion.

5 *Methodology of second language teaching*

The practising teacher will, it is assumed, have some acquaintance with the various methodological theories; his in-service training will therefore take a highly practical form and should include demonstrations of teaching procedures and of audio-visual aids, but teaching practice and demonstration lessons are not essential to this type of course. The specific methods of teaching a second language to small children should be stressed.

6 *General subjects (for untrained personnel)*

It is assumed that teachers attending the above in-service courses will be trained primary school staff; accordingly, no provision was made for general and pedagogical subjects. However, where the practising second language teacher is himself untrained, suitably modified courses will have to be given in some pedagogical subjects, including educational psychology and general teaching methodology.

REFRESHER COURSES

Continuous advance both in the theory and practice of second language teaching means that even the trained teacher cannot afford to rest; he must always be kept up to date. The educational authorities in every country should therefore arrange regular refresher courses, in addition to the initial and in-service training mentioned above. The authorities should also produce new materials in the light of these new theories and practices. The modern teacher is entitled to be accompanied by up-to-date teaching material.

TEACHER TRAINING AND THE MASS MEDIA

Television, radio, the film, etc., can be used on a large scale in teacher-training, especially in many African, Asian and Latin American countries where the vast number of teachers who need training and retraining makes imperative the extensive use of these mass media.

PROFESSIONAL JOURNALS

Journals can play an important role in training the future teacher and keeping practising teachers well informed of developments in the profession. Two types of journal are useful:

(a) local or regional newsletters for one specific second language, emphasizing the everyday classroom work, making practical suggestions to teachers and dealing with their problems;

(b) a high-level professional journal, on a regional or international basis, dealing with the general problems of teaching modern languages at the various levels and intended mainly for the teacher-trainer.

SOME RESEARCH PROPOSALS

Many of the suggestions for teacher-training mentioned above can only be tentative so long as adequate research has not been carried out. Some areas where research can profitably be undertaken are the following:

(a) the compilation of reference grammars of the second language for teaching purposes in training courses. These grammars should be in line with the advances in linguistic theory of recent years, but should take the form of pedagogical reference grammars for the use of teacher-trainers and their students, not for direct classroom application.

(b) the descriptive analysis of the mother tongue, for contrastive purposes in language teaching. Studies in contrastive linguistics are part of the students' training, both in the full college course and in the shorter in-service training. However, for the most part languages have not yet been described from the point of view of modern linguistics and until this has been done all contrastive references in the teacher-training programme must be tentative, *ad hoc*, impressionistic and as such unsatisfactory.

(c) the evaluation and comparison of the most effective methods of training second language teachers. This can take the form of the exchange of information and the scientific evaluation of achievements in both the pre-service and the in-service programmes.

(d) the application of linguistics and psycholinguistics to language learning and teaching and the effective use of these branches of knowledge in second language teacher-training. It is generally recognized that these sciences do have a very important role to play in second language teaching and learning, since they will provide the theoretical background necessary to effective practice. However, there is still need to indicate precisely where and how they can be of help, countering both the unjustified prejudices of many practical teachers suspicious of theory and also the misguided enthusiasm of others who see language teaching as nothing but 'linguistics in the classroom'.

A CENTRAL INSTITUTE FOR EACH COUNTRY

The establishment of a central planning and organizing body for each country, responsible for a specific second language or for the teaching of modern languages in general, is necessary in order to conduct the various activities outlined above. It would publish the journals, produce teaching materials, organize the different courses (in cooperation with the authorities and the educational institutions) and pass on information to similar bodies in other countries. Some countries already possess such an institute, and their experience will be a valuable guide to others.

8

The primary French pilot scheme: an English experiment[1]

PLANNING THE PILOT PROJECT

The pilot scheme for the teaching of French in primary schools was launched in March 1963. Among the factors leading to its establishment was probably a growing sense of unity with Britain's European neighbours. Thus the Annan Committee on the teaching of Russian (Great Britain, 1962), reporting in the spring of 1962, drew attention to the potential benefit for language learning in Britain if the regular teaching of a first modern language was started in good conditions and by the right methods in primary schools.

Contributory factors no doubt included the spread of audio-visual methods of language teaching in secondary schools, and the support by the Nuffield Foundation of pioneering experiments in language teaching at the primary level in Leeds and elsewhere in 1961 and 1962. The experiment in Leeds was particularly striking, even though it was undertaken in special conditions. A class of about twenty 11-year-olds of fairly high ability was given intensive instruction in French by a French bilingual teacher, Mrs M. Kellermann. In the space of one term the children achieved remarkable results in fluency and precision of speech.[2]

Encouraged by the success of the Leeds experiment and by the interest which it had aroused, the Nuffield Foundation began discussions with the Ministry's Curriculum Study Group about the

---

[1] This account of the first two years' operation of a national experiment in Great Britain sponsored jointly by the Schools Council and the Nuffield Foundation is a slightly shortened and adapted version of *Field Report No. 2*, published by the Schools Council, 38 Belgrave Square, London SW1 (Schools Council, 1966a.) We are greatly indebted to the Schools Council for permission to publish it.—Ed.

[2] For further details of the Leeds experiment see chapter 2, p. 18 above; also the 1962 Report, chapter 14, or Kellermann (1964).

establishment of a pilot project.[1] Detailed plans were drawn up for a new form of cooperative, jointly sponsored project, in which the Foundation would undertake responsibility for the preparation of a range of teaching materials to be tried out in the experiment— namely an integrated audio-visual course suitable for children beginning to learn French from the age of 8—while the Ministry would take responsibility for approaching local education authorities and inviting them to identify schools willing to participate in such an experiment. The Ministry would also make the necessary provision, partly through the local education authorities, for in-service training in Britain and France for the teachers who would take part.

WHY FRENCH?

French was chosen as the language for the experiment for a number of reasons. In the first place, French remains one of the widely used international languages; on a more practical level, the proximity of France was clearly an advantage and, however difficult it might be to provide the necessary training for primary and secondary teachers to implement an experiment in French, the difficulties presented by any other language would be greater. Moreover, it was felt that the claims of German, Russian and Spanish would be met, to a considerable extent, by the increased opportunities for the learning of a second modern language at the secondary stage, which the experiment, if successful, would open up.

On 13 March 1963, the Minister of Education, Sir Edward Boyle, announced in Parliament the launching of the scheme. He said that £100,000[2] had been set aside by the Nuffield Foundation for the development of modern language studies, and that their programme and the Ministry's pilot scheme would go forward side by side with the general expansion of modern language teaching to children at the junior stage, which had already begun in some parts

---

[1] On 1 April 1964, the Ministry of Education became the Department of Education and Science (often referred to in educational circles as 'The Department' or 'DES' or, retrospectively, still as 'The Ministry').

The Schools Council (for the Curriculum and Examinations) was set up in October 1964. The Council is representative of the education service as a whole and is a coordinating and commissioning agency for the development of curricula, examinations and related research. The Curriculum Study Group was abolished in 1964 and its staff were assigned to the Schools Council.—Ed.

[2] This sum was later increased.

of the country. He looked forward to the time when perhaps all juniors at school within the public system would start to learn a foreign language, and hoped that the pilot scheme would collect information about many important questions which would arise for teachers and administrators if this were to be so.

THE AIMS OF THE PILOT SCHEME

What are the questions which it is hoped the pilot scheme will answer?

First, it should be stressed that the scheme's aim is not to establish whether or not it is possible to teach French successfully in primary schools. Obviously it is possible. In 1959, *Primary Education* (Ministry of Education, 1959, pp. 73, *seq.*) had stated that the teaching of a modern language was possible with abler pupils in primary schools (basing its opinion on the sporadic teaching that had already taken place), but that conditions were rarely suitable. The chief question was to find out on what conditions it would be feasible to consider the general introduction of a modern language into the primary school curriculum in terms of the consequences for the pupil, the school and the teacher. The main issues can be posed as follows:

1 Is any substantial gain in mastery of a foreign language achieved by beginning to teach it at 8 instead of 11?

2 Do other aspects of educational and general intellectual development gain or suffer from the introduction of a foreign language in the primary school?

3 What are the organizational, teaching and other problems posed by such an experiment?

4 Are there levels of ability below which the teaching of a foreign language is of dubious value?

5 What methods, incentives and motivations are most effective in fostering learning of a foreign language?

The means of assessment being used to provide answers to these questions are described on page 110.[1]

PRINCIPLES OF THE SCHEME

1 *The training of primary school teachers in French*
When planning for the scheme began in 1963, there was very little

[1] See also chapter 16.

information indeed about the organizational and training problems which launching it would pose. But it was thought reasonable to suppose from the outset that, given adequate additional training both in French and in up-to-date methods, the average primary school teacher, whose qualifications in French might be limited to a pass at 'O' level,[1] acquired perhaps some years ago, and whose fluency in the language was likely, to start with, to be limited, would be able to teach the early stages well.

Initially it was a matter of guesswork to decide the minimum length of training which would have to be provided to enable such teachers to begin teaching French to 8-year-olds. In a scheme of this kind, it was important not to take any avoidable risks, and the Steering Committee for the pilot scheme took the view from the beginning that a high standard of preparatory training ought to be recognized as essential for the teachers in the scheme.

This training is described in detail on pages 102–5. It consists, briefly, of a minimum of six months' attendance at a part-time language refresher course organized locally, followed by attendance at a three-month intensive language course in France or Britain, and finally attendance at a short course on methods of presenting the language to junior pupils. Continued attendance at the local part-time language course *after* completing the three-stage training just described has been found to be advantageous; and for many teachers, success or difficulty in coping with junior classes in their third year of French, especially, may well depend on the regularity with which they have kept up their French in this way.

2 *Additional training for secondary teachers*

It was envisaged from the start that teachers in secondary schools receiving pupils for the first time with three years' experience of French would themselves need help to meet the new situation, through the provision of suitable courses; and that those secondary schools which did not already teach a modern language would need help in finding, and perhaps training or retraining, some staff. These points are discussed on pages 104 and 105.

---

[1] Secondary school examination, supervised by university examination boards and generally taken by pupils at the age of 16. The Ordinary ('O') Level is the lower stage; the next, higher stage of attainments is examined at the 'A' (Advanced) Level, normally taken by pupils at the age of 17 or 18.—Ed.

3 *Primary-secondary continuity*

From the outset it was considered essential to regard the pilot scheme as continuing for at least five years—i.e. until the children who had started to learn the language at 8 had completed their second year in secondary schools. This was, first, because the teachers in the secondary schools would be faced with a completely new situation; and second, because there was very little material available suitable for 11-year-old pupils who had already had as much as three years' experience of French. It was therefore stipulated from the start that pupils entering secondary schools from primary schools in the pilot scheme must be taught separately from beginners in French.

The need for continuity into the secondary stage was important in determining the criteria for selecting the pilot areas, and is equally relevant in any other scheme. It is very important that the pupils from primary schools where French is taught should not be dispersed over a large number of secondary schools, each of which would be receiving only small groups of pupils for whom it could scarcely hope to make proper arrangements. In the pilot scheme, therefore, when local authorities were asked to identify groups of schools interested in taking part in the scheme, it was emphasized that these areas should be compact, in the sense that the primary schools in them fed a small number of secondary schools, ideally not more than one or two, but generally about five. (In fact about 60 secondary schools will be involved in the experiment's secondary stage in the thirteen pilot areas.)

4 *A common starting age in the primary schools*

For similar reasons, it was fundamental that all the pupils taking part, at least in a given area, should start French at the same age. There was, and still is, some uncertainty what the most desirable starting point should be. While there are sound arguments in favour of introducing a language as early as possible to young children, starting a language at the infant stage means training even more teachers than doing so at the junior stage.[1] The choice of 8 rather than 7 for the starting point for the scheme was based on the belief that it would be desirable to give children a chance to settle down to junior school life before starting to learn French. A start at 8 would establish clearly enough for the purposes of the experiment

---

[1] Primary schools in England are divided into an infant stage for 5- to 7-year-olds and a junior stage for 7- to 11-year-old children.—Ed.

whether or not an earlier start provided identifiable advantages over starting at 11.

What it was emphatically hoped to avoid was the practice, which up to the launching of the scheme was becoming increasingly common, of the occasional introduction of a little French to selected pupils in their last primary year, particularly after they had taken the 11-plus examination. Such haphazard teaching of French adds to the difficulties of the secondary teachers who take on the responsibility for the pupils' French later on, without materially adding to the pupils' knowledge of the language.

5 *The integration of French into the primary curriculum*

At first there was some anxiety whether language learning might have a harmful effect upon the child-centred approach to primary education favoured by most educationists. This fear was linked to the supposition, initially widespread, that French would only be feasible in the primary school if it were taught by specialist teachers—and that the average primary school teacher was not, and could not be, adequately trained to do the work.

This question has been tackled in two ways. While it was considered that there would be many advantages if the French teacher was also the class teacher, it was also recognized that it would be possible to achieve this only in a few areas. Therefore training was provided for the primary school teachers participating in the scheme on the basis of ensuring one trained teacher of French for each stream or form entry of pupils in a school. This would mean that, when children in the second, third and fourth year of the junior school were learning French, the teacher of French would, at the most, have to be absent from his own class for two classes during the day to teach French to other classes. Similarly, in order to apply this principle as far as possible to the small schools which would have to use peripatetic teachers for French, it was recommended that no peripatetic teacher ought to serve more than two, or at the most three, schools.

Secondly, it was emphasized from the start that French should as far as possible be a fully integrated part of the primary curriculum—that is to say, connexions should be made wherever possible with other subjects such as craft, art, history and so on, and the teachers encouraged to use the same active methods as are used for other subjects.

The preparation by the Nuffield Foundation of audio-visual teaching materials specially designed for young children has of course greatly assisted in this respect.

COURSE MATERIALS

It was fundamental to the whole conception of the experiment that instruction should be based largely on audio-visual methods. Naturally, there has been no intention of preventing the able, bilingual teacher from using whatever methods he chooses, provided they are consistent with good primary teaching method. But it was equally obvious that the great majority of British primary school teachers would welcome the help of a specially designed course, based on audio-visual methods, especially if supplemented by fairly full notes in the form of a teacher's guide.

It was to meet this need that the Nuffield Foundation established the Foreign Language Teaching Materials Project.[1] The aim was to prepare an integrated range of teaching materials for an introductory course in French, suitable for children starting to learn the language at the age of about 8, and continuing for at least five years. Teachers and authorities were, however, free to choose teaching material other than the Nuffield course, if they preferred to do so. Some areas in the scheme, for instance the schools in Oxford, have themselves carried out an experiment within the experiment, using in different schools different courses, and making their own assessment of their advantages and disadvantages. Overall, 80 per cent of the schools in the pilot areas are using the Nuffield materials, the next most commonly used materials being the French-produced audio-visual course *Bonjour Line* and the US-produced teaching film series *Parlons français*.

LAUNCHING THE PILOT SCHEME

To identify the groups of schools which would be called upon to participate in the experiment, the Ministry invited local education authorities, in March 1963, to say whether they would like to take part in the pilot scheme. Authorities were told that the aim was to find about nine areas, which would between them give as far as possible a cross-section of educational conditions nationally. The areas should be compact, in the sense that they should comprise primary schools feeding a limited number of secondary schools, and

[1] Details of this project are described in chapter 13.

should be of such a size as to generate an annual age group of about 480 children. Authorities were asked also if they were willing to make the necessary arrangements for local in-service training, and to release primary teachers to attend intensive courses.

SELECTING THE PILOT AREAS

Authorities' reaction to this invitation was enthusiastic. Over half (nearly 80 out of 146) indicated interest in the scheme and put forward groups of schools willing to participate either as 'pilot' areas or as 'associate' areas. A number of other authorities, while not responding directly to the invitation to participate in the project, took the initiative in organizing local schemes of their own.

In the event the number of pilot areas was increased to thirteen. For an objective trial of the feasibility of primary French teaching and of the value of the new Nuffield materials, it was not of course strictly necessary to have anything like such a large sample of schools as even nine areas. But one aim of the experiment was to find out what difficulties arise in areas which, for instance, were short of teachers, or where school staffs were changing very quickly, or where schools were very small. It was also thought that, if there were trial areas in most parts of the country, more teachers would become aware of the existence of the experiment, and perhaps have a chance to observe it at first hand. If it were decided later on to proceed towards a general introduction of French into the primary curriculum, there would then be a solid basis of experience on which to build. At the same time, by extending its scope, more colleges of education and colleges of further education, as well as institutes and departments of education, would be brought into the experiment. In all there are 125 schools participating, involving an age group of approximately 6,000 children.

TRAINING THE PRIMARY TEACHERS

In July 1963, the Ministry told the authorities which areas had been chosen as pilot areas and invited their help as a matter of urgency in planning the training required to get the project launched by September 1964. Each area assessed the general standard of qualification in French already possessed by the teachers who would be taking part, and took steps to provide a local part-time language course to help teachers, where this was necessary, to refresh their

French and prepare themselves for the three-month intensive course in France.

1 *Local language courses*

These local part-time courses were organized round a language laboratory, in such secondary schools and colleges of education and further education as already possessed one. Their intensiveness (from about 25 up to 90 hours' preparatory work) varied considerably; as did the materials used to train teachers on these courses. In some areas the basic course used to increase the teachers' linguistic proficiency was *Voix et Images de France* produced by CREDIF.[1] Several of the course tutors devised additional material of their own to reinforce particular structures or to enlarge vocabulary. Some areas also used the primary course which the majority of the teachers were either using or about to use in their own schools. The purpose here was twofold—to familiarize the teachers with the material and to show them various interesting ways in which the material could be presented to a class.

2 *The intensive language courses*

Meanwhile, arrangements had been made for courses of three months' duration to be held, starting in the spring term of 1964, at the British Institute in Paris and at the University of Besançon. The courses were specifically designed to enable the teachers to reach the highest standard of proficiency in spoken French of which they were capable in the time and to improve their knowledge of contemporary France. The centres were asked to provide practice in French conversation on prepared topics in small groups and to ensure that the vocabulary used on the course was such as would be useful to teachers in their classrooms. Special attention was given to poems and children's stories which might be useful as class material. Each of the centres was equipped with a language laboratory; and in addition to talks, language study, work in discussion groups and other activities, the courses provided for a daily period of language laboratory work. Contact with French people outside the classroom was also held to be of great benefit.

3 *Courses in method*

When the teachers had returned from these courses, arrangements

[1] Centre de Recherche et d'Étude pour la Diffusion du Français, École Normale Supérieure de St. Cloud, 11, avenue Pozzo-di-Borgo, 92-Saint Cloud, France.

were made to attend one of three ten-day courses organized and staffed by members of HM Inspectorate. The object of these courses was to discuss possible methods of presenting the language to young children and to demonstrate the range of audio-visual language course materials which might be used. Each of the courses drew special attention to the possibilities of integrating French into different parts of the primary curriculum, e.g. through art work, photography, other visual activities, games, songs, etc. These courses also provided an opportunity for Mr Spicer, the Organizer of the Nuffield Materials Project team, to present his trial materials, which had meanwhile been given pre-trial tests in fifty volunteer schools.

Later, in the summer of 1965, three additional methods courses were held, under the same directors and with the teachers attending in the same grouping as before. These courses[1] provided an easy and useful way of enabling teachers to share their experience about the difficulties they had encountered and successes they had enjoyed in teaching the language in the first year.[2] Teachers were also able to offer fresh assessments, in the light of their own experience, of the language courses available, and particularly to discuss with Mr Spicer the first stage of the Nuffield materials.

TRAINING FOR SECONDARY TEACHERS

In December 1965, the Schools Council sponsored a conference, held at Torquay, to discuss the implications for the secondary schools of children reaching them with three years' experience of French. This conference concluded that there would be a clear need for courses for secondary school teachers, both in new methods of teaching a language (to enable them to follow up the good work done in the primary schools) and, for some teachers, to enable them to improve their fluency in the language itself, especially French. It is expected that both local part-time courses and one-term intensive courses, as for primary teachers, will be provided. It will also be possible to extend the range of these language courses

[1] Similar courses were also held in 1966 and 1967 in order that teachers might discuss the problems (and opportunities) that had offered themselves in the second and third years of the scheme.

[2] Mutual help by teachers in the various areas of the scheme has also been made possible through the circulation, once a term from autumn 1964, of a journal called *Junior French* edited by Mr A. Davis of Blackbird Leys School, Oxford, with the help of the Oxford local education authority.

to cater for other needs, if it appears to be necessary subsequently.

To enable modern language teachers in secondary modern schools to familiarize themselves with the full range of existing audio-visual and similar language courses now available, the Schools Council, since 1966, has provided courses devoted to demonstrations and discussions of primary and secondary language courses. All the modern language staff of the pilot area secondary schools are encouraged to attend these and similar courses. Attention is given, not only to teaching materials in French, but also in other modern languages, especially Russian, Spanish and German.

MODERN LANGUAGE CENTRES

In addition, the Torquay conference strongly recommended that local authorities should provide opportunities for primary and secondary teachers of modern languages to come together to discuss common problems. Obviously it is of great assistance to the secondary teachers to visit the primary schools in their catchment area to see at first hand the type of modern language teaching being provided.

So far, only a few modern language teachers' centres have been established. Generally, the venue for local courses has been the institution providing the language laboratory for the course, and this is not necessarily a suitable place to establish a teachers' centre. But the need for teachers to have access to a good local library of modern language teaching materials of all kinds will steadily increase, as the pilot scheme progresses. At present, this need is met in part, by the existence of the Language Teaching Information Centre, at Leeds.[1] A wide variety of courses, in French and other languages, is displayed there, together with different types of projection equipment, etc.

But secondary schools participating in the pilot scheme seem likely to feel the need for access to a choice of supplementary material, from a source easily accessible to them. Initially, this need may be met by schools providing their own resources, but the provision of an additional library of material, available at the area teachers' centre, seems likely to be necessary before long.

[1] The Language Teaching Information Centre, 31 Harrogate Road, Leeds 7, is supported by the Nuffield Foundation and the City of Leeds Education Committee. See chapter 13 below for further details.

THE SPREAD OF PRIMARY FRENCH TEACHING

From the beginning, provision had been made to associate with the project a number of areas in addition to those chosen as pilot areas. The principles of the scheme would be applied in the associate areas in exactly the same way as the pilot areas, and the same training facilities, on the same financial terms, would be made available to teachers in the associate areas. In addition, one set of the Nuffield Foundation's trial course materials (free to the schools in the pilot areas) was to be provided to each associate area, revised after trial in the pilot schools.

In the summer of 1964, when the organization and training programme for the pilot areas was established, all the areas which had originally applied for membership of the scheme and had not been selected as pilot areas, were admitted into associate membership. Subsequently, a few other areas also applied to associate groups of schools with the scheme, and by 1965 there were 53 areas in association with it, involving altogether about 5 per cent of the annual age group.

To provide intensive language course facilities for teachers from the associate areas, the arrangements which had been made with the centres in France (at Paris and Besançon) were continued. In September 1964, a similar course was started in London at the Holborn College of Law, Languages and Commerce and in September 1966 another at Leeds College of Commerce, primarily for the benefit of teachers unable to go to France but also to provide information about the usefulness of such a course as a substitute for the French ones. Altogether, the three first-established centres provided courses for 360 primary teachers from January 1964 to July 1965, and it is likely that about 240 teachers (mainly from the associate areas) will have attended them in the academic year 1965/6. The pilot areas have also been provided with further places on these courses, to make good losses amongst their own primary teachers trained for the scheme, due to marriage, transfer, promotion, etc.

Up to 1 January 1966, each pilot area had seconded an average of 15 teachers for training on the intensive courses, and each associated area had seconded five. (Each pilot area contains about 12 primary schools.)

SURVEYING THE NATIONAL SITUATION

During 1964, it became clear that the existence of the pilot project had been interpreted by some authorities and teachers as an encouragement to launch local experiments; and individual primary schools were continuing to introduce French for one, two or three terms at the end of the fourth year, without reference to the relevant secondary schools or full consideration of the effect on pupils' later education. The Chairman of the Steering Committee, Mr George Taylor, accordingly wrote to all authorities in May 1964, pointing out that the pilot project itself constituted an investigation into the feasibility of primary French teaching on a large scale, and that its results would be published as soon as they became available. The Committee did not suggest that experiments should be confined to schools in the pilot and associate areas of the project, but they drew the attention of the local education authorities to the principles on which the pilot scheme was based, and to the fundamental importance of adequate planning, preparation and supervision before any start was made.

Complaints from secondary teachers of modern languages about the dangers of uncoordinated primary experimentation, and the intermittent nature of language teaching in some primary schools, continued to occur. Following the establishment of the Schools Council in October 1964, an assessment was made, based on information supplied by local education authorities, of the extent of primary French teaching in the country as a whole. Although the information collected was not complete, the return showed that in 119 local education authority areas, there were nearly 5,000 primary teachers teaching French, 1,600 of them in schools in the pilot areas or associate areas or schemes locally organized by local education authorities, and about 3,300 in schools which were not coordinated in any scheme at all. In terms of schools, the survey showed that 21 per cent of the 14,000 schools in the areas involved were providing primary French of some kind.

The survey also showed that French was not being taught in any primary school in 15 local education authority areas, and that 72 per cent of the local education authorities who responded were providing local refresher language courses for some of their teachers. Similarly, although there were many schools introducing French in the fourth year of the junior school, many more were introducing it in either the second or third or even the first year.

This survey did not attempt any assessment of the quality of language teaching being provided. It did, however, collect information about the teachers in French. Rather more than 50 per cent of them had only an 'O' level qualification in French, and about one quarter an 'A' level qualification. Nearly a quarter had resided in France for more than one month continuously, and well over half appeared either to have attended a local language refresher course or to be attending one.

The Schools Council had inferred from this information that the quality of much French teaching outside the pilot scheme or local schemes must leave something to be desired, and it was proposed to make it possible for all authorities, whether in the scheme so far or not, to associate groups of schools with the pilot scheme, provided that the principles laid down for the scheme were followed in the schools concerned. An invitation to this effect was issued by the Schools Council to local education authorities in June 1966.[1]

THE SITUATION TODAY

1 *The pilot areas*
The teaching of French to all the 8-year-olds in the pilot schools in the pilot areas began in September 1964. After a year and a half's operation, the project seems to be going well. Most teachers have the impression that the addition of French to the curriculum has had a highly beneficial effect on children's attitudes to other subjects and that this is not simply due to the novelty of learning French. In some schools, teachers have reservations about the wisdom of including the least able children amongst those learning French, but the pilot scheme principle that children of all abilities should be included until a general assessment has been made of their performance is being adhered to.

As stated earlier, 80 per cent of the teachers in the pilot schools are using the trial Nuffield materials; other teachers are using *Bonjour Line* or *Parlons français*, and 2·5 per cent, mainly the bilingual teachers, are not using any commercially prepared materials at all. Many of the schools are now reaching the critical stage where writing is introduced, it having been a rule generally observed by all the pilot schools that writing should not be tackled during the first year of teaching.[2]

The provision of properly trained teachers continues to be a problem for many of the authorities. Most pilot areas are continuing

---

[1] As a result of this invitation the number of associate areas rose to 84 by the autumn of 1967.
[2] For a discussion of this practice see chapter 6 above.

to send about five teachers a year on intensive courses to ensure that they have staff available to guarantee continuity of teaching to the end of 1967/8, when the second (and final) wave of children being studied in the scheme will move on to their secondary schools. The schools will of course continue to provide French subsequently.

While it is clear to any visitor to the pilot schools that the attainment in French and enjoyment of it by most of the children are already considerable, some statistical results about their attainment in it should be available in 1968, based on three years' learning of the language by the children in the first wave and of two years' learning of it by children in the second wave. These results will be provided by the National Foundation for Educational Research, who are carrying out an intensive and thorough evaluation of the project.[1]

2 *The associate areas*

Some of the schools in the associate areas are following one year behind the pilot area programme, and some two years. Although these areas are adhering closely to the principles of the scheme, there are instances where certain departures have been made. The Schools Council hopes to continue to provide information to these areas on tackling the problems raised by the introduction of French in the primary school, derived from its experience in the pilot areas.

Advice about the organization of courses in primary language teaching methods was provided at a conference, organized by the Schools Council at Harrogate in February 1965, which was attended by representatives from nearly all the associate areas. This conference explained the principles on which the methods courses for the teachers in the pilot areas had been organized the year before, and the Schools Council's staff provided help to the associate area representatives in arranging between themselves to provide similar courses on a regional basis during 1965 and 1966.[2] By 1966 14 such courses had been run on a regional basis, involving teachers from 42 authorities. The need to provide them, of course, continues. Similarly, the Schools Council will be arranging for representatives of areas associated with the scheme to come together to discuss the

[1] See chapter 16 below.
[2] For further details of the project, with additional information for the modern language specialist, see the Schools Council's *Working Paper No. 8, French in the Primary School* (Schools Council, 1966).

implications for secondary schools, and to examine the conclusions reached at the Torquay conference on these questions.

3 *Local schemes*

It is not known exactly how many local schemes are in operation, but in addition to the few authorities, such as Leeds and East Ham, who were running schemes of their own before the pilot scheme was introduced in 1963, a considerable number of authorities decided in 1963 to set up their own schemes. Such evidence as has been obtained suggests that these are variable in quality and that consolidation on the lines described would be beneficial in some cases.

In some of these areas, the secondary schools have already begun to receive pupils from primary schools taking part in improvised schemes. By contrast with most of the pilot areas, these schools often find themselves receiving pupils from a range of primary schools with widely varying lengths of course and practices in French teaching. In these areas there is a clear need for direct consultation between secondary and primary teachers, with the collaboration of the local authority.

LOOKING TO THE FUTURE

There are, altogether, three appraisals of the pilot scheme in process. First, the statistical evaluation of the pupils' attainments in the language is being carried out by the National Foundation for Educational Research. As mentioned above (p. 109), this will lead to the production of an interim report in 1968, and a more complete report about 1972. It will set out to answer the questions mentioned at the beginning about the broad general effects of teaching French in primary schools, and provide proper evidence on which to base a decision for the future.

At the same time, members of HM Inspectorate are making a general appraisal of the scheme. Some of them are scrutinizing it from the language point of view, and others are making a general assessment of its impact on the class, the teacher, and the school. These opinions are being collected and will be analysed by the National Foundation as a supplement to its own report.

Finally, everyone taking part in the experiment, or coming into contact with it, will be making his own informal assessment. This means not only children and teachers, but parents, who are already displaying a keen interest in its progress. The pace at which the experiment has developed since it was introduced in 1963 can be partly attributed to the factors described in the first section of this chapter, but a great deal can perhaps be explained in terms of a growing feeling among parents and teachers that language learning is a need in our society and that it can make a contribution to a child's educational and psychological development, if the teaching is conceived in the right way.

It may seem that this is now so obvious that there is no need to continue to treat the teaching of primary French as a matter for experiment. But the pilot scheme was not set up to determine whether French can be introduced into the primary curriculum, but to find out the profit and loss of doing so. So far, it seems that the omens are good, and that the profit is likely to outweigh the loss. But the scheme is still in the early stages, and some of its success at present may be attributable to novelty. The Schools Council feels therefore that, at present, the aim should be to consolidate the teaching of French where a start has already been made, and not to extend it further without careful thought and without ensuring that the principles described in this report can be followed. The time for deciding whether a general advance should be made toward introducing French into all primary schools will come when the results of the formal evaluation are available, and future plans can be made based on the lessons that have been learnt.

9

Bilingual education in an American elementary school

PAUL W. BELL[1]

INTRODUCTION

In recent years national attention has been focused on the educational needs of the 'culturally disadvantaged' pupil. Unfortunately, in their zeal to identify the students who come under this classification, some educators have included all those pupils whose native language is not English. Though, fortunately, the situation is changing, all too often the potential for bilingualism has been left unexploited, as well-meaning school personnel have taken the position that the child who comes to school as a speaker of a language other than English can best be helped to achieve by 'stamping out' his mother tongue. Therefore, the child is permitted to communicate only in English. Paradoxically, after these pupils have completed seven, eight or nine years of school, having forgotten or never having been exposed to education in their native tongue, they are encouraged to study their vernacular as a foreign language.

Even the traditional foreign language programmes which have been developed in most public elementary and secondary schools reflect a basic lack of interest in developing truly bilingual students. After twelve years of study of Spanish, French, or German, the student is never really expected to be bilingual. Never is he expected to study other subjects in the foreign language. The United States, in contrast to some foreign nations, has not provided for an educated bilingual population.

BILINGUAL ELEMENTARY SCHOOLING

The purpose of this paper is to examine a school in which bilingual-

---

[1] Mr P. W. Bell is Coordinator for Bilingual Education to the Dade County Public Schools at Miami, Florida.—Ed.

ism and biculturalism are thought of as advantages and not disadvantages. The Coral Way Elementary School in Miami, Florida,
has as its goal the development of pupils who are literate, educated
bilinguals. The advantages of bilingualism are offered to English-
speaking pupils who would not normally have the opportunity to
learn two languages in childhood. In this school native English-
speaking pupils study not only the traditional curriculum, but also
study Spanish and learn to study the curriculum in Spanish. At the
same time, Spanish-speaking pupils who must learn English in order
to be successful in an American school, receive this necessary
instruction in English and in addition they are offered a programme
which will make them literate in their native Spanish. Coral Way
is a school in which all pupils have the opportunity to become
completely bilingual. It is the first public elementary school in the
United States to offer such a programme.

The question may be posed as to why Miami needs a bilingual
school. The answer can be found in an examination of the community. Miami is a bilingual area with over 200,000 native speakers
of Spanish in its population. For many years Miami has looked to
Latin America for commerce and tourism. This community has a
need for educated bilingual clerks in its stores, bilingual execu-
tives in business, bilingual doctors, bilingual secretaries, bilingual
lawyers, bilingual policemen, and even bilingual bell-hops. In short,
the bilingual has an advantage in almost every category of employment. And as important as bilingualism is locally, there will be an
increasingly greater demand for educated bilinguals nationally.

In the spring of 1963 it was, therefore, decided that one elementary school out of Dade County's more than 150, would offer a
bilingual programme. Before the school itself was chosen, certain
educational objectives were established. They incorporated assumptions developed through research and through the experiences
gained from examining our second language and vernacular programmes for the Cuban refugee pupils who had entered the Dade
County schools. The goals were these:

1 The participating pupil will have achieved as much in the way of
skills, abilities, and understanding as he would have had, had he
attended a monolingual school, and in addition will have derived
benefits which he could not have attained in a traditional school.

2 He will be approximately as proficient in his second language as
he is in his first. If he is a skilled reader in his first language, he will

be a skilled reader in his second language. If he has mastered the fundamental processes and concepts in arithmetic in one language, he will handle them equally well in the other language. If he can express himself clearly and adequately in his first language, he will be able to do likewise in the other language.

3 He will be able to operate in either culture easily and comfortably.

4 He will have acquired consciously or unconsciously an understanding of the symbolic nature of language and as a result will be able to achieve greater objectivity in his thinking processes.

5 In general terms he will be readier to accept strange people and cultures and will thus increase the range of his job opportunities.

6 He will have skills, abilities and understandings which will greatly extend his vocational potential and thus increase his usefulness to himself and the world in which he lives.

7 He will broaden his understanding of people and the world and be able to live a richer, fuller and more satisfying personal life.

INITIATION OF THE PROGRAMME

Once the goals were established, the school was selected. Coral Way was chosen because of three factors. First, it was located in a neighbourhood which was approximately 50 per cent Spanish-speaking and 50 per cent English-speaking. Second, the neighbourhood was a reasonably stable middle class community. The third factor was the interest of the staff, the administration of the school and the parents in the idea of providing bilingual education for the children of the area.

In the late spring of 1963 a series of meetings were held with the parents. The goals of the programme were explained; questions regarding the organization and the curriculum were answered. After the last meeting, the parents of the pupils who were to be in grades one, two and three during the 1963-4 school year were given the option of enrolling their children in the instructional programme or in a traditional programme. There was no screening of pupils nor entrance requirements for enrolment. However, individual counselling was provided for those who desired it. It was carefully explained that the programme was not only for the gifted or academically talented. The staff was equally careful to explain that it was expected that pupils' progress would be comparable to that of pupils in a traditional programme. Achievements would vary, as in any other class. Any parent could withdraw his child at any time it was felt that school progress was being hindered by the bilingual programme. It was further explained that in the first year only grades 1 to 3 would be involved, but that an additional grade level would be added each year until the full six-year programme was developed.

As a result of these meetings, enough children were involved to permit the creation of four classes on each grade level. Two classes were formed of native speakers of English and two of Spanish. Registration for the traditional programme was so limited that only two classes were formed, a first and second combination and a straight third grade. In general, the pupils involved in the bilingual programme reflected the normal range of the school population.

Six teachers from the faculty were selected to work in the English programme and six credentialed teachers who were native speakers of Spanish were hired to work in the Spanish programme. All of the Spanish-speaking teachers were bilingual though none of the American teachers were. Three unqualified 'aides' were added to the staff to help with clerical work and to assist in the instructional programmes in art, music and physical education. The 'aides' represented the only overstaffing of the school and their salaries were the only expenditures not provided for in all of the county's elementary schools.

THE CURRICULUM

During the summer of 1963 and again in 1964, the teachers, the aides, the principal and members of the County Bilingual Education Department were involved in a special full-day six-week workshop. Detailed plans and schedules for all phases of the curriculum and the school's operations were developed.

In seven curricular areas, special attention was given to problems resulting from the bilingual nature of the programme. Detailed linguistic sequences for English as a second language and Spanish as a second language were developed in order to incorporate the concepts of the several content areas in the curriculum. Science was given special attention because the availability of parallel texts in English and Spanish made it possible to sharpen the science concepts through their study in divergent cultural settings. Spanish as the vernacular was given special attention because no satisfactory programme was available and one had to be created. Music, art and physical education were given attention because in these areas intracultural relations would initially be the greatest. In all areas of the curriculum, the programme in the bilingual school incorporated and was in harmony with the regular Dade County programme as it appears in curriculum bulletins.

For the instruction in English, the State-adopted texts were selected. Special materials for English as a second language were provided. For instruction in Spanish, four series of texts were ordered: a Spanish basal reader series, a Spanish translation of the science series, a Spanish health series, and a Spanish modern mathematics series. All of these materials were recently published in the United States, and reflected modern American pedagogy in their approach to content. Supplementary reading and reference materials in Spanish were ordered for the library.

The principal, working with his staff and with the director of elementary education, developed a complex and comprehensive schedule to ensure the best possible staff utilization and to guarantee sufficient time blocks to carry out the curriculum.

THE TIME-TABLE

The pupils participating in the bilingual programme, both English-speaking and Spanish-speaking, receive approximately half of their instruction in each language. The time devoted to instruction in the second language for each group is staged so as to increase the proportion gradually. The time allotted to the learning of the basic skills and concepts compares favourably with the time regularly allotted in Dade County in monolingual schools, the only difference being that in the bilingual school the time is divided between the two languages. In the beginning stages the basic skills and concepts are always introduced in the first language of a child. These skills and concepts are then incorporated into the second language programme as part of a language learning experience. In this way the child reinforces the concepts and skills and at the same time advances in his mastery of the second language.

In order to ensure close correlation between the curricula in the native language and in the second language, teachers were organized into teams. Each team has one English teacher and one Spanish teacher who work with the same group of approximately 60 pupils. In the team working with native English-speaking pupils, the English team member is responsible for developing the usual English curriculum during half the school day and the Spanish teacher develops the second language programme for the same pupils during the other half of the day. In this way each teacher works with two groups of boys and girls. In the teams working with the Spanish-speaking pupils, the Spanish-speaking teacher develops the traditional curriculum and the English-speaking team member develops the second language programme. The aides provide release time for the teachers so that both teachers in a team have an extended planning period at the same time.

In Dade County first- and second-grade pupils normally attend school from 8.30 a.m. to 2.00 p.m. and third to sixth grade pupils attend from 8.30 a.m. to 3.00 p.m. However, the second-grade pupils in Coral Way go to school from 8.30 a.m. to 3.00 p.m. and during the last twelve weeks of the school year the first graders stay an extra hour also. The lengthened school day in first and second grade provides for extra time devoted mainly to the teaching of reading in the second language which begins after a foundation of vernacular reading has been established. For many pupils this means that reading instruction in the second language begins as early as the thirteenth week of the first grade.

PRELIMINARY RESULTS

A preliminary examination after the programme had run for two years indicates that the pupils are making progress comparable to that made by previous classes which were involved in a mono-lingual programme. Perhaps a better indication of the success of the programme can be seen in the fact that after one year of offering the bilingual programme, the parents of the pupils who were in traditional classes requested that their children be moved into the bilingual programme, thereby making it unnecessary to provide regular classes in the primary grades. In the course of the first two years only three or four parents requested their children to be withdrawn from the programme. Parents have also reported that their third graders are helping their high-school aged brothers and sisters with their Spanish lessons.

The evaluation by the teachers has also been generally favourable. One first-grade teacher who has taught in the school for years summed up the teachers' attitude when she was asked 'How do you explain the pupils' good progress when only half the day is spent studying English?' Her answer was, 'I seem to be planning better and wasting less time. The pupils also seem to be more highly motivated to learn.'

It should also be emphasized that the pupils actually spend as much time with educational experiences in each curricular area as they would in a traditional programme. In fact, in reading they spend more time totally, since they have at least one hour in vernacular reading and an extended period of second language reading. The total time spent in science, social studies, arithmetic, health, art, music and the other aspects of the curriculum equals or exceeds the time spent in these areas in a monolingual school. Study in these areas, with concepts introduced in the native language, then developed in the second language, does not produce interference, but reinforcement.

FUTURE DEVELOPMENTS

In terms of curriculum, it is anticipated that in the following year of the programme the language of instruction for units developed in grades three, four and five will not depend on the first language of the pupils. Groups will be mixed and the units will often be developed in the language which best fits the content. For example, mixed groups of Spanish- and English-speaking pupils may study a unit on Latin America developed in Spanish and taught by the Spanish-speaking teacher. At another time the same group may study colonization of the New England area in English with the native American teacher. The fourth grade may be studying the early history of Florida in Spanish and modern Florida history in English. Regardless of the medium of instruction the underlying concepts of man's adjustment to his environment, the development of democratic principles, the interdependence of man will be developed.

Plans are presently under way to start additional bilingual schools in Dade County. Their success will depend to a large extent on three factors: 1 The programmes must be designed and tailored to fit the school and the school community. 2 The teachers must be educated in their first language and trained in the use of modern pedagogical practices; and 3 Ample time must be provided for detailed planning and correlation of the instructional programmes.

The pupils in Coral Way are rapidly becoming bilinguals who are distinctly 'culturally advantaged'. They are learning to operate effectively in two languages and in two cultures. These boys and girls are broadening their understanding of other people. They are being prepared to live satisfying lives and to contribute to their community and their country.

10

'Frühbeginn des Englischunterrichts': the Berlin primary school pilot project

PETER DOYÉ[1]

INITIATION OF THE PILOT PROJECT 'FRÜHBEGINN DES ENGLISCHUNTERRICHTS'

In 1963 an expert committee formulated a pilot project that was to start at Easter 1964 in six classes of six different primary schools in West Berlin. The aim of the study was to assemble data on the problem of the optimum age for beginning second language learning. English was chosen as the second language since approximately 97 per cent of all Berlin children learn English as their first foreign language. The question of the age at which experimental teaching should begin was not easy to decide. There is much to be said for a beginning in the first grade, when children enter the primary school, but in view of all the problems of a completely new situation which a child has to face at his school entry (e.g. establishing himself in a new social group, getting accustomed to a new environment, and becoming acquainted with his teacher, etc.), it was decided that our experiment should start in the third grade, when most of the children are 8 years of age.

Six third-grade classes with 187 children (91 girls and 96 boys; about 30 pupils per class) were chosen. The sample was selected according to sociological criteria only. The classes chosen had to be representative of the social composition of Berlin primary school classes. Therefore we took 'normal' primary school classes from six different areas of our town. They were by no means a selected *élite*.

The question of whether the English lessons should be given by

---

[1] The author of this chapter, Peter Doyé, who is now Professor of English at the Pädagogische Hochschule, Braunschweig, Federal Republic of Germany, was one of the initiators and, until 1966, planning consultant of this project. See also Doyé (1966).—Ed.

the classroom teacher or a specialist teacher of English was decided in favour of the former, for the following reasons:

1 Only the classroom teacher knows his children well enough to teach each of them individually, which is particularly necessary at this early age.

2 Only the classroom teacher can integrate the English lessons flexibly into the normal curriculum of a third grade.

This last argument must be understood in relation to the time available for the foreign language instruction. We had 90 minutes per week at our disposal. Instead of dividing them into two full lessons of 45 minutes each (i.e. the normal length of a lesson in West Berlin schools), we split these 90 minutes into six units of 15 minutes each, one for every day of the week. Thus the children were in daily contact with English and the teachers were free to fit in these 15-minute periods at any time of the school day.

The decision that the classroom teachers should give the English lessons restricted the choice of teachers who were suited for participation in our project. They had to possess the following qualities: (a) experience in teaching younger children, (b) mastery of the English language, (c) knowledge of modern foreign language methodology, and (d) experience in teaching English to beginners in the fifth grade. It was not difficult, however, to find six teachers who possessed these characteristics, since English has been a compulsory subject in all West Berlin schools since 1946, and we could therefore draw from a large reserve of qualified teachers in the primary schools.

In order to prepare the experiment a study group was formed, under the chairmanship of Oberschulrat Klawe, the Director of the experiment, with experts from the Pädagogische Hochschule, Berlin, and the Pädagogisches Zentrum, and the 14 teachers who were to take part in the project in the following two years. In this study group a general plan was developed consisting of the principles of the whole enterprise and a guide, for the use of the six 'pioneer teachers'. We avoided going too far into details in this guide, so that the teachers would not feel hampered in their individual approach. We did not prescribe any definite teaching method although we determined rather strictly *what* was to be taught (see pp. 122, *seq.*).

It must be mentioned here that this foreign language instruction beginning in grade 3 was to pursue no other aims than those established for the 'normal' English course starting at grade 5 laid down in the *Bildungsplan für die Berliner Grundschule*:[1] to develop elementary skills (within a limited vocabulary) in the understanding, speaking, reading and writing of English. We proceeded on the assumption that these pupils would attain *greater* proficiency in these skills than pupils following the conventional course beginning at grade 5.

EXECUTION OF THE PROJECT

The experiment began at Easter 1964, after the parents of all 187 participants had given their consent.

From the beginning the teachers used the direct method. The classes were conducted exclusively in the foreign language. According to a decision of the study group and following the example of other projects (FLES for example)[2] all six teachers worked only orally during the first year of the experiment and postponed the introduction of written symbols until the second year of study. Thus a concentration on the two basic skills of listening and speaking was made possible.

Doing without reading and writing demanded considerable ingenuity on the part of the teachers. To maintain the interest of these 8-year-olds and, at the same time, not to be overwhelmed by their exuberance was quite an achievement. The teachers employed a great number of activity methods (e.g. games, rhymes, riddles and songs).

This need for flexibility and variety had its counterpart in the need for systematic procedures. The teachers found out very soon that in this situation a strictly systematic approach was indispensable for two reasons:

1 Although the children learnt the language rapidly through 'natural' or playful devices, they also forgot it rapidly.

2 The children had very little opportunity to practise outside the classroom what they had learnt at school, since they possessed no written or printed material that could have served as a basis for such practice.

Looking back on the experience of the first two years, we can say

[1] Published by the Senator für Volksbildung, West Berlin, 1962.
[2] FLES is the abbreviation commonly used in USA, for Foreign Languages in Elementary Schools. See chapter 2, p. 17.

5

that all participating teachers have succeeded in combining liveliness with systematic teaching.

The content of the course had been decided at the beginning of the experiment. The study group drew up a list of topics to be treated in all classes. The criteria for the selection of these topics were:

(a) The interests of 8-year-old children

(b) The importance of the topic for later use in real-life situations

(c) The possibilities of presenting and explaining the subjects to 8-year-old children.

The topics were:

1 Toys
2 The school and the classroom
3 The family
4 Parts of the body
5 Clothing
6 Food and drink
7 At the table
8 In the street
9 Animals
10 A child's daily routine.

In spite of our intention to leave as much freedom to the individual teacher as possible, we went as far as determining a compulsory *active vocabulary* for all participating classes. This vocabulary was selected in accordance with the ten topics listed above and on the basis of available linguistic statistics. The word list that served as a norm of selection for our vocabulary was the Minimum Adequate Vocabulary of Michael West, which is an adaptation of the *General Service List of English Words* (West, 1953) to the requirements of the spoken language (West, 1960). Of the items of our word list[1] for the third and fourth grades 95 per cent are contained in the Minimum Adequate Vocabulary. The rest were chosen because of their relevance to the needs and interests of these young children.

Our word list consisted of 80 words for grade three and another 70 words for grade four. As the whole active vocabulary of the children should, however, comprise 150 words at the end of the third grade and 250 words at the end of the fourth grade, the teachers were free to add 100 other words of their own choice. It must be emphasized

---

[1] Copies of this list and further details of instruments mentioned in this report can be obtained directly from the author.

here that we did *not* prescribe the passive vocabulary. We found this neither necessary nor desirable as it might have hampered the teachers too much.

What we did determine, however, were ten basic patterns to be learnt in the third grade. These patterns belong to a group of chief English sentence patterns, according to the findings of A. S. Hornby, who has analysed the structural groundwork of the English language and graded it on methodological principles (Hornby, 1959).

The teaching materials that were employed in our project consisted mainly of tangible objects in the immediate environment of the pupils and of toys which the children brought to school. The teachers added a variety of realia from Britain or the USA, such as pictures, flags, stamps, charts, maps, posters, coins, souvenirs, picture books, picture postcards, etc.

Some of the classes worked with flannel boards, others with flashcards. From time to time a record player or a tape recorder was used to let the children hear the foreign language spoken by native speakers or to acquaint them with the original version of English songs and rhymes. As already mentioned, written material was not used until the fourth grade.

PRELIMINARY RESULTS

These preliminary results refer only to the first year's work. We have undertaken a similar evaluation of the work done in the second year, but the results are not yet available.

The third-grade results were obtained by means of detailed reports from the six teachers, and through an objective test.

Teachers' reports
The teachers were asked to keep continuous anecdotal records of their work and to write a report at the end of the year, based upon these records. It was agreed that the reports should be drafted in a standard form, which had to include the following points:

(a) Situation of the school and the class with detailed information about the children's social background, age, sex, etc.
(b) Selection of subjects, i.e. the topics treated as well as the vocabulary and patterns taught.
(c) Teaching methods followed in conducting the project.
(d) Materials used.
(e) Results and conclusions drawn from the first year's work.

The main conclusions can be summarized as follows: highly successful 53 children; successful 88 children; and only moderately successful 46 children.

The teachers reported unanimously that most of their pupils liked the English lessons. The majority preferred them to the lessons in other subjects and often complained about the shortness of the teaching units in English (15 minutes).

The test

In addition to the subjective evaluations by the teachers we also assessed the results by means of an objective test. Lacking a formal standardized test for 8- to 9-year-old children, we had to construct a test ourselves. It consisted of four parts:

Part I   Vocabulary
Part II   Pronunciation
Part III   Answering questions
Part IV   Free oral production

In part I the children's vocabulary was tested by presenting them eight flashcards with objects, numbers or actions on them, which they had to name. The words were taken from the compulsory vocabulary for grade three and selected as a random sample of the total list. One mark was given for each object, number or action named correctly, regardless of pronunciation, as long as the utterance was intelligible.

In part II the children had to repeat four sentences—spoken by the examiner—each of which contained two difficult sounds. Only these sounds were scored, so that the maximum attainable was again eight points.

In part III the children had to answer four questions. For each sentence two points could be scored for a meaningful response that was free from mistakes in grammar and pronunciation, one point for a meaningful response with not more than two mistakes in grammar and pronunciation and zero for a response with more than two mistakes.

In part IV they had to describe a picture representing a simple scene in an English house. This part was most difficult to evaluate, as free oral production is a very complex skill with several different components. For the scoring of this skill we adopted the system that is used in the Speaking Tests of the Modern Language Association

of America[1] and scored the items on the following criteria: vocabulary, structure, pronunciation and fluency. Sixteen points were
attainable in this part.

The maximum sub-scores were:

Part I	8 points
Part II	8 points
Part III	8 points
Part IV	16 points
Total	40 points

The mean raw scores that were actually attained were:

Part I	6·79 points
Part II	6·64 points
Part III	5·91 points
Part IV	7·67 points
Total	27·01 points
Standard deviation	3·8 points
Highest score	37·5 points
Lowest score	16·5 points

CONTINUATION AND EXTENSION OF THE PILOT PROJECT

The preceding data refer to the first year of our experiment (1964–5).
Meanwhile this first group of children has completed the second
year of English (1966). The scope of the aural-oral skills was
extended and the skill of reading introduced.[2] At the end of the
second year a test similar to the one described on p. 124 but with
more complex items was administered and the results suggested
that considerable progress had been made.

At the beginning of the third year writing and work with a
textbook are introduced.[3] From that time on the children have five
lessons a week (45 minutes each), as is the case in a 'normal' course
beginning in grade five.

The project was not only continued with the first group, but was
also extended to more schools. At Easter 1965, another 240 children
in eight classes starting learning English in grade three, and at Easter

[1] MLA—Cooperative Foreign Language Tests. Educational Testing Service,
Princeton, New Jersey.
[2] For reading we used the working scripts of a course called *Hallo!* Mary Glasgow
& Baker Ltd, London.
[3] *Peter Pim and Billy Ball* I/1. Cornelsen Verlag, West Berlin.

1966 the same number of children were added so that in the school year 1966/7 about 660 children participated in this project.

Let us finally come back to our initial question of the optimum age for beginning the study of a second language. If our experiment is to contribute to a solution of that question, it is not enough to show that the children participating in our project have reached satisfactory results. We must discover how these results compare with those obtained in a 'normal' course beginning in the fifth grade, i.e. at the age of 10.

We have accordingly made the following arrangement: In each of the six schools of our first group (the 187 children that have meanwhile reached the fifth grade) we selected one parallel class, which most nearly matches the experimental class, and asked the six teachers to undertake the normal fifth grade courses in these classes too, in addition to a continuation of the *Frühbeginn* course in their experimental classes. After two years, at the end of the sixth grade, we hope to ascertain, by means of an objective test, whether the corresponding groups have obtained different results and what these differences indicate.[1]

---

[1] The general question of research on starting a language at different age levels is discussed by J. B. Carroll in chapter 5, pp. 59, *seq.* above.

11

Teaching German in an English primary school: a personal record

ERIKA SIPMANN[1]

INTRODUCTION

In the first year I taught at two primary schools. A third school in a neighbouring rural district was added in the second year. The German classes were mostly made up of the brighter 'A stream' children. This fact had bearing on the methods which could be employed and on the rate of progress. But the selection of pupils aroused criticism, and subsequently a wider distribution of intelligence and ability was aimed at.

In the first year I taught one group of 8- to 9-year-olds, one group of 9-year-olds and two groups of 10- to 11-year-old pupils. In the

[1] The writer of this chapter, Miss Erika Sipmann, is a primary school teacher in West Berlin. She went to England before the completion of her own training to be a German *Assistentin* in an English grammar school. In the course of her stay in England the local education authority in whose area she was serving, East Sussex, organized language teaching experiments in primary schools and invited Miss Sipmann to teach German in two and later in three schools to children varying in age from eight to eleven. Miss Sipmann taught German in these schools for two years (1962–4). After that she returned to Germany to complete her own training and to qualify as a certificated teacher. Before she left she wrote a report of her work mainly for the benefit of her successor taking over the German teaching in primary school classes.

Miss Sipmann was by all accounts a most successful teacher. The report she had prepared was the basis of a paper she submitted to the 1966 Hamburg meeting. The study in this chapter is based on this paper. It is included in this volume as an illustration of the kind of situation of language teaching to young children that primary teachers in many countries have faced in the sixties and the way a lively and inventive teacher has responded to this task. It is not intended as a 'model' of teaching to be followed by others. Miss Sipmann is a young teacher. Her own ideas even today are still developing and she herself is highly critical of some of the aspects of her work in East Sussex. But her account is detailed and lively and therefore offers the reader a concrete picture of a teaching experiment as it is seen by a thoughtful practitioner.—Ed.

second year three new groups were added, one of 8-year-olds and two of 9-year-olds. Of the groups who started first only two had a second year of German in the primary school, as the 10- to 11-year-old children left after the 11-plus examination to go on to secondary schools. Those children who started to learn German when they were 8 will have had the advantage of three years of foreign language instruction by the time they leave the primary school.

Following the recommendations of the British Bilingual Association (1962) no group consisted of more than fifteen children. A period of 35–40 minutes daily was assigned to each group in the first year. This, however, was felt to be too long. The periods were therefore reduced to 30 minutes in the second year.

In two schools a small classroom was made available for the teaching of German. In the country school only a corner of the dining-hall could be set aside for this purpose. Going into a special room meant stepping out of the ordinary routine of school life and into a 'German' atmosphere. This and the fact that their teacher taught no other subjects and could therefore more easily be identified with the language had, I feel, positive psychological effect. The children were, however, conscious of the fact that they were learning a foreign language. They learned and used it with the same delight as they might learn and use a secret code in order not to be understood by outsiders. A number of parents showed their interest by attending a special German evening class in order to keep up with their children.

Much has happened in the field of primary school language teaching since this case-study was first written. It was originally intended for my successors. When I began I had no information on the grading of German grammatical structures or on the choice of vocabulary for primary school children. In this respect I was left more or less to my own devices. On methods I had learnt a great deal from my training as a teacher of English at the Pädagogische Hochschule, Berlin, and from discussions with other teachers at various conferences, particularly from the recommendations made by Mrs Kellermann[1] and others experimenting with the introduction of French in the primary school. Looking back I realize that, although I tried to the best of my ability to grade the language material, my approach was largely intuitive.

[1] See 1962 Report, chapter 14 on the work by Mrs Kellermann, and also Kellermann (1964) and references in chapters 2 and 8 above.

AIMS OF THE COURSE

My teaching efforts were guided by the following aims:

1 To form in the minds of my pupils a concept of the foreign language as a medium of expression that exists independently and in its own right and not solely in terms of the mother tongue. To form an attitude that regards the foreign language as a meaningful instrument for the expression of thoughts, feelings and actions.

2 To teach a reasonable mastery of sounds and intonation.

3 To impart the understanding and correct use of a limited selection of common structures.

4 To teach relevant vocabulary items pertaining to everyday situations encountered by children.

5 To impart some knowledge of the country, its people, their customs and way of life, creating a vivid picture of the country, so that the children would feel more familiar and more at home if ever they went to Germany.

But most of all it seemed to me to be important that the children should enjoy learning German and that their initial enthusiam should be kept alive.

PLANNING THE COURSE

In planning the course I was guided by the following criteria:

1 The situations should arise from the children's environment.

2 They should allow visual presentation including mime.

3 They should allow dramatization.

4 The situations should call for an everyday and, in the first instance, concrete vocabulary.

5 A maximum opportunity for practising a particular structure had to be given.

6 A revision of structures and words previously learned should be possible.

The order in which language material was introduced and the rate of progress were determined by the situations themselves and by the practical experience of teaching. They therefore varied somewhat with each group.

Situations were grouped under topic headings. These centred

thematically mostly around the Familie Müller. The children of Herr and Frau Müller were called Ina and Udo. The German publishing house, Moritz Diesterweg, kindly made us a present of a sufficient number of copies of the *Deutsche Auslandsschulfibel: Ina und Udo.*[1]

This book was used later on to supplement the oral work when the reading stage had been reached. It contains a simple vocabulary and simple structures which are repeated throughout. Although this textbook is really designed to teach reading, it can also be used to teach German. We also made good use of a small number of copies of *Der Kinderduden.*[2]

CONTENT OF THE FIRST YEAR COURSE

The content of the course may be summarized as follows:

1 Winter Term

Topics: *Unsere Klasse*
            Mein Spielzeug
            Unsere deutschen Freunde
            Wir rechnen
            Der Herbst ist da
            Mein Hampelmann
            Das Datum
            Wie spät ist es?
            Das Christkind ist da

Songs: *Alle meine Entchen*
            Es ist eine Mutter
            Schwesterchen, komm tanz mit mir
            Vom Himmel hoch, o Englein, kommt
            Stille Nacht (*1 Strophe*)

Linguistic skills: By the end of the winter term I expected the children to have formed a rough conception of singular and plural in regard to nouns and verbs, and to have developed some feeling for the changes brought about by gender in the nominative and accusative

---

[1] *Ina und Udo*, Deutsche Auslandsschulfibel, Verlag Moritz Diesterweg, Frankfurt am Main.

[2] *Der Kinderduden*, Bibliographisches Institut, Mannheim.

case. I expected them to have good number comprehension, to tell the time correctly and to be able to use dates.

2 Spring Term

Topics: *Der Winter ist da*
            Meine Kleidung
            Meine Anziehpuppe
            Udo ist krank
            Frühlingswetter ist launisch
            Am Morgen

Songs: *Schneeflöckchen, Weißröckchen*
           Kuckuck, Kuckuck! Ruft's aus dem Wald
           Bruder Jakob
           Laurentia, liebe Laurentia mein

Linguistic skills: By the end of the spring term I expected the children to have acquired a better feeling for German word order and to differentiate the various forms of the present tense. We mainly worked on using the already available sentence patterns in new situations. The children improvised plays and little scenes with the language material they had learnt.

3 Summer Term

Topics: *Zu Hause bei Ina und Udo*
            Udo kommt zu spät zur Schule
            Kommt essen, Kinder
            Wer will fleißige Handwerker sehen
            Wir sind die Musikanten
            Wir gehen baden

Songs: *Der Schneider hat 'ne Maus*
           Wir sind die Musikanten
           Wer will fleißige Handwerker sehen
           Lachend, lachend

Linguistic skills: The summer term mainly aimed at teaching the use of the accusative and the dative after prepositions. There was much scope for repeated use of already available patterns in little scenes.

By the end of the year the children were expected to be able to comprehend a simple story with the vocabulary that had been introduced during the year, to answer questions about their immediate surroundings such as school, home, toys, friends and their various activities. Much attention was given to good pronunciation and intonation.

CONTENT OF THE SECOND YEAR COURSE

1 Winter Term

Topics: *Wir fahren mit der Eisenbahn*
           Am Zeitungskiosk
           Auf der Straße
           Weihnachten in Deutschland
           Ein Krippenspiel

Songs: *Heissa, Kathreinerle*
           Der Schaffner hebt den Stab
           Bunt sind schon die Wälder
           Horch, was kommt von draußen rein
           Weihnachtslieder zum Krippenspiel

Linguistic skills: The main emphasis was on the handling of the accusative and the dative cases. We played a number of games such as guessing an object with a minimum number of questions and 'I pack my suitcase', which required the free use of different patterns. German coinage was introduced.

2 Spring Term

Topics: *Wir gehen einkaufen:*
               Im Lebensmittelladen
               Im Obst-und Gemüseladen
               In der Bäckerei
           Ina und Udo gehen in den Zoo
           Wir können alles messen
           Eine Erdkundestunde
           Auf dem Postamt

Songs: *Scherzlieder*
               Mein Hut der hat drei Ecken
               Ein Hund ging in die Küche
           Es tönen die Lieder
           O du stille Zeit
           Lustig, ihr Brüder

Linguistic skills: By the end of the term the children were expected to be able to use German money and measurements and to conduct a shopping conversation. We also did some work on the geography of Germany.

3 Summer Term

Topics: *Ein Besuch auf dem Land*
            Märchen: Rotkäppchen
               Hänsel und Gretel
               Die Prinzessin, die nicht lachen wollte
               Der Rattenfänger von Hameln
            Eine Reise auf dem Rhein
            Wir besteigen eine Burg
            Wir hören eine alte Sage (Die Lorelei)

Songs: *Hänsel und Gretel*
            Die Lorelei
            Im Frühtau zu Berge
            Der Mond ist aufgegangen

Linguistic skills: By the end of the term the children were expected to know the past tense and the past participle of some common verbs and to be able to use the simple future. To encourage oral composition the children were required to listen to stories and to retell them. These compositions were sometimes written down though accuracy in spelling was not expected.

VISUAL AIDS

In the absence of commercially produced visual aids we had to fall back on our own resources. In a way this was perhaps a good thing as we were able to suit our particular needs. Whenever possible we tried to make use of real objects. The children readily brought their toys. Their mothers and sometimes the infant department provided us with things such as cutlery, crockery, a clock, clothes for dressing up, etc. Together we produced a model shop, road, farm and zoo. From Germany I obtained a sufficient amount of German toy money and measuring tapes. Many of the visual aids, however, were pictures and friezes which I made myself, and which were mainly used to convey a story or situation. As these pictures were the primary means of understanding it was important to make sure that they told their story clearly in order to avoid any confusion or ambiguity. They were large and colourful, very simple yet essentially realistic and always aimed at representing some aspect of life in Germany.

Pictures, however, are static. Objects can be handled. The children can do something with them as they speak. This is more interesting for them and seems to have positive effect on learning and remembering. Today I prefer therefore using picture segments to be assembled and moved about on a flannel board whenever pictorial representation is called for. In this context mime was found to be one of the most effective ways of putting meaning across and of practising structures, since it satisfies the children's need for activity.

As the course progressed the need for film strips or cartoon films made itself felt. The visual aids at our disposal, although adequate in the initial stages, were less satisfactory when the language became more complex.

TEACHING THE STRUCTURE

For English-speaking children German is a difficult language. There are such structural peculiarities as the genders, the cases, separable verbs, etc., which do not occur in English, but are necessary in German to form even the simplest sentences. A feeling for these as vehicles carrying meaning had to be developed.

No formal grammar was to be taught and structures were practised in sentence patterns. But I found that the repeated use of a structure in a pattern must be motivated. Pattern drill cannot be practised with young children for its own sake. Situations were therefore found which called for the repetition of patterns in as natural a way as possible.

In the beginning only one part of a pattern was changed, e.g.

Das ist ein Auto.
Das ist ein Reifen, etc.
Ich habe ein Auto.
Ich habe ein Heft, etc.
Ich habe einen Reifen.
Ich habe einen Roller, etc.[1]

Gradually the number of changes increased:

Ich trage einen Rock.
Ina trägt ein Kleid.[2]

[1] Topic: *Mein Spielzeug.*
[2] Topic: *Meine Kleidung.*

Ich ziehe meiner Anziehpuppe ein Kleid an.[1]
Ich stehe um 5 Uhr auf.
Meine Mutter steht um 7 Uhr auf.[2]

Different contexts and vocabulary ensured variety. The children loved using these patterns. It gave them confidence. Gradually a flexible fund of readily available patterns accumulated and enabled the children to assimilate new patterns more quickly. All patterns recurred frequently until they were used quite automatically.

One mother who attended my evening class for the parents of the pupils told me that her 8-year-old son spotted several mistakes in an essay she had written because to him 'it didn't sound right'.

The pace was determined by the achievements of the slowest of the group. Before the children were required to ask each other questions the answers to such questions were well practised. The children were then given plenty of opportunity to ask each other questions. They enjoyed doing this. It gave a new incentive to practice.

Was ist das?	*Das ist ein Buch.*
	Das ist ein Heft.
	Das ist ein Ball, etc.
Hast du eine Puppe?	*Ja, ich habe eine Puppe.*
	Nein, ich habe keine Puppe, etc.
Wie spät ist es?	*Es ist 7 Uhr.*
	Es ist halb acht.
	Es ist fünf vor neun, etc.
Woraus ist der Rock?	*Der Rock (er) ist aus Stoff.*
Woraus ist die Bluse?	*Die Bluse (sie) ist aus Seide.*
Woraus ist der Tisch?	*Der Tisch (er) ist aus Holz,* etc.

In instances such as in the second example I preferred my pupils to answer in complete sentences, although it is common usage to answer only with 'yes' or 'no', in order to give more opportunity for using the pattern. I know the controversy on this point. Today I would perhaps avoid questions calling for 'yes' and 'no' answers of this type altogether. On the whole I tried to keep the language as natural and idiomatic as possible.

In a more informal teaching atmosphere where the teacher tries

[1] Topic: *Meine Anziehpuppe.*
[2] Topic: *Am Morgen.*

to give the pupils plenty of opportunity to use the language they are learning a variety of situations arise which prompt the introduction of incidental language material. Thus when the children were drawing I wanted them to ask their friends for crayons in German. So I practised:

> *Bitte, gib mir einen roten Buntstift.*
> *Bitte, gib mir einen blauen Buntstift.*
> *Bitte, gib mir einen gelben Buntstift,* etc.

A feeling for the relation between gender and endings or cases and endings was slow to grow. It took an even longer time before the children were capable of abstracting the structural elements and transferring them to other language situations.

Although no formal grammar was taught, it seemed occasionally advantageous to make the children aware of certain rules. For example, the use of prepositions followed by the dative had been practised in a variety of patterns such as:

> *Das Radio steht auf dem Schrank.*
> *Die Vase steht auf dem Tisch.*
> *Das Bild hängt an der Wand.*
> *Die Uhr hängt über dem Bett.*
> *Ina spielt mit einem Ball.*
> *Hans spielt mit einer Katze.*

The children readily realized what had happened. I told them that *mit, auf, in, an, unter, über, neben* and *zwischen* are '*Zauberwörter*' (magic words). Later I described prepositions followed by the accusative as '*Pfeilwörter*' (arrow words). Such explanations had to be in English, but I could see no harm in this.

USING THE PATTERNS IN MEANINGFUL SITUATIONS

In the beginning of the course structures were taught and practised by manipulating and talking about objects which the children brought to class. As soon as enough patterns had accumulated I tried to make them become part of a story. At this point I introduced the Familie Müller. Their children Ina and Udo first, then their parents Herr und Frau Müller, then the friends Dora, Emil, Anni and Peter. New structural elements were now embedded in a story. The use of structures in patterns arose now from building up or talking about a story.

The best way, I found, to use language material naturally was to dramatize the stories. Acting a story seems to provide the best motivation for speaking. In order to be able to set a scene or play whenever we desired the seating arrangement had to be very flexible. Usually we sat in a circle, but the chairs could easily be stacked away in a corner. With the aid of a few props and a few sketchy costumes any situation could be staged. The children were more or less left to improvise these little scenes with the language material that was available to them. They showed a great deal of imagination in doing this and derived more fun out of it that way. Acting a story provided an opportunity for teaching new expressions, especially idiomatic ones. Nowadays I would also use puppets to give the children still another opportunity to speak.

Here is an example showing how a scene was developed.

Topic: *Am Zeitungskiosk.*

Situation: *Frau Müller geht zum Zeitungskiosk*

It was intended to practise the use of '*möchten*' in a simple sale conversation and to give yet another opportunity for dealing with German money. A variety of German newspapers, magazines, and books had been laid out on a table. Above it was a sign reading: *Zeitungen und Zeitschriften.* Various sweets and their prices had been listed on the blackboard behind them.

Some of the pattern practices which arose from the situation are listed below:

Was ist das? *Das ist ein Kiosk.*

Das ist eine Zeitung.

Das ist eine Zeitschrift, etc.

Was kostet die Zeitung? *Sie kostet . . . DM.*

die Zeitschrift? etc.

dieses Buch? etc.

Ich kaufe eine Zeitung, eine Zeitschrift, ein . . .

Hans kauft ein Buch, eine Karte . . .

Hans möchte ein Buch, eine Karte . . .

Am Kiosk kann man . . . kaufen.

Dialogues such as the following developed spontaneously:

Frau Müller geht zum Kiosk

Frau Müller: *Guten Tag.*

Verkäufer(in): *Guten Tag. Was darf's sein?*

F.M. *Ich möchte eine Zeitung.—Ich möchte eine Morgenpost, bitte.*

V.	*Und sonst noch etwas?*
F.M.	*Ich möchte eine Zeitschrift und zwei Eis. Ina, möchtest du ein Buch?*
Ina	*Ja, bitte, Mutti. Ich möchte ein Buch.*
V.	*Dieses Buch ist sehr lustig. Es heisst 'Vater und Sohn'.*
F.M.	*Ina, möchtest du dieses Buch?*
Ina	*Ja, Mutti.*
V.	*Ist das alles?*
F.M.	*Ach, Vati möchte eine Karte von Süddeutschland. Haben Sie eine Karte von Süddeutschland?*
V.	*Ja, sicher. Hier!*
F.M.	*Danke, das ist alles. Was macht das?*
V.	*Das macht DM. 8,50.*
F.M.	*Hier sind 10 Mark.*
V.	*8,50, 9,00, 10,00 Mark. Danke. Auf Wiedersehen.*
F.M. und Ina	*Auf Wiedersehen.*

Being improvised the dialogue differed each time, but it was nearly always just as fluent and idiomatic.

The work was supplemented by songs and games. Games, especially competitive ones, were very popular with the children. They were a most useful means of revising without making it too obvious. Below I have listed some of the many we played.

Games:
Competitive mental arithmetic.
Ich sehe was, was du nicht siehst (I spy)
Hide-and-seek with objects.
Guessing an object with a minimum number of questions.
Wortketten (Kinderkleid—Kleidertasche—Taschenuhr, etc.)—and many others more.

Singing games:
Wir sind die Musikanten
Wer will fleißige Handwerker sehn
Wir fahren mit der Eisenbahn
Schwesterchen, komm tanz mit mir
Mein Hut der hat drei Ecken—and many more.

READING AND WRITING

At the beginning work was kept purely oral, but later all groups, some sooner than others, expressed the wish to see and write the

German they knew. At this stage each child was allowed to keep a German book into which songs and stories could be copied. The children illustrated them most beautifully and took great pride in them.

At first writing was confined entirely to copying. Later the children were allowed to make up sentences within given patterns of various kinds. In the second year they began writing little compositions, i.e. they retold stories. Although accuracy in spelling was not expected, it was found that there were not too many spelling mistakes. This was probably due to the fact that the vocabulary had been seen and written correctly many times before.

PRONUNCIATION AND INTONATION

It took me a little time to realize which of the German sounds were particularly difficult for English-speaking children and to find ways and means of teaching their correct pronunciation. This may account for the fact that the second set of beginners mastered the sounds more quickly. It is a fallacy to assume that children can hear their own mistakes or readily perceive the difference between what they have said and the correction by the teacher. It was therefore, occasionally necessary to explain how certain sounds are produced.

Most of my pupils were very good at imitating intonation even to the extent of copying the personal peculiarities of the teacher. The repetition of sentences in patterns seems ideally suited to teach good intonation.

Whenever possible I brought in other native speakers or played records to give the children practice in listening to other voices. Occasionally the tape recorder was used to practise pronunciation and intonation.

CONCLUSION: PUTTING GERMAN TO USE

The children were eager to use the German they had learnt. Some parents told me that their children spoke German outside school when they played and even taught their younger sisters and brothers. By the end of two years they had acquired a very good basic vocabulary. New words could often be explained in terms of already available vocabulary. The children could understand and retell a simple story. They were able to use most of the patterns they had learnt with ease. Most of them had acquired a good accent.

The head teacher of one of the schools made it possible for the

German groups at her school to spend ten days on the Rhine in August 1964. We arranged well in advance for the children to correspond with boys and girls of their own age from the town we planned to visit. This definitely gave the children a new impetus to learn German. It was possible to find pen-friends for the children of the other schools, too. Letters and visits are exchanged to this day.

On several occasions the children entertained their parents with little scenes, plays and songs. As far as I can judge German made a real impact on the lives of these children and also on the schools as a whole. It created a keen and lively interest in Germany and the Germans and generally broadened the educational horizon.

12

'Bonjour Line': an audio-visual course in French for foreign children

CATHERINE GOLDET[1]

INTRODUCTION

When the *Centre de Recherche et d'Étude pour la Diffusion du Français* (CREDIF) began work in 1960 on the problem of teaching French to foreign children, it attempted to meet a particular need which has been increasingly felt over the last ten years in various countries, i.e. teaching a second language in the primary school. It might seem rather a hazardous undertaking to work out a method for use with children of widely differing backgrounds and needs, sharing only the fact of not being French; but, on the other hand, the need to help teachers by producing such a course seemed imperative.

CREDIF had already perfected *Voix et Images de France*, an audio-visual course for adults; the course for children was therefore able to benefit from the experience gained from this previous work and use the same linguistic basis, namely Stage One of *Français Fonda-mental*. The work leading to the creation of *Bonjour Line* has been directed within the CREDIF team by Madame Hélène Gauvenet. In introducing the method to the reader, we propose to show how it was conceived, what pedagogical principles guided its creation and, most important, how it can be used in primary schools.

PURPOSE

It should be stressed at the outset that this course is aimed at children who are taught at school in their native language: it is

---

[1] Mademoiselle Catherine Goldet, a language specialist at CREDIF, has been responsible for research, development and training in connexion with *Bonjour Line* and is a collaborator of Madame H. Gauvenet, the author of the course.—Ed.

definitely not intended for a particular élite and makes no claims
to make children bilingual. Its aim is simply to teach the basic
mechanisms of the French language in the primary school, since all
the research done in this field has shown that a foreign language is
acquired very much more easily at the age of 8 or 9 than at 12 or 13.

This course is intended for children not below the age of 8,
i.e. it is for school children who have already mastered reading and
writing in their own language. Its aim is to avoid the dangers of
prematurely teaching two very different phonetic and orthographic
systems simultaneously, while introducing a foreign language at a
time when the child is still receptive enough to learn a new system.
Moreover, a series of psychological experiments carried out in
French primary schools (with 6- to 11-year-olds) has shown that a
child under the age of 8 cannot yet properly grasp the logical
relationships between a succession of pictures which tell a story.

Faced with a set of pictures a child who is too young just points
to things, and later describes them or else projects himself into the
situation and invents a story. Since the *Bonjour Line* course has as its
starting point a story told in pictures it is suitable for children who
are over the age of 8 and, consequently, able to follow the progression of a series of meaningful pictures.

LINGUISTIC CONTENT

When determining the linguistic content of *Bonjour Line* we followed
Stage One of *Français Fondamental*. This vocabulary and grammar
was, as I may remind the reader here without giving a complete
account of its history, produced under the direction of Monsieur
G. Gougenheim of the Sorbonne. Stage One of *Français Fondamental*
comprises 1,445 words and constitutes neither an artificial language
different from 'normal' French nor a closed language: it contains
those words and grammatical items which appear most frequently
in the spoken language and which are consequently the most
useful. Also a study of recordings of children's conversations has
enabled us to verify that the structure words children use are the
same as those appearing on the *Français Fondamental* list. On the
other hand the nouns used by children go beyond this list, which
is hardly surprising, since the use of nouns depends on a criterion
of availability (*disponibilité*) within a centre of interest, and a child's
centres of interest are, of course, quite different from those of an
adult.

This explains the presence in *Bonjour Line* of some nouns which are not found in the vocabulary of *Français Fondamental*. We composed stories for *children*, and the subject matter called for the child's special vocabulary. We chose simple sentence structures, in order to respect a pedagogical progression and also because it would be absurd to use complex sentences in the second language when the child is hardly able to manage such sentences in his native language.

We may add that, although we have aimed at linguistic and grammatical accuracy, we have been even more concerned to place the child in a world corresponding as closely as possible to the preoccupations of his age group: we feel it is important that the child should enjoy the stories he is presented with and that they should encourage him to express himself as spontaneously as possible in the foreign language. In short we had to motivate the learning process and make the 'language bath' into which we want to place the child as tempting as possible. To do this we have appealed to the child's imagination, to his love of adventure and to his capacity for immediate attachment to any heroes of his own age with whom he can easily identify himself.

The course introduces a group of children who are caught up in a series of adventures and whose experiences, in their lives or in their dreams, are presented to the young pupils in the various units of the course. In this way the dialogue is placed in a situation.

PRESENTATION AND STAGING

Bonjour Line is an audio-visual course, 'audio-visual' being, apparently, the magic formula for painless foreign language learning! Certainly, film strip and tape used together can help the teacher quite considerably, but above all they must be used to ensure the comprehension of linguistic points. The film strip is made up of a series of pictures (great care has been taken with the drawing of these) and provides a situation for the dialogue played on tape: in this way the child grasps a series of situations which 'trigger off' the sentences of the dialogue. This is the basic idea of any valid audio-visual teaching method.

What we aim at is giving the child a series of new notions and new habits which will enable him to respond to a given situation in a new way which is different from that in his native language but analogous to it. The starting point of every lesson is, therefore, a concrete situation. We want the non-French-speaking child to get to know our language and our country directly, through situations involving children who work and play and talk in their language just as he would in his own.

Bonjour Line has three parts at present:

Part I consists of 25 lessons plus 3 revision lessons and 9 exercises in pictures. In these lessons approximately 500 words of *Français Fondamental* are taught. In our view this should correspond to the work of one school year.

Parts II and III. These two parts comprise a total of 26 lessons and 9 exercises in pictures. Each of these lessons is much longer than those in the first part and contains more teaching-points. These two parts represent approximately two years' work.

The teaching of the written language is provided for only in the second part. We know, however, that in some countries (especially North Africa) the school curriculum requires reading and writing to be taught before the end of the first part, in the first year of French.

In any case it appears to be dangerous to teach the spoken and the written language simultaneously from the start. One principle is definite: the sounds of French should be correct and firmly fixed, before the written code is taught. Without this time lag there is little hope of the child ever achieving an adequate pronunciation. This would be all the more regrettable as the developmental stage of the young child offers a special advantage for the acquisition of the spoken language, and by introducing the written word too soon, all the benefit derived from learning a foreign language at an early age would be lost.

Plan of one lesson: Each audio-visual lesson consists of two parts:

    1 the lesson as such
    2 the 'quiz' (*jeu des questions*).

The *lesson* is a dialogue involving characters who reappear in other episodes and, from lesson 9 of Part One on, become the heroes of one continuous story. These characters are children placed in situations which enable us to introduce a certain number of grammar points and certain centres of interest: the house, meals, animals, means of transport, etc. From the beginning of the second part a continuous story enables us to deal with these centres of interest in a particular context of civilization, since the adventures of our heroes take them across France.

Let us look, for example, at lesson 7 of the first part. Here are some extracts from this lesson:

Michel: *Je vais à la fête. Et toi?*
André: *Moi aussi, je vais à la fête.*
Michel: *Tu as de l'argent?*
André: *J'ai un franc. Et toi?*
. . . .
J'achète un billet.
Michel: *Moi aussi.*

Our pedagogical aims in a dialogue such as this are immediately clear: the teaching of the tonic subject pronouns *toi, moi* (*toi aussi, moi aussi*) and the verb *aller,* one of the most frequent French verbs, and this in a dialogue arising quite naturally from the pictured situations.

The *quiz* (*jeu des questions*) is a dialogue between a model teacher and Line, the good pupil who always answers the questions correctly. The quiz between Line and the teacher provides a means of teaching question-and-answer exchanges (which form the basic mechanisms of conversational speech) and this naturally so. This quiz also allows for the exploitation of interesting points in the lesson. For example:

Quiz (*jeu des questions*) for lesson 7.

Professeur: *Où va Michel?*
Line: *Il va à la fête.*
Professeur: *Où va André?*
Line: *Il va aussi à la fête.*

LESSON PROCEDURE

We may remind readers that the teacher's book gives advice on teaching points for each lesson: naturally the teacher will adapt these to the needs of his own programme. Here, however, are the main points of our method. It is essential that the child should have fully understood, first the general meaning of the story, then the particular meaning of each of the sentences, before memorizing them. Only this procedure will enable him to use them again in a similar context and then in other situations, the aim being the pupil's mastering of the fundamental mechanisms of the language.

This is why we start by showing the film strip in its entirety in conjunction with the tape, so that the child can grasp the whole of one episode; and thus his knowledge of the whole can help his understanding of each element in the dialogue.

Next we take each sentence in conjunction with its picture and explain it globally without dealing with individual words: to do this we call on previous knowledge and of course we use the picture as much as possible, never the native language which is no help to the pupil, on the contrary may well confuse him.

When this stage is completed the pupil has to repeat the lesson, sentence by sentence, and to memorize it, because only after complete memorization of each sentence will the child be able to use again, in a different context, the linguistic data he has learned. This memorization stage must on no account be neglected, as it is in a sense the corner stone of the lesson.

We now come to the most important stage, the exploitation of the lesson, which is the goal we set ourselves to reach. It is now a question of using all possible means to make the child use what he has learned, that is, to make him show in practice that he has mastered the structures and understood their use. Here the teacher's role is extremely important: it is the teacher who must ask questions and direct them so that the pupil expresses himself as well as he possibly can. To do this he will also of course use games, mime, songs and the like. The quiz is used in much the same way as the lesson and allows the lesson itself to be more profitably exploited.

At a later stage we use a certain number of moving films made by CREDIF which, while bringing in new material not found in the course, allows for the re-utilization by the child of scattered items of the language acquired through the audio-visual lessons.

READING AND WRITING

We have not ignored the problem of reading and writing. On the contrary, as from the second part of *Bonjour Line*, we make our pupils read and write. Once the phonemes and intonation patterns have been taught we can go to reading, then on to the progressive study of the most common spellings of the different French sounds. Readings and dictations have been recorded and the pupil also has a workbook with a number of written exercises. We do not feel it is necessary to enlarge on this aspect of the course here since the introduction of reading and writing depends on the demands of the school curricula of different countries. The only point which seems essential to us is that of a phasing which must be observed in the teaching of a language, namely the acquisition of oral mechanisms *before* the introduction of the written language.

CURRENT DEVELOPMENTS

The reader should not be left with an impression of dogmatism: *Bonjour Line* aims at being an open, living method, and this openness is emphasized by its use in the most different contexts, with children of varying ages (although the optimum age for starting is eight, some start a little earlier or even later) and by teachers whose training differs enormously.

CREDIF is very conscious of the fact that the tool it has provided is used in very different ways. This is why we brought together thirty users of the *Bonjour Line* method, French and foreign, for a training course at Montpellier in July 1966, in order to examine with them a number of problems and analyse the solutions individual teachers have applied in their own country. This led us to a joint review of the methodology of *Bonjour Line* and the modifications different users have had to make in order to fit *Bonjour Line* into varying school requirements. Some of the modifications suggested seemed to meet identical difficulties and we are therefore working on some changes in the first part.

We know too that the learning of a second language at primary school level raises the problem of improving the teacher's own performance in that language. Several countries are working on this problem and producing suggestions. We ourselves intend to produce some supplementary material to make the teacher's work easier.

On the other hand it is clear that such a widely used method cannot claim to meet *every* individual requirement. We hope on the contrary that teachers, as their training improves, will make the appropriate adjustments and in so doing apply one of the basic principles of good teaching, i.e. to use materials and techniques in such a manner that they become integrated into their own personal way of teaching.[1]

---

[1] Since the writing of this chapter, further research and experimentation have taken place. As a result, Lesson 12 of *Bonjour Line I* has been modified, Lessons 8A and 26 have been added, new practice materials and notes for teachers have been developed. A new edition of *Bonjour Line I* is under way and should be ready for publication early in 1969.

13

The Nuffield foreign languages teaching materials project

A. SPICER[1]

AIMS AND ORIGINS OF THE PROJECT

Among the objects of the Nuffield Foundation is 'the advancement of education', and over the last several years the Foundation has sought to achieve this objective in a variety of ways. Many research projects, large and small, designed to stimulate and encourage a reappraisal of the whole approach to the teaching of many of the established school subjects, have received the Foundation's support. To this end, teaching materials projects have been set up for secondary school physics, chemistry and biology, and for both primary and early secondary school mathematics, junior science and languages.

In so far as these various curriculum development projects have anything in common, it is perhaps a shared concern to participate in the revitalizing of the whole teaching approach in classroom and laboratory. It seems generally agreed that, in many school subjects, the syllabus content needs bringing up to date, and that the methods of presentation of these subjects are in need of considerable revision.

Much traditional teaching—influenced by examination pressures— bore the stamp of what might be called the *grammarian's* approach: the pupils were not so much taught a skill as drilled in mechanical rules. Thus, in the teaching of foreign languages, a child was required to learn tenses and rules of grammar before applying them in written or spoken communication; in science to assimilate facts and reiterate definitions before seeing what relevance they have to

[1] Mr A. Spicer was the Organizer of the Nuffield Foreign Languages Teaching Materials Project and has now been appointed Director of the Schools Council Modern Languages Project, and the Nuffield Project. Further information about these Projects can be obtained from the Director, Nuffield Schools Council Modern Languages Project, University of York, York, UK.

experimental investigation; in elementary mathematics to learn tables, formulae and theorems by rote before having to think mathematically.

Present thinking is largely in favour of reversing this established order. The aim is now to get the children talking and thinking in a foreign language before formalizing its grammatical rules; to acquire an understanding of scientific problems at first hand before having to formulate scientific generalizations; to grapple with concrete situations involving mathematical thinking before coming to the logical relationships which underlie mathematics. The emphasis, in other words, is on the achievement of a working understanding of the subject rather than on the memorization of formal knowledge about it.

Each of the Nuffield projects aims to put across this approach— and, at the same time, attempts to raise minimum teaching standards—by providing, for all teachers who wish to use them, a full range of teaching materials: extensive teachers' guides, visual aids, practical apparatus, students' handbooks, and the like. Before these materials are made generally available, however, they are tried out widely under classroom conditions and then revised in the light of this experience. The case for innovation is more easily made (and the innovation itself more readily accepted) if it can be shown to be both practicable and effective.

The Foreign Languages Teaching Materials Project represents, in fact, only one aspect of the Foundation's interest in the teaching of languages. The whole problem is being attacked on a wide front, and Foundation-supported schemes range from the preparation of language teaching materials to the construction of alternative examinations at 'O' level. Grants have been made for pilot experiments in primary school French teaching in various parts of the country; for in-service training of teachers on special study courses abroad; for a survey of language teaching in the primary school and for a report on modern languages in the grammar school; for research into teaching methods, involving the special provision of language laboratories and audio-visual equipment of different kinds, and for research into the language development of children. This list is not exhaustive but is sufficient to indicate how the whole problem both of raising the standard and extending the scope of language teaching in Great Britain is being tackled simultaneously in many different ways.

Many other organizations and individuals in Great Britain have also been engaged in research and development in the field of foreign language teaching, and wherever possible the Foundation has cooperated with them and in particular with the Schools Council.[1]

In 1961, the same year that the Ministry of Education set up its Curriculum Study Group, the Nuffield Foundation, by sponsoring meetings of science teachers to discuss ways and means of revitalizing the approach to teaching science in school, took the first steps to initiate what was to become a series of Curriculum Development Projects. In the following year, both the Curriculum Study Group and the Foundation extended their inquiries into the field of foreign language teaching. As a result of these inquiries, it was decided to set up two parallel and associated projects, one sponsored by the Foundation and the other by the Ministry. The Foundation took responsibility for the preparation of teaching materials for French in the primary school; and the Ministry undertook the administrative arrangements for the introduction of this new subject into the primary curriculum, for the conduct of the experiment and, in association with local education authorities, for the training of the teachers.

The decision to set up these linked Foreign Language Projects marked the beginning of a quite new form of joint enterprise and cooperation between the Ministry and an independent organization. In fact this experiment in cooperation may well turn out to be as important a development as the foreign language experiments themselves.

In 1963 preliminary work on the two projects began. During this year the Foundation appointed an Organizer for the Project, established a Consultative Committee and commissioned a pilot survey of foreign language teaching in the primary schools. It should perhaps be pointed out that, although it was agreed that the materials to be produced by the Project would be made available to the Pilot Scheme schools, LEAs[2] and schools were naturally free to choose for themselves whatever materials they wished to use. It was also agreed at this time that the Project's time-table for the production of materials should be geared to the time-table of the Pilot Scheme. In this way, schools deciding to use the Nuffield materials would be assured of a continuous supply of materials throughout the five-year duration of the Pilot Scheme. This was a decision of great importance for the Project, as it would inevitably

[1] See chapter 8 above.   [2] Local education authorities.

entail a restriction of the experimentation, research and revision that could be carried out in the time at the Project's disposal. Although the full implications were perhaps not completely understood at the time, it was nevertheless a decision which was taken knowingly and willingly in view of the agreed need to provide the maximum assistance for the teachers in schools participating in the experiment. This decision was all the more willingly accepted in view of the fact that the association with the Pilot Scheme would make it possible for all materials to be tested in a large number of schools. The Pilot Scheme would also ensure a constant flow of information from the teachers using the materials in actual classroom conditions. Another factor which influenced the decision was the fact that few, if any, of the French materials then available had been specifically designed for use in British primary schools by non-specialist teachers and with large classes.

Soon after the formal establishment of the Project in September 1963, it was decided to extend its aims beyond the provision of French materials for the Pilot Scheme schools. The aims of the Project were then defined as follows:

(a) to provide integrated teaching materials in French to cover the age range 8 to 13;

(b) to provide integrated teaching materials in Spanish, Russian and German for the age range 11 to 13;

(c) to undertake as much research and experimentation as was possible in the time available in those fields of study which would be likely to provide data and information relevant to the production of teaching materials;

(d) to provide information to teachers and others interested in foreign language teaching.

With these aims in view, the Project was organized into several sections, and each was given a specific task. The first sections to be established were the Headquarters, French and Information Sections. These were followed by the Research, Spanish and Russian Sections, then the Publications and finally the German Section. The Information Section operates, jointly with the City of Leeds Education Committee, a Languages Centre, including recording and copying studios.

In this way it was hoped that the main aims of the Project might be pursued simultaneously and to the mutual advantage of each section. Needless to say, in attempting to advance simultaneously on all fronts, it could not be expected that a uniform rate of progress could be maintained. Moreover the commitment to produce materials in a constant flow and to a tight schedule meant that teaching materials had sometimes to be produced before the results of research could be known. Nevertheless, this situation was not without its advantages. Materials were being produced, information and help was being provided to the teachers in the Pilot Scheme, and research was being carried out. In this way, enthusiasm was maintained and nothing was held up. All concerned were well aware that as a result of practical experience in the field, drastic revision of materials and techniques would constantly have to be made, but that at each revision more information would be fed in from the results of the continuing research.

The Project is led by an Organizer, seconded to the Foundation, who is responsible to the Director and Trustees of the Foundation for the successful completion of the programme. He is assisted by teams of practising teachers, linguists and other specialists seconded for full-time work on the Project. Each of the sections is under the leadership of an Associate Organizer, and the services of the Headquarters, Research, Publications and Information staff of the Project are available to each team. Each of the writing teams includes teachers, artists, and native speakers of the language concerned. The staff of the Project also benefit from the advice and guidance of Consultative Committees, whose members cover a wide range of relevant knowledge and experience.

A very important part is played by the teachers who are testing the courses in schools all over the country. In the case of the French materials the testing is carried out in the schools of the Pilot Scheme, together with certain other schools who have been associated with the Project from the beginning. In the case of the other languages, the schools testing the materials have been invited to participate or have volunteered to help in the experiment. These teachers provide an extremely valuable feed-back of criticisms, suggestions and new ideas both through the questionnaires which they return after completing each unit, and by personal contact made with members of the writing teams at special meetings and conferences and during school visits.

THE SCHOOLS COUNCIL CONTINUATION PROJECT

In 1967, the Schools Council decided to continue the work of the

Nuffield Project by financing the production, testing and revision of a further three years' teaching materials in French, Spanish, Russian and German for pupils of 13–16 years of age. In the case of French, two sets of materials will be produced, one for faster learners, and the other for slower learners; for the other languages one set of materials only will be produced. In this way the Nuffield and Schools Council materials, taken together, will provide an integrated course of eight years' duration for French and of five years for Spanish, Russian and German.

The Schools Council Project will be based in York and will work in close association with the Language Centre of the University of York. Work began on the Russian and Spanish materials in 1967 and will begin on German in 1968 and on French in 1969.

The Continuation Project will follow the policy of the Nuffield Project in that its materials will be produced by teams of teachers, linguists, native speakers and artists and will be thoroughly tested in schools prior to publication. Schools at present testing Nuffield Courses have been assured of continuity in the supply of draft materials and many have agreed to continue to test and report on the continuation materials.

THE FRENCH SECTION

The Section is at present engaged on the production of a five-year Introductory French Course for 8- to 9-year-old beginners covering the last three years of the primary school and the first two years of the secondary school. The Course, which is entitled '*En Avant*'[1] is being tested in association with the Schools Council's Primary French Pilot Scheme.

Work on Stage 1 of the Course was begun in October 1963, and the first draft was tried out from January to July 1964 in 50 volunteer primary schools in England, Scotland and the Channel Islands. These schools contributed greatly to the success of the experiment by sending in their criticisms and suggestions, many of which were incorporated in the revised draft of the Course. The testing of the second draft was begun in September 1964 by 151 primary schools, the original volunteers being joined by nearly a hundred of the schools taking part in the Pilot Scheme. The final 'near-printed'

[1] The publishers are Messrs E. J. Arnold & Son Ltd, Butterley Street, Leeds 10, from whom further information can be obtained.

draft of Stages 1A and 1B is being used in a further group of Pilot Scheme Schools (Associated Areas).

Stage 3, which is intended for use in either the last year of the primary school or the first year of the secondary school has now been tested in schools, and was revised in the summer of 1967, ready for publication in January 1968. Stage 1A was published in August 1966, Stage 1B in December 1966, Stage 2 in February 1967.

The teaching materials used in Stage 1 include tape recordings, flannelgraph figurines, flashcards, wall charts and games. The teacher is provided with a handbook containing the text of the lessons, teaching notes and additional information and suggestions for widening the scope of the Course. The written word is not introduced until Stage 2, when the main visualization is provided by coloured posters and flashcards.

Stage 3 continues the development of the reading process, moving from 'reading recognition' in Stage 2 to true reading. Writing, too, is further developed. The main visualization is again by means of posters and reading sheets. There are also readers and children's workbooks.

Stage 4 will continue the development of reading and writing. The visualization will be provided by film strips. There will also be readers, workbooks and worksheets. The first draft was ready for use in the schools in September 1967.

It is intended that the primary school stages of the Course should be suitable for use with large classes and by non-specialist teachers. The main aims are to teach children to speak, read and write French rather than to teach them *about* French. The compilers of the Course have attempted to present the teaching points systematically, step by step, and in the initial stages are more interested in securing fluent control of a comparatively small number of the patterns of the language rather than of a large vocabulary. While presenting material in a systematic, graded fashion, great importance has nevertheless been attached to actable dialogues or 'situations', to games and to songs. For the teachers too, there are detailed notes on how to make use of '*En Avant*', though it must be emphasized that these are intended as suggestions for their guidance, not as overriding instructions which would prevent them from employing their own method of presentation or using their own teaching techniques.

The materials are based whenever possible on research (*Le Français Fondamental* and the Project's own research programme);

but when this has not been possible the teams have relied on the intuition and experience of practising teachers and the example of relevant teaching materials.

The selection of the various situations, sentence patterns and vocabulary items, together with their sequencing and grading, is determined by various criteria among which frequency of occurrence, relevance, the interest of the children and 'teachability' claim most attention.

An item's frequency, based on the number of times the item occurs in actual language events, is one of the most powerful of these factors and the French materials will incorporate most of the frequency-determined items of *Le Français Fondamental* (*1er Degré*). The Nuffield team has not, however, attempted to introduce items following the order of frequency indicated in the CREDIF word lists. The decision to include an item in the Nuffield course may be dictated by its frequency, but its actual point of introduction is determined by other criteria.

The appropriateness of a particular item in the commonly-occurring situations of home, school or classroom determines its relevance, despite its possible lack of qualification for inclusion on other terms. This category would include utterances like '*Essuie le tableau, s'il te plaît*'. Such items would probably not occur together in an analysis of children's vocabulary any more than blackboard-cleaning itself would figure in a survey of their interests and the utterance would therefore be difficult to justify from the point of view, for example, of frequency. But it has such positive and practical value in its own right that its inclusion is justified nonetheless.

Children's interests are examined from two angles. Within the Project, statistics have been acquired concerning the frequency with which certain topics of conversation and composition have been mentioned. The most frequent of these have been termed 'centres of interest', and are taken into active consideration during the establishment of the situations of the course. In addition, teachers both inside and outside the Project can accurately estimate, in the light of their own experience, whether or not a particular situation will catch and hold a child's attention.

In a similar way, teachers in the Pilot Scheme leave the Project in little doubt as to whether an item is teachable or not. Neither they nor the pupils find all the items easy, but the inclusion of such less teachable items only occurs where the demands of the language must have priority. To English children the idea of gender in inanimate nouns is foreign and therefore a potential source of confusion, but such is the importance of the items *le/la/un/une* to the French language that the concept is presented at the very beginning of the Nuffield course.

Within such limitations the Project aims to provide as authentic a model of the contemporary French language as possible.

When the five-year course has been completed in 1969, the French section will begin work on the production of the continuation materials for pupils aged 13–16. At this point two sets of materials will be produced, one for faster learners, and the other for slower learners.[1]

THE SPANISH SECTION

This section was established in September 1964 at a comprehensive school, the Thomas Bennett School, Crawley. Pre-testing of the draft course was carried out at this school in association with a small number of other schools. In 1965 the Section moved to Leeds. Since then thirty schools have been testing the revised materials.

One of the main objectives of this introductory course, which is entitled '*Adelante*', is to ensure that it must be suitable for average and less able pupils. For this reason units are short and new material is introduced in very small amounts and thoroughly practised.

The material has been divided into three stages, which represent the oral, reading, and writing stages of the course. It is probable that for less able pupils, these three stages will take longer than two years to complete, but the aim is that the teachers should be free to proceed at the pace that is most appropriate to their pupils.

The composition of the three stages is as follows:

Stage 1 is an entirely oral stage of 20 units which introduces the pupils to a selection of the patterns of the language. Visuals take the form of flashcards, cut-outs and wall-pictures. Each unit also contains a simple dialogue situation based on known material which is suitable for re-enacting by the pupils. Games, activities and songs are included as well as background cultural information.

Stage 2 represents the reading stage. New linguistic items are introduced orally as before, but pupils are now introduced gradually to the written forms of already familiar language. Special reading

[1] Further information may be obtained from the Organizer (French), Mr N. Patrick, Nuffield Schools Council Modern Languages Project, University of York, York, UK.

material is provided in this stage, which also introduces the use of film strip presentation. Like Stage 1, Stage 2 consists of 20 units, and every fifth unit is a revision and recapitulation unit of the material of the previous four units.

Stage 3 is similar to Stage 2 except that it introduces simple written composition. It marks a transition to a form of presentation which is increasingly audio-lingual.

After Stage 3 further materials will be available which will lead up to a suitable version of the 'O' level examination or to the CSE (Certificate of Secondary Education).[1, 2]

THE RUSSIAN SECTION

This section was established in September 1964 and was based on two schools, Winchester College and the Thomas Bennett School, Crawley. In 1965 the section moved to Leeds.

An introductory two-year audio-visual course entitled '*Vperyod*' has been designed primarily for pupils beginning Russian in the secondary school at the age of 11. The main aims of the course are to teach pupils to speak, read and write Russian. The development of reading and writing skills follows the development of oral ability. Great importance has been attached to grading, and each unit of the course introduces a limited amount of new material which can be readily assimilated.

Each selected language pattern is presented audio-visually in a short recorded text, illustrated by film strips, picture sheets, flannelgraph figurines, or flashcards. The new material is then developed through various forms of oral practice, including question-and-answer games and activities, and audio-lingual drills. The newly-learned pattern is then incorporated in a recorded 'situation' or dialogue which the pupils can re-enact after listening and repetition practice. Each unit of the course also contains teacher's notes, which include suggestions on method, cultural background information related to the subject matter of the unit, and songs. Short readers, integrated with the structural progression of the course, are provided for the

[1] For details on these examinations, see chapter 8 above, page 98, footnote [1].
[2] The publishers are Macmillan & Co. Ltd, Little Essex Street, London WC2. Stage 1 was published in September 1967, Stage 2A in April 1968 and Stage 2B in December 1968. Further information about the Spanish Section may be obtained from the Organizer (Spanish), Mr D. Rowland, Nuffield Schools Council Modern Languages Project, University of York, York, UK.

development of reading. The pupil's workbook is supplied as an aid to the development of early written work, and is followed by the gradual development of carefully guided written composition.

Pre-testing of the draft course was carried out with 11-year-old pupils at the Thomas Bennett School. Since September 1965, thirty schools have tested the revised drafts of the course. Stage 1 was published in September 1967, Stage 2 in March 1968 and Stage 3 will be published in December 1968.

In September 1967 the Russian Section began work on the production of further course materials designed for pupils of 13–16.[1]

This was established in September 1965 at the Language Teaching Centre of the University of York. Since January 1966, some 36 schools have taken part in the initial testing of the draft version of Stage 1. A further test has taken place from September 1966. The published version of Stage 1 will be available in September 1968, and Stage 2 a year later.

Language material is being selected for its suitability for communication between 11-year-old pupils of average ability and their German fellows, and is being taught by methods of which the primary aim is to develop fluency in speech. Reading is introduced half-way through the first year and writing at the beginning of the second year.

New material is introduced in dialogue form, recorded by German native speakers and illustrated by film strips. The use of the language is developed by means of flashcards. Oral practice in questions and answers, games and activities including '*Basteln*', songs, etc., are used to develop fluency in the new patterns of the language.

Each unit includes short recorded dialogues for learning by heart and acting. The visuals accompanying these dialogues serve to put pupils in various German situations in which they have to use a particular language pattern. They also provide a wide variety of authentic, photographed, cultural background information. Each unit includes teacher's notes, taped audio-lingual drills and a

---

[1] The publishers are Macmillan & Co. Ltd, Little Essex Street, London WC2, and Percy Lund, Humphries & Co. Further information on the Russian Section may be obtained from the Organizer (Russian), Mr D. Rix, Nuffield Schools Council Modern Languages Project, University of York, York, UK.

reference page summarizing the patterns and vocabulary introduced in that Unit.[1]

THE RESEARCH SECTION

The Research Section of the Project is currently engaged on the
production of testing materials. Tests are being constructed to
assist the teacher in the evaluation of the progress of his pupils,
and also to provide the language teams with a clearer indication of
the progress of the schools who are trying out the draft materials.

It is also intended that the research team should assist the language
teams in the trial and validation of alternative teaching procedures
to those generally suggested in the draft materials. In this way it is
hoped to strengthen the experimental nature of the courses being
produced.[2]

THE CHILD LANGUAGE SURVEY

From the beginning of the Project, it was felt that a French course
could not be satisfactorily produced without some knowledge of the
linguistic habits of the children in the two language communities
concerned. Precise information was also needed on the grammar,
vocabulary, and centres of interest of French children in the relevant
age groups. After a conference with CREDIF in November 1963,
a joint pilot survey was proposed, with the Project being responsible
for the English side and CREDIF for the French: information
would then be exchanged in either raw or processed form, depending
on whether agreement could be reached about the model of analysis
to be employed. To date the Survey has collected the corpus of
written and spoken children's language on which the analysis is
being based. Some 80 hours of speech and 1,500 pages of written
material are being sampled and analysed to provide the information. Pilot analyses of these children's interests and grammatical
selections have been completed, and computer programmes are now
being devised as the next step in a statistical statement of the grammar. An experimental lexical study is also being undertaken. Close

[1] The publishers are Messrs E. J. Arnold & Son Ltd, Butterley Street, Leeds 10,
UK. Further information on the German Section may be obtained from the
Organizer (German), Mr A. Peck, Nuffield Schools Council Modern Languages
Project, University of York, York, UK.
[2] Further information on Research may be obtained from Mr W. Prescott,
Nuffield Schools Council Modern Languages Project, University of York, York,
UK.

contact has been maintained with CREDIF throughout, and as the Project has expanded, similar reciprocal arrangements with other countries are being made.

Although in its early stages the French course has not been able to profit fully from the Survey, later stages should derive considerable benefit from it.[1]

PUBLICATIONS SECTION

One of the first tasks of the Research Section of the Project was to produce a catalogue of available French teaching materials. This catalogue has now been republished in a revised form. Another early piece of research undertaken was a *Report on Foreign Language Teaching in British Primary Schools* in 1963 by C. M. Lazaro. These two publications were followed by others dealing with such subjects as language laboratories (Moore and Antrobus, 1964), the use of puppets in language teaching (Rowlands 1965), audio-visual French courses suitable for primary schools (Nuffield Foundation, 1965), language teaching films (Antrobus, 1966), primary school French readers (Naylor, 1966), and a survey of Russian teaching in schools in Great Britain (Sollohub 1967).[2]

The production and distribution of draft materials is now being undertaken for the Spanish, Russian and German sections, as well as for the French, while the Project's series of Reports and Occasional Papers is being continued.

INFORMATION CENTRE

A French Teaching Information Centre was established in Leeds in 1964 at 31 Harrogate Road, Leeds 7, in accommodation provided by the City of Leeds Education Committee. Here a collection of audio-visual and other course materials, supplementary aids, readers, reference books and periodicals is available for inspection.

The Centre has now been extended to become a joint Nuffield and City of Leeds Modern Languages Teaching Information Centre. The Information Centre now contains teaching material for Spanish, German and Russian, and for some of the other languages

[1] The Nuffield and CREDIF child language surveys are the subjects of two separate chapters. See chapters 14 and 15 below. Further information may be obtained from Mr R. W. Rutherford, 31 Harrogate Road, Leeds 7.

[2] A full list of publications is obtainable from the Publications Officer, Mr J. M. Scholefield, Nuffield Schools Council Modern Languages Project, University of York, York, UK.

taught in Leeds. Facilities for listening to records and tapes, and for looking at films and film strips have been extended and the whole range of materials for inspection is continually being expanded. The Centre is also concerned with the organization of modern language courses for teachers.

The Centre already deals with a large number of postal requests for information on many aspects of language teaching, and members of the Project staff have acted in a consultative capacity to architects, education authorities, manufacturers of language teaching equipment and others interested in the development of teaching facilities. More than 2,000 visitors, including many from overseas, have been received at the Centre in the last three and a half years.[1]

[1] Inquiries should be addressed to the Information Officer, Mr D. Nicholson, Nuffield / City of Leeds Modern Languages Teaching Information Centre, 31 Harrogate Road, Leeds 7, UK.

Linguistic and
educational research

14

The Nuffield child language survey

R. J. HANDSCOMBE[1]

ORIGINS

The Nuffield Child Language Survey is part of the Nuffield Foreign
Languages Teaching Materials Project, whose history and present
position are outlined elsewhere in this volume by its Organizer,
Mr A. Spicer.[2]

The project itself was originally established to provide an audio-
visual course of French for United Kingdom school children aged
8–13. From the beginning, the team members were aware that if
the language of such a course was to be up-to-date, appropriate
and interesting to the children, they would need a great deal of
information. They needed to know as much as possible about the
way of life of children in both Britain and France in order to be
able to present the language material accurately, and they also
needed to know particular details of the grammar, vocabulary and
centres of interest of the children in both communities so that the
language itself would be acceptable to them. Despite the ever
increasing interest being shown in child-orientated research programmes, there was little information of the latter sort available.

A conference with CREDIF took place in November 1963 to
work out ways of meeting the deficiency. A joint pilot survey of
children's language was proposed, with CREDIF conducting the
French investigation and the Nuffield Project assuming responsibility for English. Any information so obtained would then be
exchanged.

---

[1] The author was, until 1967, the Associate Organizer (Research) in the Nuffield
Foreign Languages Teaching Materials Project in charge of the Child Language
Survey. This chapter is based on an article in a recently published Council of
Europe volume of studies.—Ed.
[2] See chapter 13.

This conference also suggested ways of collecting material. The research workers would concern themselves with both written and spoken language. They would use various sources, including conversations between children and adults, between children and other children, existing and 'commissioned' written work, like diaries and compositions, *psycho-drames*, and spontaneous speech acquired by surreptitious recording.

THE ENGLISH CORPUS

Dr Ruqaiya Hasan of Edinburgh University was invited to undertake the English survey. Two factors immediately affected her choice of recording method with regard to the spoken material. Any analysis presupposed transcription, and transcription within a fixed time limit. Interest had also been expressed in the possible deduction of a teaching model of pronunciation. The essential criterion in each case was one of intelligibility.

After consultation with the Phonetics Departments of Edinburgh and Leeds Universities, it was decided that, in the circumstances, the south-east of England would be the best place to record. So that the results would not be regionally biased it was also recommended that control recordings should be taken elsewhere. Eventually eight schools around London were chosen for the main corpus, with five from Yorkshire supplying the control.

There remained one further consideration. It was always envisaged that the results of the Survey would be made available for teaching purposes. As the classroom situation almost always presupposes the presence of an adult teacher, it was thought wise to concentrate on those recording situations where an adult either took part in the conversation or remained present while the children talked. This had one immediate result. Experimental recordings had shown that surreptitious recording was exceedingly difficult. It was now abandoned except as a further means of control.

The method finally chosen saved much time and labour with little loss of naturalness and spontaneity on the part of the children; Dr Hasan decided to combine the techniques of 'uncontrolled interview' and 'free-play'.

Two hundred and forty children formed the population, 60 from the four age groups 9–12 inclusive. They were divided into groups of three, sometimes three boys, sometimes three girls, sometimes mixed, depending on the school. The children's teachers made sure that there was a wide range of intelligence and usually tried to choose children who already knew each other well both in and out of school. This meant that two possible sources of tension—being compelled to take part in something, and a feeling of isolation—were avoided, and it was also made clear that the children were not being examined, compared or tested in any ordinary sense.

Each group was recorded for about an hour. The procedure was to tell the children something about the length of the recording and its nature, and to concentrate on putting them at their ease. After a few minutes the tape recorder was switched on. This was always in full view, but as most of the children were accustomed to being recorded (either at home or in school or both), what little nervousness there was seldom lasted for long. The early minutes were mainly concerned with a standard identification procedure in which the school, the serial number of the group, and the names and ages of the children would be announced.

For the next 40 minutes the children talked freely among themselves, and the adult interviewer too took an active part. There were no aids, in the shape of pictures or other visual cues, but anything in the immediate or more remote extra-linguistic situation could be made relevant, like a badge, a poster on the wall, or a film showing locally. Usually there was no shortage of conversation. In the interests of transcription, however, it was sometimes necessary for the interviewer to intervene, to prevent two children from talking at once if they became excited, or to ask one to speak a little louder.

After 40 minutes a break was called, and then for the last 20 minutes or so the children imagined themselves in a situation of their own choosing (it is interesting to note, in passing, that their usage often interpreted 'situation' as 'predicament') and acted out the incidents of it as if they were taking part in a sort of impromptu drama for radio. This was called 'free-play' and corresponded to the *psycho-drames* recommended in the Survey's terms of reference.

As each set of tapes was completed it was returned to the Survey's headquarters in Leeds for transcription. Here the importance of intelligibility cannot be overstressed. There is a total of 80 hours of speech to transcribe. The Survey's full-time Transcription Secretary is quick and accurate, and yet it usually takes about 24 working hours to transcribe one hour of 'easy' recording into normal orthography, including hesitations and repetitions. On the other hand, a 'difficult' tape can take anything up to 70 hours, with after that another 24 spent on checking and correction. The three examples that are printed in the appendix to this chapter are of about average difficulty, and give a brief indication of the language in the spoken section of the corpus. (See pp. 172, *seq.*)

A preliminary examination of the tapes had shown which topics the children had talked of most and allowed some estimate to be made about which ones they had pursued and found interesting. A list of 19 composition titles was drawn up. This was then circulated to all the children who had already taken part in the recording. They were asked to choose the five titles that appealed to them most and to write at least a page about each. Once again, the help of their teachers was freely given in collecting and supervising where necessary. The resulting 1,500 compositions now form the major part of the written section of the corpus.[1]

THE ANALYSIS

The Nuffield Child Language Survey is concentrating mainly on grammar. Many language investigations in the past have tended to focus their attention on vocabulary. This may have been simply because grammars capable of dealing adequately with spoken language have been slow to develop, or it may indeed be that the most direct way of characterizing the difference between the language of adults and children is by means of vocabulary comparison, where, presumably, the slang of childhood will be observed gradually giving way to the jargon of the adult world while a common core remains the same.

Such investigations would certainly highlight the most obviously unique features of children's language, for nothing is more unique than children's slang. But at the same time nothing is more transitory. A vocabulary study based on frequency of occurrence alone would be very much conditioned by the date of the survey, and would thus lack a certain dimension and, in consequence, authority when its information came to be applied.

All language changes. The ideal survey would delineate both the unique and shared features of child and adult usage, however transitory they were, over a never-ending period of time. It would prepare dictionaries of slang, carefully dated. But the Nuffield Child Language Survey is not, and in its terms of reference never can be, an ideal survey. Its attention must first be turned to the most widely shared and most stable patterns of the language.

[1] All the written material has now been transcribed and published in two volumes (Handscombe, 1967; 1967a).

Of the Survey's three focal areas, grammar, vocabulary and centres of interest, grammar has the most stability, the highest proportion of shared features and a language of its own in which these features can be described and compared.

Dr Hasan was familiar with a model of grammar that lent itself smoothly to the task of describing children's language. Based on the work of the late Professor J. R. Firth, it had been developed by many British linguists, prominent among whom is Professor M. A. K. Halliday of University College, London. Before she left to join another Nuffield project in the Communication Research Centre, Dr Hasan completed the *Grammatical Analysis Code* (Hasan, 1964), a document which summarized the main descriptive categories of English and made it possible to make some 2,000 positive ('the clause is . . .') or negative ('the clause is not . . .') statements about each clause and its constituent units, and was designed for use with a computer. One thousand clauses have already been analysed in these terms and some interesting results obtained. The Survey intends to examine some 20,000 clauses along similar lines, 5,000 (in all probability) from each of the four years 9–12. It is hoped that this will lead to a fairly comprehensive statement about these children's grammatical patterns.

But this is not to say that the two remaining focal areas will receive no attention whatsoever. As far as children's interests are concerned, a start has already been made with the publication of a volume called *Topics of Conversation and Centres of Interest in the Language of 11- and 12-year-old Children* (Handscombe, 1965). This was written primarily to provide course compilers with details of the actual topics talked about by these children during the course of the recordings. Because they were slightly older children, the recording technique was modified, with the hour being split into three twenty-minute periods, the first devoted to uncontrolled interview and the last to free-play as before, but with the middle period allotted to free exchange between the children while the interviewer was absent. A great many topics were mentioned, naturally enough. Those that were dwelt on at length or which occurred frequently were called 'centres of interest'. Both the topics of conversation and centres of interest were listed in the appendices to the volume. Table 1 is an example of such a list.

It may be quite true that we should enter more fully into the children's environments if we want to know in detail about what interests them. We should meet and talk to their parents and friends,

Table 1. The active interests inside the home of 11- and 12-year-old children[1]

$$11 \begin{cases} 35 \text{ boys} \\ 22 \text{ girls} \end{cases} \qquad 12 \begin{cases} 32 \text{ boys} \\ 28 \text{ girls} \end{cases}$$

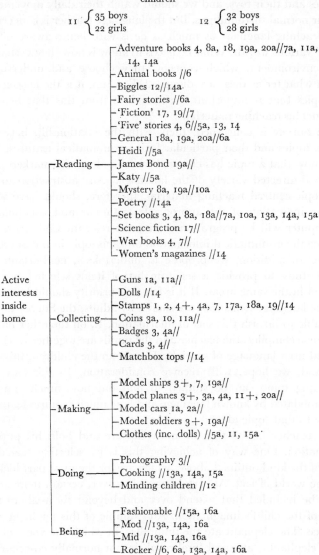

Active interests inside home

Reading
- Adventure books 4, 8a, 18, 19a, 20a//7a, 11a, 14, 14a
- Animal books //6
- Biggles 12//14a
- Fairy stories //6a
- 'Fiction' 17, 19//7
- 'Five' stories 4, 6//5a, 13, 14
- General 18a, 19a, 20a//6a
- Heidi //5a
- James Bond 19a//
- Katy //5a
- Mystery 8a, 19a//10a
- Poetry //14a
- Set books 3, 4, 8a, 18a//7a, 10a, 13a, 14a, 15a
- Science fiction 17//
- War books 4, 7//
- Women's magazines //14

Collecting
- Guns 1a, 11a//
- Dolls //14
- Stamps 1, 2, 4+, 4a, 7, 17a, 18a, 19//14
- Coins 3a, 10, 11a//
- Badges 3, 4a//
- Cards 3, 4//
- Matchbox tops //14

Making
- Model ships 3+, 7, 19a//
- Model planes 3+, 3a, 4a, 11+, 20a//
- Model cars 1a, 2a//
- Model soldiers 3+, 19a//
- Clothes (inc. dolls) //5a, 11, 15a

Doing
- Photography 3//
- Cooking //13a, 14a, 15a
- Minding children //12

Being
- Fashionable //15a, 16a
- Mod //13a, 14a, 16a
- Mid //13a, 14a, 16a
- Rocker //6, 6a, 13a, 14a, 16a

[1] Boys before //; girls after. The numbers refer to the various groups of three children in particular schools. 12-year-olds are marked 'a'; the unmarked groups are 11-year-olds. A 'plus' sign ('+') shows that the topic has been pursued at length or frequently by a particular group. 'Mod', 'Mid' and 'Rocker' refers to certain styles of teenage behaviour and dress.

we should investigate their bookshelves, their collections, their pictures and their toys, and we should watch their daily movements in their normal surroundings. But the language teacher is concerned with teaching language as much as he is with being aware of his pupils' various worlds. What he needs to know is how they verbalize their environment, which concepts they choose and understand and in what terms these are discussed. For him, it is the *language* of the topics that is important, because it is from this that he can construct his teaching material.

The Survey is concerned, then, with the relationship between certain topics and their particular lexico-grammatical features. We only know that a topic has changed when we hear the markers of a new field-directed variety of the language.[1] Any abstraction to do with topic-centred teaching material, therefore, should have with it some indication of the appropriate grammar and vocabulary. A computer will be programmed with the relevant Code cards to produce the grammatical information on each topic in the Survey's sample. In addition, we propose to undertake a field-orientated lexical study to provide a separate list of items selected by the children in the same areas. If it is felt that priority should be given to those language items that are shared by adults, the Survey hopes to be able to furnish this sort of information. If, on the other hand, the course compiler, the teacher and the pupils are together working to build up a language of special relevance to the children, this too can (and, we hope, will) receive consideration. In this case an interesting topic can be studied to find out how much can be accommodated by known language and how much requires features unique to that topic alone.

The teacher knows that he must capture and hold his pupils' imagination. One way of achieving this is by selecting teaching items of the kind outlined above, which are for the most part locked into the world of fact. At certain ages, however, certain items may surely be included that extend over and beyond the real, to the world of the child's imagination. An example of this might be the sentence 'The elephant ate the umbrella', in which the vocabulary items 'elephant', 'ate' and 'umbrella' do not normally co-occur in this grammatical structure.[2] The idea itself, though, may be

---

[1] The term 'field-directed variety' is derived from a work on linguistics and style by Enkvist, Spencer and Gregory (1964), published as No. 6 in this series.

[2] Such an approach to language teaching is the suggestion of Mr Andrew Wright, the Project's Senior Artist.

sufficient to stimulate a whole host of more conventional language in order to arrive at such a concluding sentence. It is doubtful whether the Survey could go into much detail about such rare collocations, but it is possible that an examination of the free-play material would provide clues as to how to go about it.

PRESENT POSITION

The Survey has now completed its collection of language with the exception of some of the control texts. Over half the spoken material has been transcribed, and eleven volumes of transcription have been published and circulated in mimeographed form to other research workers both in Britain and abroad.[1] The sampling methods have been tested and decided. Contact has been made with the necessary computer techniques and experimental programmes are in the process of being devised.

The shape that the final grammatical statement will take has not yet been fixed. It may be helpful here to show two of the tables from one of the Survey's recent publications *The First 1,000 Clauses: A Preliminary Analysis*, as these will probably be taken as guiding lines.[2] The first (Table 2, p. 170) concerns 'tense' selection in the various verbal groups of the first 1,000 clauses. Seven hundred and seventy-eight of these clauses contained verbs, while 222 were 'minor' clauses without verbal groups, the sort that frequently occurs in the question-response situation. The 'Code Number' column on the left refers to that section in the *Grammatical Analysis Code* under which the information was originally recorded.

The recording situation may account for the high number of verbs with 'simple presentness', amounting to 50 per cent of the whole, for such selection is probably one characteristic of the various topics selected by the children in that situation.

The next table (Table 3, p. 171) shows the relative popularity of linking features in the clause.

The most popular linking features in this small sample are items belonging to the 'initial adjunct' class, which includes 'and', 'but' and 'or', for example. A very long way behind in second place is that variety of linking exemplified in 'He came *and saw me*', where in addition to the initial linking adjunct, the subject of the second verb is missing.

[1] Published as Occasional Papers Nos. 5, 7, 9, 10, 13, 14, 15, 18, 19, 21 and 22 (Hasan, 1965; Hasan and Handscombe, 1965-6). For the written material see p. 165, footnote [1].
[2] Published as Occasional Paper No. 11 (Handscombe, 1966).

Table 2. 'Tense' selection in the verbal group[1]

Code number	Tense and example	Frequency
08	Simple present lexical verb ('takes')	212
03	*Simple present grammatical verb	180
07	Simple past lexical ('took')	71
13	Past in present ('has taken')	67
52	Present modal ('can take')	41
02	*Simple past grammatical verb	38
01	Partial lexical verb (infinitive without 'to', e.g. solo headword in the second verbal group 'I saw him go')	34
53	Present modal sequent ('could take')	20
78	Present present-participle ('taking')	16
77	Present infinitive ('to take')	14
10	Simple future ('will take')	14
18	Present in present ('is taking')	12
Others		59
	Total	778

It is also interesting to note that of the 672 clauses with subjects, 50 per cent selected their subject-word from members of the personal pronoun sub-class in the singular ('I', 'you', 'he', 'she', or 'it') and 24 per cent from the plural of the same sub-class ('we' and 'they'): in other words, 80 per cent of all the headwords in the subject were personal pronouns.

As a preliminary step towards the lexical analysis, all the formal items expounding the grammatical unit 'word' in the first thousand clauses have been listed. Table 4 (facing p. 172) represents part of this list.

The verbs in this list are given mainly a traditional tense description while the word-classes are defined according to the categories of the *Grammatical Analysis Code*.

[1] The two entries marked * include both the lexical and grammatical uses of the verbs 'to be' and 'to have' (the difference between the lexical and grammatical use of 'to have' is illustrated in 'He *has had* lunch, *has* he?' where the 'has' is grammatical in both the tag and the independent clause, while the 'had' is lexical). This was done in order to provide information on the total occurrence in the sample of these two verbs: the analysis in future will follow the definition in the entry, and these present figures will be revised. One immediate result would be that the entries in 08 would be even more numerous.

Table 3. Linking features in the clause

Code number	Linking feature and example	Frequency
01	A$^{\&}$ initial: I shouted *and* he came	158
21	A$^{\&}$ –S: He protested *and* (*he*) came	11
20	–S –pP: He will climb the mountain, (*he will*) come home safely and . . .	7
03	A$^{\&}$ final: I ordered him to come: he came *moreover*	6
16	–S: He caught a plane, (*he*) came yesterday and . . .	5
25	A$^{\&}$ –S –pP: He will climb the mountain *and* (*he will*) come home safely	5
18	–S –P: He put the car in the ditch, (*he put*) himself in hospital, and . . .	3
	Various combinations of the above	19
	Total	214

(Abbreviations: A$^{\&}$ = linking adjunct; –S = subject omitted; –pP = verb partially omitted; –P = verb completely omitted)

Despite the quantity of information embodied in *A Preliminary Analysis*, the sample in itself is too small to allow any significant deductions or recommendations to be made. Its purpose, on the other hand, has been fulfilled: the Survey is reasonably satisfied that it can comply with its aims in producing a satisfactory description of these children's English. Ways of discovering and displaying lexical information are still being explored.

CONCLUSION

The 1962 report of the Hamburg Conference on the teaching of foreign or second languages to younger children recommended certain areas for research. One of these recommendations was that

'Research must be conducted to expand our knowledge of the normal course of development of the child's learning and use of his native language, particularly with respect to phonology, grammar, and vocabulary. Studies should be made of children in different countries, learning different types of languages, preferably on a co-operative basis so that comparable methods may be employed.' (Stern, 1967, p. 103.)

Throughout its life, close and very friendly liaison has existed between the Nuffield Child Language Survey and the Survey conducted by CREDIF at St Cloud, about which Mme Leclercq writes elsewhere in this volume. As a result of this cooperation, the Nuffield French team has been able to make use of much unique material. Recently an exploratory visit was made to Madrid to seek ways of establishing a similar reciprocal arrangement. With the expansion of the Nuffield Project to include courses in the Spanish, German and Russian languages, the exchange of information in the Survey's original terms of reference has gained an even greater urgency and significance.

Appendix

Samples of children's speech recorded and transcribed by the Child Language Survey.

1 Well . . . hm . . . a few weeks ago there was . . . there was a little family of mice living under the bush in our garden it's a large bush . . . they call . . . we call it the jungle bush and . . . he . . . and Binky found them one day and the hi . . . it's funny because they made little burrows in the ground an' he . . . he dug his paw down an' he was bur . . . he was . . . hm . . . fishing out little mice by the dozen and at last there came . . . hm . . . er . . . he . . . a rather large mouse about half the size of a rat and he bit Binky's paw and it started bleeding . . . hm . . . so we took Binky in and he never went near there again . . . it was funny because he seemed to talk . . . he seems to talk to the next door neighbour's cat called Tinker . . . they're very great friends and he l . . . he seemed to ask Tinker if he could dig out the mice for him so next day Tinker came down and he looked over his shoulders to see if nobody was watching because I was watching from the french windows . . . hm . . . I hid behind the curtain because I like watching puss . . . cats doing anything and he'd . . . he put his paw down this hole and he managed to drag the rat out by its tail and he squashed it with his paw . . . he banged it down with his paw but he didn't actually really squash it an' he carried it by the tail and went up to Binky who was watching by the barrel . . . there's an old barrel in our garden which we put . . . whi . . . which we've rolled down on the side and put straw in for . . . er . . . for the cats to rest in 'cos they like that . . . Binky was sitting by the barrel and Tinker brought the rat up to . . . ooh . . . it was half mouse half rat . . . up to him . . . and he laid it down on . . . he laid it down next to Binky's nose and then Binky did a sort of little dance as if to say . . .

'Oh I'm so pleased you've done this . . . aren't you clever and I'm clever too because I caught lots of little mice' . . .

Transcript 2a (9-year-olds from Kent) Pp. 88–9.

2 We're in the higher stream and . . . hm . . . the . . . Sheila can't get moved now because . . . hm . . . you see once we're placed . . . once we're placed we have to work like that because they si . . . hm . . . they put you in these streams whether you . . . they think you're going to pass, whether you've got a hope to pass and . . . hm . . . whether they don't think you'll pass. 3J is the ones that get into 5X and should pass I mean . . . hm . . . 3TG will go into . . . er . . . 4TG and they think they'll pass because we're in . . . er . . . a high stream A and . . . hm . . . and they think . . . hm Sheila should pass as well because . . . hm . . . she's in 3A.

Hm . . . Mummy likes hm . . . Mummy thinks the . . . the streaming is good because hm . . . because of the ones that they don't get mixed up with the ones that won't pass and the ones that will pass so the ones that will pass want a little more coaching and the ones that won't pass . . . they don't think'll pass they . . . hm . . . they won't get as much helping as . . . hm . . . they would as if they were in . . . hm . . . the same class when the ones that wouldn't pass would be . . . would have to . . . er . . . get up to the work that the ones that would pass would be . . . as they'd all be having to do the hard work when some of them could do the hard and some could do the easy.

Ibid. Pp. 12–14.

3 Well why do you think . . . why do you think people do wrong things?
Erm . . . er . . . they might be poor or something . . .
Yes . . .
Erm . . . they might not like a person . . .
I think it's because they can make a profit on things . . . they can get . . . erm . . . a load of lead and melt it down and sell it to a manufacturing firm to make lead things and they make a profit from it . . .
And . . . erm . . . I think they do it partly because people have been blackmailing them and they want the stuff to pay for what they're being blackmailed . . . instead of going to the police or or something like that . . .
X. (the adult interviewer): Hm . . .
But they always know they're going to be caught . . .
Really they . . . they nearly always get caught . . . it's about two out of a hundred what don't get caught . . .
No I wouldn't say so . . .
No I wouldn't say so . . .
It's not many what don't get caught . . . in the end though we caught . . .
ev . . . every criminal will be caught . . . erm . . . because they'll do a job

say . . . erm . . . burgle a house or something then they'll go away for about two years and then decide 'Oh I'm getting poor after that burglary so I'll s . . . I'll do another' . . . well then they'll do . . . do the job . . . they'll catch him . . . say . . . this time . . . and then they'll make him pay for the last job . . . and this . . .

X. Hm hm . . .

That they've done . . . and so they'll be caught in the end . . .

But how can they prove that he did the l . . . the job before?

Well I expect when he's caught he'll say 'Well I did it' you know . . . if they say 'It's the same kind of burglary' and if they follow up the clues what they had before . . . and they used . . . they . . . they should find out . . .

Transcript 2d (9-year-olds from Yorkshire) Pp. 124–5.

15

The CREDIF child language survey

J. LECLERCQ[1]

AIMS OF THE SURVEY

In November 1963 the Nuffield Foundation and the *Centre de Recherche et d'Étude pour la Diffusion du Français* decided to undertake two parallel investigations of child language, in England and France respectively. The first stage of the project entailed collecting recordings of conversations between children aged from 9 to 13. This corpus was then to be analysed with a view to obtaining a detailed breakdown of (a) topics and (b) linguistic features. Similar research is to be carried out in the field of written language. It is hoped that these surveys will produce results applicable to the teaching of foreign languages to children.

INFORMANTS AND RECORDINGS

The children's conversations were recorded in Paris and its suburbs and in two provincial towns. The greater part of these recordings was made in primary and secondary schools attended by children from varied social backgrounds. Some children were recorded in their homes, to provide us with a basis for comparison.

The total population will consist of 312 children divided into four age groups: 9-, 10-, 11-, and 12-year-olds. We hope to have more or less equal numbers of boys and girls. The children are divided into groups of three for each recording session. Thus, we plan a total of 104 recordings, divided roughly equally between groups of boys, groups of girls and mixed groups. Each conversation lasts for thirty to forty minutes.

At present the CREDIF has finished the recording and transcription of conversations between 9-year-olds, and a selection of

[1] Madame Leclercq, the author of this chapter, is the research worker in charge of the French (CREDIF) Child Language Survey.—Ed.

these has been published.[1] Fifteen conversations from each of the three other age groups have been recorded and transcribed. The recordings were planned to be completed in 1967.

TECHNIQUES EMPLOYED

(a) *Free conversation*

We feel justified in calling the first part of our recordings 'free conversation' in so far as the interviewer working for the survey asked only the minimum number of questions, intervening only at the beginning and when conversation lagged.

Previously the interviewer had asked the teacher to choose self-confident children from the top two-thirds of the class. More often than not the children formed their own groups according to personal affinities. The interviewer then asked them to talk about things that interested them, as if it were playtime. Most of the children took full advantage of the situation; some even began to sing. All spoke freely about their teachers and classmates. On one tape conversation even turned to rather improper subjects. In view of this it seems unlikely that the children were inhibited by the presence of the adult interviewer.

However, from the outset we felt that it would be necessary to make some recordings unknown to the children, so as to collect samples of absolutely spontaneous language. On an experimental basis we used this procedure to record three groups of children. (These conversations are not included in the selected transcripts.) As the children were free to move around the room, much of these recordings consists of language used fully in context, and sometimes proves very difficult to interpret. (Ideally we should have installed a hidden television camera as well as a microphone and tape recorder.) However, the non-contextualized language on these tapes did not differ from the language recorded in the presence of an interviewer.

(b) *'Game'* (*Role-playing*)

The second part of our recordings is referred to as the 'game'. After thirty minutes of free conversation, the interviewer asked the children to choose an episode in their everyday life and recreate it through dialogue—to 'act out' a familiar situation. First of all,

[1] *Enquête sur le langage de l'enfant français.* CREDIF—ENS, Saint-Cloud; also Nuffield Foreign Languages Teaching Materials Project, Reports and Occasional Paper No. 20. October 1966 (CREDIF, 1965; Nuffield Foundation, 1966).

he proposed some specimen situations such as the end of the school day, a picnic, a visit to the zoo, etc., but the situation to be acted out was always chosen by the children themselves.

We must admit to a few cases of failure, when in spite of their efforts the children did not manage to enter into the 'game' and reverted to ordinary conversation. In general, though, this exercise appealed to the children.

By choosing these two investigation techniques, we hoped to establish comparisons between language in and out of situation.

CENTRES OF INTEREST

In the preface to the selected transcripts of conversations between 9-year-olds, we present a statistical breakdown of the subjects treated most frequently by the informants. This analysis was based on the number of words (grouped in units of 50) connected to a given *theme*. On this basis we were able to distinguish between 34 centres of interest, which we grouped under four main headings: home life; school life; outside activities; and personal interests and preoccupations. We shall limit ourselves here to mentioning that the subjects most frequently treated by boys and girls are school work and classroom life. Apart from this, the activity of story-telling through allusion to television or cinema films occupies as important a place in boys' conversations as that of school work, whereas it is almost totally absent from girls' conversations.

LINGUISTIC STUDY

The CREDIF has no coding system adequate for an exhaustive analysis of the text. So far, mechanical treatment of the corpus has not been envisaged. However, we have carried out partial studies of text samples from 9-year-olds, and at present we have produced counts of structures used for direct question forms and subordinate clauses.

This pilot study covered fifteen conversations, representing a total of about 82,000 words, or nine hours twenty minutes of playing time.

The results of this pilot study have been compared with those obtained during the preparation of *Le Français Fondamental* (163 conversations, a total of about 300,000 words) and will soon be compared with similar studies of samples from the other age groups.

Other studies focusing on coordination and *reprise* (repetition and cross-reference) of subject and object are envisaged before long.

It goes without saying that we also plan to study the structures most frequently used by the child, so as to define the degree of complexity of sentences used by children of a given age; in other words, our aim is to define the types of sentence produced and to study the internal organization of these sentences. At this point, however, we are faced with the problem of dividing up the corpus. What should we adopt as a unit? Where does the spoken sentence begin and end? How far can prosodic features be used as criteria for marking the limits of the sentence? And what are the coordinating elements used by the child? We give as an example the following transcription, chosen at random from a conversation between 9-year-olds:[1]

Les Beatles c'est des chanteurs anglais, ils sont quatre puis ils ont les cheveux longs.

Are we to treat this utterance as two sentences or three? *Puis* can hardly be taken as an adverb of time in this context, so should we consider it a coordinating element? This example, which was chosen to show one of the difficulties facing us in the segmentation of our corpus, should also explain why we have decided to begin with studies of detail, in the hope of progressively widening our terms of reference. In this field, where exploration has barely started, we should be unwise to try to run before we can walk.[2]

---

[1] For longer excerpts from the transcripts see the appendix to this chapter.

[2] As this chapter summarizes only the earlier stages of this research, it may be appropriate to draw attention briefly to some of the latest developments in the survey:

  1. A book of the transcripts of conversations of 10-year-old children was published in January 1968. These transcripts have been coded for certain prosodic features.
  2. A syntactic analysis by computer has been developed by CREDIF. A preliminary analysis of 3,000 clauses is under way. The results of this analysis should be available in the autumn of 1968.

Appendix

Excerpts from transcripts of the talk of 9-year-old French children.

—t'as déjà vu au cinéma . . . heu . . . comment déjà?

—oh moi au cinéma j'ai vu . . . heu . . . la révolte des Apaches.

—Moi j'ai vu . . . comment? Tu sais le truc, le Renard, là? comment i(l) s'appelle? C'est John Williams qui chante la chanson . . . je me rappelle plus, mais . . . c'était un beau film c'était des renards et il avait . . . le . . . le chasseur il l'avait pris dans un piège et après . . . hein? et après le monsieur . . . et puis il l'avait mis dans une cage où y avait plein de . . . y avait plein . . . de . . . de vaches autour et après . . . heu . . . se . . . son père il est venu et il a . . . il a enlevé . . . une barrière, alors les les . . . vaches, i(l)s ont détruit la maison et la mère elle a pu s'enfuir mais elle a presque été tuée alors . . . heu . . . après i(l) y a un monsieur, i(l) ont . . . heu . . . non, avant i(l)s ont été dans une maison, i(l)s ont traversé un trou où y avait un ravin en bas, puis la mère elle avait peur, alors . . . heu . . . le père il è . . . il l'a rassurée parce qu'i(l)s avaient vu une maison, alors i(l) fallait traverser ça, alors après, i(l)s ont fait des petits et il a été chercher . . . des bêtes pour les donner à manger et i(l) i(l) cherchait un terrier après, alors y avait un . . .

—il est méchant la bête? si . . . ça gratte, ça fait un trou dans la terre.

—les castors?

—non

—les taupes?

—oui une taupe, et après, i(l)s, i(l)s voulaient la déloger pour se . . . loger dedans, mais alors i(l)s ont continué leur chemin parce qu'e(ll)e voulait pas leur donner leur . . . logement alors après, i(l)s ont continué, i(l)s ont trouvé un trou et là y avait un un type (ou tigre) qui était en haut et i(l) voulait prendre les petits, alors après le chasseur il est venu, il a tué le tigre (ou type) et après il a tué les . . . les renards, il a . . . il les a élevés puis il les a . . ., il leur a donné à manger, il les a logés, et après i(l)s sont partis les renards c'est la fin . . . c'est un beau film.

[I is 9 and D 10 years old]

I—Qu'est-ce que tu veux pour Noël?

D—Oh j'sais pas, j'ai demandé un sac

I—moi j'ai demandé une, tu sais une boîte du, du petit . . . heu . . . magicien, et j'ai demandé une petite poupée adorable et sa boîte à bijoux.

D—j'ai demandé aussi une poupée tu sais qui a un haut de corps en tissu, comme ça on peut la mettre comme un vrai bébé, puis j'ai demandé une chaîne en or, puis j'sais pas, j'avais envie d'une écharpe, d'une écharpe, et d'une ceinture . . . pour mon pantalon.

I—moi j'vais aller . . . heu . . . demain, aux grands magasins là

D—moi aussi moi le matin

I—oui moi aussi en même temps parce que j'vais aller chez le dentiste

D—ce soir j'vais aller coucher chez Mamie

I—j'aurai un appareil dentaire, ça va pas être drôle

D—c'est pas rigolo tu sais, le mercredi, quand j'vais . . . chez Papy, coucher, ah le, le matin i(l) faut, pour aller dans la salle de bains, i(l) faut, faut passer, tu sais, comme ça, parce que y a les, y a les gens qui travaillent, alors, ah! la! la!

I—t'aimes bien quand c'est Noël?

D—oh oui, mais j'préfère les grandes vacances, y a bien plus de vacances.

I—oui mais quand même moi j'aime bien, parce que on, on, on se réunit entre nous, puis on se fait des cadeaux . . . heu . . .

D—moi c'que j'préfère à Noël c'est le réveillon.

I—oh oui, et le réveillon du 1er janvier j'aime bien.

D—moi j'aime bien aussi, c'est la nuit de Noël . . . heu . . . pour aller à la messe, tout ca, j'aime bien [inaudible] le dimanche, mais enfin c'est pas pareil la messe de Noël surtout a St Raphaël, le jour de Noël, et quelques jours après et quelques jours avant, y a . . . des petits santons c'est toute une grande crèche qui fait au moins à peu près toute cette pièce et alors c'est que des petits santons mais quand on met . . . heu . . . 50 francs j'crois ou quelque chose comme ça dans un petit ange qui tend que(l)que chose, dans une petite boîte, alors tous les petits santons se mettent à travailler, mettons le bûcheron coupe son bois, tout ça, c'est très mignon.

I—ah oui, ah ben moi je vais passer Noël à la X mais j'ai pas très envie d'y aller à la X, parce que c'est chez ma tante,

D—oh X, oh j'l'aime pas tellement

I—moi non plus

16

The evaluation of the primary French pilot scheme in Great Britain

CLARE BURSTALL[1]

The rapid spread of modern language teaching at the primary level has focused attention on the urgent need for research in this area. It is not enough, however, to advocate research or even to carry it out: a research study must be properly designed, use objective methods of assessment, and be capable of replication. Studies of second language learning have often been extremely unsatisfactory in design, execution and evaluation. Many have used so restricted a sample that they are of merely local interest; the 'tests' developed during the course of such studies are frequently of unknown validity and reliability; and reports of experimental teaching tend to value anecdote above statistics. No questions are answered by inadequate research.

Second language learning at the primary level has raised problems of educational policy which can only be resolved by research on a national scale. It must be recognized, however, that research on this scale requires considerable financial support, the whole-hearted cooperation of teachers and administrators, and a high standard of professional skill on the part of the research staff. At the present time, the only large-scale project of this kind in progress, known to the author, is that associated with the Pilot Scheme for the teaching of French in British primary schools. This study will therefore be described in some detail, as an example of a national research project carried out in intact classes within the normal school environment.

[1] The author, Mrs C. Burstall, is the Senior Research Officer responsible for the project described in this chapter. The work is carried out at the National Foundation for Educational Research in England and Wales, 79 Wimpole Street, London W1, UK.—Ed.

THE PILOT SCHEME

As was shown in chapter 8 the Pilot Scheme was initiated by the Ministry of Education in 1963, in response to a growing dissatisfaction with the scope and outcome of modern language teaching within the state educational system. The long-term evaluation of the scheme was undertaken by the National Foundation for Educational Research (NFER). A research team was appointed in April 1964, to carry out a longitudinal study of two consecutive cohorts of pupils. These children were to be followed through from the beginning of their second year in the primary school until the end of their second year in the secondary school. The fieldwork of the study was therefore expected to extend over a seven-year period, involving approximately 13,000 children. The work of the NFER team has been concentrated initially on the following main areas of inquiry:

1 Do other aspects of education and general intellectual development gain or suffer from the introduction of French teaching in the primary school?

2 Are there levels of ability below which the teaching of French is of dubious value?

3 Is any substantial gain in mastery achieved by beginning to learn French at the age of 8?

4 What methods, attitudes and incentives are most effective in promoting the learning of French?

5 What organizational and teaching problems are posed by the introduction of French teaching in the primary school?

THE EXPERIMENTAL SAMPLE

One hundred and twenty-five primary schools were selected for inclusion in the Pilot Scheme. These schools were situated in thirteen different administrative areas of England and Wales, chosen to provide a representative sample of the educational conditions existing throughout the country. The initial task of the research team was to establish the general characteristics of the schools in the sample, so that an appropriate experimental design could be formulated. The Head of each Pilot Scheme school was therefore contacted in May 1964 and asked to complete a questionnaire which asked for detailed information regarding:

1 The size, type, and internal organization of the school.

2 The percentage of grammar school places obtained by the pupils of the school during the previous three years.

3 The general socio-economic background of the school as indicated by parental occupation.

4 The existence of possible bilingual influences in the pupil's home environment.

5 Previous French teaching in the school, if any: age groups taught; teacher's training and qualifications; time allocated to French teaching; type of French course followed, etc.

6 Proposals for teaching French from September 1964 onwards: age groups and numbers of pupils to be taught French; teacher's training and qualifications; time to be allocated to French teaching; type of French course to be followed, etc.

On the basis of the information obtained in response to this questionnaire, the schools participating in the Pilot Scheme were assigned to one of three experimental groups, according to their size, type and history of French teaching:

Group 1. Schools where no French would have been taught to the school population which would be in existence from September 1964. Most of these schools had no history of French teaching and intended to teach French to second-year juniors only in September 1964, thereafter adding an age group each year.

Group 2. Schools where French had been and/or would be taught to several age groups. In some of these schools French was already being taught throughout the school. It was not therefore possible to evaluate the initial impact of the introduction of French teaching in Group 2 schools, but it was hoped to observe the effects of 'sustained impact' and also of teacher experience.

Group 3. Small rural schools with fewer than three junior classes. These schools ranged in size from 16 to 160 pupils on roll. Although Group 3 schools constituted almost a third of the total sample, they were concentrated in three administrative areas: West Sussex, Dorset and Bedfordshire.

THE EXPERIMENTAL DESIGN

1 The effect of the introduction of French on the general level of attainment

The evaluation of the Pilot Scheme includes an investigation of the effect of the introduction of French on general attainment in the primary school. It was therefore necessary to establish an accurate picture of the general level of attainment in the schools participating in the Pilot Scheme as rapidly as possible, to enable a subsequent assessment of the effect of the introduction of French on general attainment. Since this assessment was to be restricted to the primary stage of the experiment, it was decided to administer a general attainment battery to all children in the experimental sample both at the beginning of their second year and at the end of their fourth year in the primary school. The same battery would also be administered to suitable control groups.

The problem of selecting appropriate controls varied according to the experimental group. In Group 1 schools, for example, the fourth-year pupils, who would not be taught French during their primary school career, were to act as internal controls. They would be given the battery of general attainment tests at the end of their fourth year in the primary school; the same procedure would then be repeated the following year with the succeeding fourth-year classes. The scores obtained in this way would be compared with those of the French-taught pupils when they in turn reached the end of their fourth year in the primary school. If the introduction of French teaching had affected general attainment either positively or negatively, this effect would be reflected in the mean scores of the fourth-year pupils.

It was not possible to set up a similar system of controls in Group 2 schools, since, in most of these schools, the teaching of French had already been extended to several year-groups. Since the French Project intended to make use of the same general attainment battery as that used in the NFER investigation into the effects of streaming in junior schools,[1] however, it was possible to set up an external control group for Group 2 schools within the 'streaming' sample, using only those schools in which French would not be taught. The fourth-year pupils in these schools were to act as an internal control group for the Group 2 pupils.

The class structure of Group 3 schools precluded any system of internal control groups. Many of the schools in this group had only one class for the whole of the junior age range, so that it was impossible to select a group of pupils to act as controls. Each Group 3 school was therefore individually matched with a control school which resembled the experimental school as closely as possible, but in which no French was taught. Those pupils who fell within the experimental age range in Group 3 schools and their matching

[1] For further details of the tests making up the general attainment battery see Barker-Lunn (1967).

controls would thus be given the general attainment battery at the beginning of the experiment and would subsequently be re-tested for general attainment before transferring to the secondary school in 1966.

The general attainment battery was administered to the first experimental cohort in October 1964. This cohort consisted of all children in Group 1 and Group 2 schools who fell within the age-range 8·0–8·11 on 1 September 1964 and all children in Group 3 schools who fell within the age range 8·0–9·11 on that date. A wider age range was selected for testing in Group 3 schools, because of the extended age range in each class. The same general attainment battery was administered in October 1965 to all children in Group 1 and Group 2 schools who fell within the age-range 8·0–8·11 on 1 September 1965. These children (approximately 6,000) constituted the second experimental cohort.

The general attainment testing schedule is shown in outline below:

October 1964: General attainment testing of experimental age group in all Pilot Scheme schools. (First cohort.)

June 1965: General attainment testing of all fourth-year children in Group 1 schools. (Control classes.)

October 1965: General attainment testing of experimental age group in Group 1 and Group 2 schools. (Second cohort.)

June 1966: General attainment testing of all fourth-year children in Group 1 schools (control classes). Re-testing of experimental age group in Group 3 and matching control schools.

June 1967: Re-testing of all fourth-year children in Group 1 and Group 2 schools. (First cohort.)

June 1968: Re-testing of all fourth-year children in Group 1 and Group 2 schools. (Second cohort.)

In September 1967, the children in the first experimental cohort transferred to the secondary school, to be followed in September 1968 by the second cohort. The final statistical analysis of the general attainment data, to be carried out in the autumn of 1968, will conclude this phase of the project.

2 *Low-ability children*

When the Pilot Scheme was outlined in 1963, the schools taking part in the experiment were encouraged to offer instruction in

French to all children in the appropriate age range, whatever their level of ability. It was recognized, however, that the question of teaching French to the whole ability range would come under review in the course of the experiment: 'whether or not there is a level of ability below which it is inexpedient to go is something which will, we hope, be shown as the scheme progresses.'[1] This policy was later endorsed by the authors of the Newsom Report, who recommended that children of all levels of ability should be given the opportunity of learning a foreign language: 'there is too little experience nationally of trying to teach a foreign language over the whole, or most, of the ability range for anyone to gauge the limits and possibilities'. (Great Britain, 1963.)

In the majority of Pilot Scheme schools, French has been taught to the whole ability range since the beginning of the experiment in September 1964; in a few schools, however, children of low general ability have been withdrawn from the French classes. Classroom observation led to the hypothesis that the teacher's attitude towards the teaching of French to children of low ability might have a determining influence on the extent to which such children experienced success or failure in learning French. A scale measuring positive and negative attitudes towards the teaching of French to the less able child was therefore developed. The final version of the scale was put to use in June 1966. The data were analysed in relation to the children's scores on the general attainment battery and on the French tests, in an attempt to discover whether children of equal ability appear to reach different levels of proficiency in French as a consequence of a positive or negative attitude on the part of the French teacher.

At this stage of the analysis, the experimental evidence suggests that children of low general ability reach the highest level of achievement in French when they are taught in heterogeneous groups in schools where the teaching staff have a favourable attitude towards the teaching of French to the whole ability range. Further analysis of the data relating both to teacher-attitude and to class composition will be undertaken in connection with the intensive study sample described below.

3 *The effect of length of exposure to French on level of proficiency*
As the study progresses, assessments will be made of the level of

[1] Press statement issued jointly by the Ministry of Education and the Nuffield Foundation on 13 March 1963.

proficiency in French attained by groups of secondary school pupils who were introduced to French at the age of 11+, so that comparisons may be made with the French scores obtained by the children in the experimental groups. Outline proposals for the evaluation of the secondary stage of the Pilot Scheme include:

(a) A comparison of the two experimental cohorts at 11+ and 13+ with two groups of secondary school pupils who have been taught French for the same length of time (i.e. for three or five years), but who are aged respectively 14+ and 16+.

(b) A comparison of the two experimental cohorts at 13+ with secondary school pupils of the same age, but who have only been taught French for two years.

It is hoped that the Pilot Scheme, if successful, will lead to the earlier and easier introduction of a second modern language at the secondary stage, on a wider scale than has previously been the case.

4 Organizational and teaching problems

A detailed study is being made of the organizational and teaching problems posed by the introduction of French teaching in the primary school. A great deal of background information on time-table and staffing difficulties has already been supplied by the teachers participating in the experiment and is being supplemented by observational data provided by members of HM Inspectorate.

5 The development of oral French tests

In all Pilot Scheme schools French is taught initially by predominantly oral methods: the language is viewed primarily as a means of communication and the written symbols are not introduced until a later stage of instruction. As there were no suitable measuring devices available, it was necessary for the team to develop oral French tests in the early stages of the project, in order to obtain an objective assessment of the level of proficiency in French attained by the children in the experimental sample. The first tests to be constructed were tests of listening comprehension (Test LCA) and oral production (Tests OPA and OPB).

(a) *Test LCA*. Test LCA is a group test of listening comprehension, designed for children who have reached a particular stage of instruction in French—in this case, the purely oral stage—and not for children who have attained a specific chronological age or school grade. The final version of the test contains 65 multiple-choice items, of which five are used as practice examples. The items are recorded on magnetic tape by a native French speaker, to ensure a standardized presentation. Each item consists of a brief but complete statement, spoken smoothly and clearly in French at normal conversational speed. The items reflect the common content of the audio-visual courses in use in the Pilot Scheme schools.

The complete set of test materials consists of a master tape, a teacher's instruction manual, and a pupil's test booklet. The test booklet contains 260 black and white drawings, arranged in 65 sets of four. The child's task is to scan the appropriate set of four pictures while listening to the tape-recorded statement, and to identify the picture which corresponds to the statement. The three 'distractors' are composed in such a way that the child cannot identify the correct picture unless he understands all the elements of the spoken sentence, since it was considered essential to avoid testing recognition of isolated vocabulary items. For instance, in the practice example '*C'est un chat blanc*', the first picture in the series shows a white dog, the second a black cat, the third a white cat and the fourth shows two white cats and a black dog. Each set of pictures is numbered and each picture is identified by a letter: 'A', 'B', 'C' or 'D'. The child indicates his answer by writing the appropriate letter in a numbered box at the right-hand side of the page. The position of the correct picture in each set of four was determined by the use of random number tables. The test items are presented in a random order of difficulty.

The administration of Test LCA, including instructions, takes approximately 30 minutes. Each item is spoken once only and is followed by a pause of 10 seconds, during which the child writes his answer. A five-minute break is provided half-way through the test. The first five items of the test are untimed practice examples and serve to familiarize the child with the test procedure. All the instructions for the test are given in English: the test can be administered without difficulty by a class teacher who has no knowledge of French.

(b) *Test OPA.* Test OPA is an individually administered test of phonetic accuracy. The aim of the test is to provide a measure of the child's ability to reproduce accurately the sounds of spoken French. The test comprises 12 items, recorded on tape by a native French speaker. Each item consists of a short but complete and meaningful utterance (e.g. '*La neige tombe.*'), which the child is instructed to repeat. Each item is spoken once only and is followed by a pause of approximately seven seconds, during which the child's response is recorded. Each response is scored on a four-point scale.

All instructions are given in English and the test is preceded by untimed practice examples. Each vowel, semi-vowel and consonant of standard spoken French occurs at least once during the test, and care has been taken to present a variety of intonation patterns. The vocabulary items and structural elements which compose the test items are aurally familiar to the children in the experimental sample.

(c) *Test OPB.* Test OPB is an individually administered test of oral production. The aim of the test is to provide a measure of the child's ability to produce an appropriate response to an oral stimulus in French. The test consists of 12 items, preceded by 4 practice items, recorded on tape by a native French speaker. Each item is in the form of a simple question (e.g. '*Que fait la petite fille?*') which refers to a black and white illustration, mounted on card. There are four such picture-cards, one of which is used as a practice-card, to familiarize the child with the test procedure. Each question is spoken once only and is followed by a 15-second pause, during which the child's response is recorded. The child is instructed to give his response in the form of a complete phrase.

Each response is scored separately for structure/vocabulary and for intonation/pronunciation, using four-point scales. Provision is also made for 'bonus' points. One 'bonus' point may be added to the child's score for any item, if the child has been able to expand the expected minimal response.

The initial construction of these tests was preceded by a content analysis of the various audio-visual French courses in use in the Pilot Scheme schools, to establish which elements of the French language were common to all courses. Graded vocabulary and structure lists were subsequently produced and were used as a basis for item construction, so that the tests would not have a bias in favour of any specific French course. The tests were then extensively pilot-tested in England, France and the States of Jersey, and have twice undergone revision after item analysis. The pilot tests carried out in France were particularly useful in bringing to light certain ambiguities in the pictorial material of Test LCA. The final versions of the tests were administered to the children in the experimental sample in June 1966. Test LCA was administered to all the children in both experimental cohorts (approximately 13,000). Tests OPA and OPB were administered to a random sample of approximately 600 children. The random sample was confined to the children in the first experimental cohort (i.e. children who had been learning French for nearly two years).

(d) *Test RCA*. Test RCA is the most recent to be developed. It is a group test of reading comprehension, devised for the experimental age range and with reference to the teaching methods employed in Pilot Scheme schools. The construction of test items was preceded by a content analysis of the teaching materials used in the third-year French classes. Members of the research team also visited many of the schools in the sample to observe the introduction of reading and to discuss the construction of a suitable test of reading comprehension with the teachers concerned. The first draft of the test was given pre-pilot classroom trials in February 1967. The test was then revised in the light of classroom experience and, in March 1967, was subjected to a full schedule of pilot-testing in England and the Island of Jersey. After item analysis and revision the final version of Test RCA was administered to the first experimental cohort in June 1967. At the time of testing, the children in this group had been learning French for almost three years.

The final version of Test RCA is in three sections, each section preceded by printed instructions in English and appropriate practice examples to familiarize the pupil with the type of item contained in that section. The first section consists of 20 multiple-choice comprehension items of the type used in testing listening comprehension, except that, in Test RCA, the items are printed below the picture-sets in bold face type rather than recorded on magnetic tape. As in Test LCA, the pupil's task is to examine each set of four pictures and identify the picture which corresponds to the printed item. The pupil indicates his answer by writing the appropriate identification letter in a numbered box at the right-hand side of the page in his test booklet. The position of the correct picture in each set of four was determined by the use of random number tables. The item 'distractors' are composed in such a way that the pupil cannot identify the correct picture unless he understands all the elements of the printed sentence: he cannot select the correct picture by responding merely to a key word in the item statement. The content of the items reflects the common content of the audio-visual courses in use in Pilot Scheme schools. The second section of the test contains 20 sentence-completion items, in which the child's task is to identify the word necessary to complete the sentence. A choice of four words is given: the child simply places a tick beside one of the words. No element of writing ability is involved since he is required only to identify the correct word, not to copy it. The final section of Test RCA consists of a passage of continuous prose, followed by 10 multiple-choice questions designed to test comprehension of the content of the passage. Again, the child has simply to indicate his answer by writing the appropriate identification letter in the space provided. This section of the test is considerably more difficult than the two preceding sections and is intended to 'stretch' the most able pupils in the sample. The administration of Test RCA, including the instruction period, takes approximately 30 minutes. All the instructions are in English and the test can be administered without difficulty by a class teacher who has no knowledge of French.

Further French tests will be developed by the research team as required. It was originally anticipated that a test of written expression in French would be administered to the whole of the experimental sample while the children were still in the primary school. As the experiment progressed, however, it became clear that such a test would be inappropriate at the primary stage, at least as far as the first cohort was concerned, since very few children in this group would have had any experience of writing in French before transferring to the secondary school. At the time of writing, it appears probable that the children in the second cohort will be introduced to writing in French while still in the primary school; it is therefore planned to administer a complete battery of French tests to the second cohort in June 1968. This battery will be used to measure attainment in the four basic skills of listening, speaking, reading and writing: the tests making up the battery will be based on those already developed by the research team, but will be suitably revised and extended in range.

6 Intensive study sample

When the results of the test programme carried out in June 1966 became available, an intensive study of a small group of children was initiated. Two sub-groups were selected from the main sample: a group of 'under-achievers' (i.e. children whose foreign language scores were markedly inferior to their general attainment scores) and a group of 'over-achievers' (i.e. children whose foreign language scores were markedly superior to their general attainment scores).

These two groups will be matched for age, general level of attainment, socio-economic background, school environment, etc., and will then be studied in depth. The study will include an investigation of such factors as the relationship between general attainment and linguistic ability, the child's interaction with teacher and peer-group, the influence of parental attitude and socio-economic background on the development of linguistic skills, and the importance of personality characteristics in second-language learning. An attempt will be made to identify those factors which accelerate or retard the acquisition of a second language in childhood. The children taking part in this small-group study will be followed through into the secondary school. Measuring devices, such as attitude scales, questionnaires, and tests of linguistic ability, will be developed as required.

17

The main stages in the development of language tests

CLARE BURSTALL[1]

Any investigation of second language learning at the primary level must entail the objective assessment of the four basic linguistic skills: listening comprehension, oral production, reading comprehension and written expression. At the present time, there is an almost complete lack of attainment tests suitable for primary school children who have been taught a second language by audio-visual methods. Since test development is a lengthy process, this situation is unlikely to change in the immediate future. It may therefore be useful to outline the main stages in test development and to illustrate some of the problems peculiar to the assessment of oral skills at the primary level.

1 CONTENT ANALYSIS

Attainment tests, whatever their subject-area, must be constructed with reference to specific course or programme objectives. The first stage in the development of an attainment test is therefore the definition of these objectives by means of a detailed analysis of course or programme content. Once the test has been developed, it can only be used to measure the attainment of the educational objectives so defined.

2 ITEM CONSTRUCTION

Test items must be constructed within the limits imposed by the definition of course objectives. A greater number of items must be constructed than will be needed for the finished test, since a con-

---

[1] The present chapter by Mrs Clare Burstall gives guidance on the construction of language tests. A fuller treatment of research procedures including tests is to be found in Part II of this volume, the research guide contributed by Professor J. B. Carroll.—Ed.

siderable 'margin of discard' must be allowed. In general, the more complex the items of the behaviour which the test is intended to measure, the greater the necessary 'margin of discard', although much will depend on the skill and experience of the item writer.

At the primary level, items intended for use in oral tests should be kept short, since lengthy items tend to have poor discrimination indices. The total test should be as short as the limits of reliability allow. If the test is designed to measure the child's comprehension of the target language, each item should be in the form of a complete and meaningful utterance. Isolated words or incomplete phrases do not make satisfactory items: 'a pupil's ability to translate individual words out of context is a poor measure of the pupil's skill in using the language' (Johnson *et al.*, 1963). When a multiple-choice technique is employed, it is essential to compose plausible 'distractors', so that the child cannot answer the item correctly merely by responding to a key word in the item. In multiple-choice tests which involve pictorial material, the optimum number of response choices for each item has generally been found to be four: if only three response choices are presented, the guessing factor is too high; if there are more than four, the younger child has difficulty in scanning them all.

The construction of good test items is an extremely exacting task. The item writer must have a thorough grasp of the subject-matter being tested; he must be familiar with the educational characteristics of the group for whom the test is intended, in order to set a suitable level of item difficulty; and he must also possess considerable verbal ability, since each item must be totally un-ambiguous and capable of functioning as an isolated unit. If no single individual combines these qualities, it is usual for item construction to be undertaken on a group basis.

3 PILOT TESTS

The next step in the development of a test is the administration of classroom trials. The draft items are made up into a pilot test, which is then administered to a sample of children representative of the age range and ability of the children for whom the test is ultimately intended. The administration of the pilot test will reveal defective or ambiguous items and will bring to light any technical difficulties or deficiencies in the formulation of the instruction manual. It will also provide information regarding the possible range of performance on the test.

Where tests of second language attainment are concerned, it is essential that the pilot test should be administered to a representative sample of native speakers of the language under study. This is particularly important when the test contains pictorial material with a cultural content or when it is necessary to establish the potential range of responses to a series of oral stimuli. The test performance of native speakers will also indicate whether any of the items are measuring extraneous factors. During the development of Test LCA, for example, pilot-testing carried out in France brought to light the fact that many 8-year-olds were failing the item '*Il est huit heures et quart*' because they had not yet learnt to tell the time from a clock-face, although they fully understood the meaning of the spoken phrase. A similar finding was reported by Johnson and his co-workers (1963). They discovered that a series of test items designed to test comprehension of the Spanish for 'left' and 'right' failed because the children could not correctly identify drawings of right and left hands: 'children who had no difficulty determining right from left, either practically or linguistically, failed this test on the basis of their inability to distinguish left from right in a mirror image'. In both these cases, children were failing listening comprehension items for reasons other than inability to comprehend. This might not have been detected if the items had not been pilot-tested on a native sample.

4 ITEM ANALYSIS

When the first draft of a test has been pilot-tested and scored, the test items are submitted to a detailed analysis. The purpose of item analysis is to determine the level of difficulty and the discriminating power of each item in the test. The level of difficulty of an item is established by calculating the percentages of children who answer the item correctly: items which fall outside the required range of difficulty are discarded. The discrimination indices of the remaining items must then be calculated. Various statistical techniques have been devised for this purpose, based on a measure of agreement between performance on the test as a whole and performance on the individual test item. In broad terms, an item discriminates effectively when those children who score high on the test as a whole tend to answer it correctly, whereas those with a low total score tend not to do so.

When an item fails to discriminate effectively, it must be discarded. In the case of orally-administered tests, however, it is often fruitful to probe the cause of failure, since the item itself may not be defective. A low discrimination index may be caused by ambiguity in accompanying pictorial material or by a momentary fault on the magnetic tape, both of which are easily rectified.

If the test employs a multiple-choice technique, a further analysis of the wrongly chosen alternative items must be carried out. If a large proportion of children—particularly children with a high total score—consistently choose the same wrong alternative, the 'distractors' are not working efficiently and should be revised or replaced.

The order in which test items are arranged may have a decisive influence on test performance. This is particularly true in the case of tape-recorded group tests, where the child's performance is paced by the master-tape. In this situation, a random order of presentation has much to recommend it. In the original version of Test LCA, for example, the items were arranged in an approximately ascending order of difficulty. When the items were scored, it was found that the later items in the test were frequently omitted or answered erratically, and it proved impossible to distinguish between the effects of fatigue and of item difficulty. A further consequence of the original ordering of items was that children who obtained a low total score became restless and discouraged during the early stages of the test, but were obliged to continue listening to the tape until the end of the test period. These difficulties were eliminated by presenting the items in a random order of difficulty.

After item analysis, selected items are assembled into a revised version of the test, which is then administered to a further representative sample of children, in circumstances which approximate as closely as possible those in which the final test will be administered. Some of the original test items will have been revised and others discarded: the whole process of item analysis must therefore be repeated when the second draft has been scored. The final version of the test may then be assembled.

5   TEST ADMINISTRATION AND SCORING

The objective assessment of oral skills enta ls the administration of language attainment tests in a standard form. Tests of listening comprehension, reading comprehension and written expression present relatively few technical problems, since they are capable of large-scale administration by non-specialist staff. Tests of oral production, on the other hand, present formidable administrative difficulties and inevitably require specialist scoring. This type of test must usually be administered on an individual basis and therefore tends to be restricted to a sub-sample of the experimental population. It is essential, however, that present research should include an assessment of oral production, since little is yet known about the correlation between listening and speaking skills at the primary level.

No matter how much skill has gone into the construction of a test, the results will be worthless unless a standard procedure for test administration and scoring has been strictly observed. The provision of clear instructions for the administration of the test, for both teacher and pupil, is an essential part of test construction. The instruction manual must be pilot-tested as carefully as the test itself, since it must be completely comprehensive and unambiguous. The administration of the test will be greatly facilitated if it is possible to arrange 'briefing' meetings at which the test procedure may be fully discussed with the teaching staff concerned.

If the test is intended for use in the primary school, it is advisable to include a provision for the repetition of instructions, so that the length of the instruction period can be adjusted to suit the needs of different ability-groups. It is also essential that the test itself should be preceded by a sufficient number of practice examples to familiarize the children with the test procedure. At the primary level, all instructions should be given in the child's mother tongue, to avoid test errors caused by failure to understand the instructions.

The test materials themselves must also be presented in a standard form. For oral tests, the provision of a standard master-tape is the most effective method of ensuring a uniform presentation. The master-tape should be recorded by a native speaker of the language under study. The use of a standard master-tape means that only one form of the spoken language may be employed, although it does not rule out the possibility that dialect forms of the second language may be studied within the framework of a major inquiry.

Objective tests may be scored either by hand or by machine. The relative merits of manual versus machine scoring will not be discussed here: the interested reader is referred to Chapter 10 of the handbook *Educational Measurement*, edited by E. F. Lindquist (1963). In the context of primary education, the main disadvantage of machine scoring is that it entails the use of electrographic pencils to complete separate answer sheets: young children do not always possess the necessary degree of manual dexterity to perform this task successfully.

The main problem in the scoring of language attainment tests lies in the development of objective techniques to score tests of oral production. Tests of this type demand specialist scoring: the items are usually scored according to a rating scale, each point on the scale being defined in terms of specific behavioural elements. Test OPA, for example, which is designed to measure phonetic accuracy, is scored according to the following four-point scale:

0 = omitted, incomplete or inaudible response.

1 = inaccurate response (i.e. attempt made to repeat whole phrase, but at least one error in pronunciation).

2 = fairly accurate response (i.e. whole phrase repeated with reasonably good intonation and no serious error in pronunciation).

3 = excellent response (i.e. whole phrase repeated with native accuracy).

Descriptions of other rating scales devised to score tests of oral proficiency will be found in the research reports of Andrade *et al.* (1963), Johnson *et al.* (1963), Otter (1965), and Pimsleur (1961). It is, of course, impossible to eliminate all traces of subjectivity from the scoring of individually administered oral tests, but, with well-defined rating scales, high inter-judge reliabilities may be obtained.

If test scores are to be used for comparative purposes, the test must be standardized on a representative sample of children who fall within the appropriate age range. 'Raw' scores can never be used for purposes of comparison, since the average raw score and the spread of scores about the mean will vary from one test to another. The raw scores must therefore be converted into standardized scores, which may then be used to compare each child's performance on the test with that of a representative sample of children. It must be emphasized that tests are standardized on the basis of a specific set of instructions for administration and scoring; any deviation from the original procedures will inevitably invalidate comparisons with established norms.

CONCLUSION

The current increase in modern language teaching at the primary level and the development of new methods and materials have stimulated the demand for research into the major problems of second language acquisition. Recently reported investigations have suggested potentially fruitful approaches to the study of second language learning, which should encourage coordinated research efforts on both a national and an international scale. To be of real value, however, such research must conform to high standards of professional skill in its design, execution and evaluation.

PART II: RESEARCH GUIDE

Guide for the Collection of Data pertaining
to the Study of Foreign or Second Languages
by Younger Children

by J. B. CARROLL
Educational Testing Service, Princeton, N.J., U.S.A.

Contents

1 Purpose of this Guide[1]

One of the most pressing problems facing educators in many countries in the world today is that of the teaching of foreign or second languages to young children. Answers are sought to such questions as: how early in the child's schooling should such languages be taught? Should such languages be taught to all children, or only to selected children? How much time should be devoted to such teaching? What methods and materials should be used? What methods of examining should be employed?

In April 1962, there was an international meeting of experts at the Unesco Institute for Education in Hamburg, to pool opinions and experiences on such matters. The report of that meeting is now available in both English and French (Stern, 1963, 1965, 1967). The meeting was concerned with three main questions:

1 What arguments and evidence, if any, justify teaching of second languages to children of primary school age?

2 What experience and experimental evidence has accumulated in different countries in regard to such teaching? What methods and teaching materials have been developed? What results have been attained?

3 What are the main problems which need further examination? What investigations in connexion with the teaching of foreign languages in the early years of schooling are now required?

With regard to the first question, the conferees recognized, first, that there were many sound educational reasons for desiring that children should acquire competence in foreign or second languages rather early in their educational experience. In many countries early acquisition of a second language is necessary or at least highly desirable in order to enable the child to communicate with his fellow nationals in the same country (whether in the immediate vicinity or in more distant parts of the country), or to enable him

[1] *Acknowledgements.* Thanks are hereby expressed to Dr Moshe Anisfeld, now of Cornell University, Ithaca, NY, for his help in preparing a preliminary draft of this material. In particular, I have drawn heavily from his drafts for the appendices.

I am indebted to the Literary Executor of the late Sir Ronald A. Fisher, FRS, Cambridge, to Dr Frank Yates, FRS, Rothamsted, and to Messrs Oliver & Boyd Ltd, Edinburgh, for permission to reprint an abridged form of Table III from their book *Statistical Tables for Biological, Agricultural and Medical Research.*

to learn from the more readily accessible educational materials couched in a second language. More generally, it was stated that 'the political, economic and cultural interdependence of the world today demands a crossing of language and national barriers in the earliest phases of schooling'. Psychological and neurological evidence was cited to suggest that the learning of second languages is easier, at least in some respects, for a person when he is a child than when he reaches adolescence or adulthood.

With regard to the second question, abundant evidence was assembled to show that the early teaching of second languages is practical and feasible, provided that teaching methods and materials are properly selected. It was concluded that 'there is sufficient evidence available in different countries which leads to definite suggestions on how to make this work effective'.

With regard to the third question, it was concluded that the research evidence left many issues not completely or satisfactorily answered. A number of such issues were mentioned with the hope that ways would be found to attack them more systematically through appropriate surveys and experiments. The reader is referred specially to chapter 19 of the above-cited report, 'Research problems concerning the teaching of foreign or second languages to younger children', by the present author.

It is the purpose of this Guide to spell out some of the ways in which research surveys and experiments can be done to provide more definitive answers to the questions raised at the Hamburg meeting. The Guide is published on the assumption that under the auspices of Unesco or other agencies it will be possible through international cooperation to collect a series of data and to sponsor certain experiments that may shed light on these questions. It is also assumed that some sort of international committee and a central directorate will be established to guide this international project, somewhat on the pattern of the 'International Project for the Evaluation of Educational Achievement' now in progress under the aegis of the Unesco Institute for Education in Hamburg.[1]

There is ample precedent for international studies of educational progress under varying conditions. The forerunner of the above-mentioned international study of educational attainment was a pilot study of educational achievements in certain school subjects in twelve countries, reported by Foshay et al. (1962). Recently there

[1] For other references to the International Project for the Evaluation of Educational Achievement (IEA), see also chapter 2, p. 19.

appeared, also, a comparative study of children's attainments in French among selected schools in England, Holland, and the Flemish-speaking areas of Belgium (Halsall, 1963–4).[1]

Research can be, and is, conducted at various levels of sophistication and rigour. At the lowest level, there is 'teacher-conducted' research, often performed without any formal design or control and with only the most elementary statistical treatment of data. At approximately the same level, there is what is sometimes called 'action research', in which a teacher, or more often a group of teachers or an educational organization, undertakes to introduce an innovation and evaluate its effects on a solely impressionistic basis, by the sheer impressiveness of the outcomes, without regard for the possibility that the effects may be due to the shock of novelty or change itself, or to the effort and enthusiasm with which the innovation is introduced. This Guide is not concerned with these relatively unsophisticated types of research, if they may be called research at all. Rather, it is concerned with studies and experiments that are carefully planned, with due regard to the logic of scientific method and the validation of findings against possible alternative explanations of them.

Formal studies of the latter sort may be classified into (a) surveys and status studies, on the one hand, and (b) controlled experiments, on the other.

Surveys and status studies are designed to assemble observations and other kinds of data concerning on-going programmes of teaching. If these data and observations are collected in a sufficiently large number of situations and on a sufficiently *uniform* basis, it is thought possible to draw inferences regarding many problems relating to second language teaching through the comparison of results obtained in different situations, for there is no doubt that the results will indeed vary. The importance of *uniformity* in the collection of such data cannot be over-emphasized, because it is necessary to collect the *same kinds* of data, using the *same methods* of data collection in order that the comparisons among different teaching programmes in different schools in different countries can be made on an equitable basis, i.e. so that any contrasts or differences that are found arise solely from the situations being studied and not from the methods of data collection.

[1] Halsall, Elizabeth. 'A comparative study of attainments in French', *International Review of Education*, 1963–4, 9, 41–59. Halsall's study must be regarded as somewhat inconclusive, due to the absence of adequate measurements and controls.

Therefore, a primary purpose of this Guide is to specify uniform procedures whereby data can be collected for comparative surveys. Of course, there are limits to the extent to which the procedures can be truly uniform, because they must be carried out in different languages and in different cultural situations. Nevertheless, one must have faith in the possibility that special care and attention can minimize the loss in the process of translating materials into different languages or using these in different cultural situations. It is suggested that persons or organizations cooperating in this investigation follow very carefully the guidelines set forth here. Materials patterned on these guidelines should, if possible, be submitted to the central directorate for review before they are used. If it is necessary to make departures from these guidelines, information on such departures can usually be circulated among the different countries, and the central directorate can issue supplementary instructions which will bring all procedures again into conformity.

The essence of a controlled experiment in education is to determine the effect of specified procedures of training, teaching, or selection upon learning or some other aspect of behaviour. The magnitude of these effects cannot properly be assessed unless all conditions other than the particular experimental treatments under study are carefully and systematically controlled. Controlled experiments will ordinarily be carried out in particular local situations and it will not always be easy to obtain uniformity over several countries. This is because the conditions under which experiments are carried out will often depend very much upon local customs, laws, and educational practices. Efforts should be made, however, to maintain whatever degree of uniformity may be possible, even in the case of controlled experiments.

A secondary purpose of this Guide, therefore, is to give suggestions to teachers, educational administrators, and others who are in a position to plan and conduct experiments in particular local situations and to report the results to a central directorate for collation and dissemination. A major section of the Guide is reserved for this.

2 To whom this Guide is addressed

The Guide is addressed to four groups of persons interested in problems of second language teaching and willing to cooperate in studies:

1 To persons in national or regional ministries, bureaux, or departments who would be able to supply summary information concerning the teaching of foreign or second languages to children in the country, region, province, or state of their jurisdiction. The attention of such persons is drawn particularly to section 6 of this Guide pertaining to the kinds of information and data they might be able to furnish. These persons may in some cases also take responsibility for coordinating the flow of information from the second group of persons to whom this Guide is addressed (see next paragraph).

2 To headmasters, foreign language supervisors, and foreign language teachers in local schools who have conducted, or are conducting, programmes whereby young children (pre-school, nursery, kindergarten, or in the first six grades) are taught foreign or second languages, and who would be willing to supply information on these programmes and to collect systematic data from the pupils and teachers involved, according to the schedule suggested in section 7 of this Guide.

3 To persons who volunteer to participate in international committees for the design of tests and other instruments to measure children's proficiency in several of the commonly taught second languages, such as English, French, Arabic or Hindi. The attention of such individuals is drawn especially to section 9.

4 To persons who would be in a position to conduct educational experiments in the teaching of foreign or second languages to young children, and who could report the results of such experiments to the central directorate of the investigation. The attention of such individuals is drawn especially to section 10 of this Guide.

3 Questions to which answers are sought

The primary purpose of the surveys and studies envisioned by this Guide is to obtain information that would help in drawing conclusions as to the best policies and procedures to recommend concerning the teaching of foreign or second languages to young children.

As mentioned in section 1, the investigations to be conducted divide themselves into two main types: (a) broad survey and 'status' studies of on-going teaching programmes, from which conclusions might be drawn by comparing the results obtained under different situations or with different kinds of students; and (b) experimental studies that would determine the effects of specified procedures of training, teaching, or selection upon learning or other aspects of behaviour. Some kinds of questions can be answered more readily or conclusively by the former type of investigation, while other questions can be answered better by the latter type of investigation. In general, the survey or status study is the more feasible means of answering questions about broad policies concerning educational matters, while the experimental study is the method of choice in studying questions concerning detailed procedures of teaching. Nevertheless, it should be recognized that many kinds of questions must be approached both by survey studies and by experimental methods.

In this section, we will consider the kinds of questions to which answers are sought by means of surveys and status studies. Some of the questions more readily handled by controlled experimentation are listed in section 10, below.

In the Unesco publication cited earlier (Stern, 1963, 1967 (English); 1965 (French)), the present writer has already supplied a lengthy list of research problems concerning second language teaching to children. From that list, with certain appropriate changes of phraseology, the following problems seem amenable to solution by international survey studies (the numbers in [ ] refer to the numbers used by the writer in the Stern publication, pp. 103–9 in the English version and pp. 134–40 in the French version).[1]

[2] What progress do children make in acquiring a second language when they receive no formal instruction in it, but learn it through informal contacts with other children or with adults?

[4] Are better results obtained when two languages are introduced simultaneously as first or native languages, or are they better when the introduction of a second language is delayed until after L1 is firmly established? (It is assumed that in some countries or regions, it is customary to have children learn two languages simultaneously as first languages; comparisons can then be made with the many situations in which a second language is introduced only after L1 is firmly established.)

[5] Are better results obtained when two L2s are introduced

---

[1] As previously mentioned (see p. 10, footnote [1]), in this listing, and elsewhere in this Guide, L1 denotes the first or native language, and L2 denotes a second or foreign language.

simultaneously, or are they better when the two languages are introduced successively?

[6] In situations in which it is desirable to present L2 as soon as feasible in formal schooling, are results dependent upon how soon L2 is used as the medium of instruction for school subjects other than the L2 itself?

[10] What are children's rates of progress in acquiring second language proficiency under different educational policies and in different cultural situations? (Tabulations should be made for children starting at different ages, in different countries, learning different languages and in different motivational settings. Account is also to be taken of the amount of time—clock hours—devoted to language teaching, and of the methods of instruction.) It should be emphasized that questions falling under this rubric are the main object of the survey and status studies contemplated under this investigation.

[11] To what extent are foreign language skills and knowledge retained after instruction and practice in the language cease?

[12] How effective are different time-tables of instruction at different age levels, i.e. different time-periods of contact at any one time (10-, 20-, 30- or 45-minute periods) and different frequencies of contact periods (twice a day, once a day, every other day, twice a week, etc.)?

[13] Does learning a second language in childhood make learning still another foreign language easier at some later age?

[14] What are the different systems of foreign language teaching that exist in each country? How do educational policies differ with respect to goals of instruction, age of beginning language instruction, duration of language instruction, methods of instruction, etc.?

[16] Is there any simple but meaningful way of categorizing the various teaching methods and procedures in common use?

[17] How do textbooks and other teaching materials in different countries and regions reflect educational policies and procedures?

[20] What different results are obtained when the introduction of the written language is made at different stages of language instruction? Are better results obtained when the written language is introduced at the outset, or are they better when it is introduced only after competence in the spoken language is fairly well established?

8

[21] To what extent does using the L2 as a medium of instruction in other subjects boost competence in that language?

[24] To what extent are better results obtained through the use of such teaching aids as films, tapes, language laboratories, teaching machines, and the like?

[25] What are the effects, if any, of L2 teaching on proficiency in the first language? Are there benefits, or are there adverse influences? Particular attention should be given to the effects of L2 learning on reading, writing, and spelling in the first language.

[26] What are the effects, if any, of L2 teaching on the learning of other school subjects? Are these effects accounted for solely by considerations of the amounts of time available for learning, or by other factors?

[27] Are 'slow learners' particularly affected by foreign language learning? Is foreign language learning a special hindrance to them, or is it a benefit?

[28] What variations occur among the different countries in systems of recruiting, training, and qualifying teachers of foreign languages for children? Are these variations reflected in the quality of the results obtained in teaching?

[29] What kind of results are obtained when the child is taught L2 by the regular classroom teacher (whose competence in L2 may be minimal), as compared to results obtained when special teachers are used for foreign language instruction?

[31] What attitudes do nationals of different countries have toward problems of second language learning, and towards the learning of specific languages (particularly, languages of 'wider communication' such as English, French, Arabic, Swahili, etc.)?

4 Language learning situations to be studied

There is a wide variety of situations throughout the world in which children learn second or foreign languages. Among the background factors that might make these situations differ in critical ways are the following:

1 LINGUISTIC FACTORS: the extent to which L2 differs from L1.
The following cases may be distinguished:

Case 1.1. L1 (the native language) and L2 (the second or foreign language) are different, but coordinate dialects of the same language.

Case 1.2. L2 is a 'standard' language, while L1 is a 'creolized' or otherwise 'substandard' variant of it.

Case 1.3. L1 is a colloquial or vernacular form of a language, while L2 is a literary standard language (e.g. Classical Arabic).

Case 2.1. L1 and L2 are different languages, although in the same language family.

Case 2.2. L1 and L2 are in different language families.

These cases are described in more detail in Stern (1967, pp. 95–7; and 1965, pp. 126–7). It is probable that international studies should focus on Cases 2.1 and 2.2, since Cases 1.1, 1.2, and 1.3 represent educational problems that are mainly of local or regional concern. Nevertheless, international studies should not completely exclude concern with Cases 1.1, 1.2, and 1.3 because there are possibilities for collecting information on these cases that would be of common interest to many countries facing such problems. The problem of teaching 'standard' languages to children whose L1 is a colloquial, substandard, or creolized language is of wide interest to many nations.

2 LEVEL OF ATTAINMENT EXPECTED

3 DEGREE OF CONTACT WITH THE SECOND LANGUAGE (ASIDE FROM EDUCATIONAL CONTACTS). The spectrum of possibilities includes:

Case 1. L2 is used either as a first language or as an acquired language in the immediate family or household of the child.

Case 2. L2 is used by a population in close geographical contact with the family, such that the child frequently hears L2 spoken by other children and/or by adults, and/or frequently sees written material (e.g. street signs, postmarks, newspapers, etc.) in L2.

Case 3. L2 is used only by a special group of individuals (e.g. a religious society, a servant class, a class of white Europeans, etc.) and is heard only occasionally by the child.

Case 4. L2 is the language of a population residing at a long distance from the child, and is practically never heard by the child.

The survey should include study of each of these cases.

4 MOTIVATION FOR LEARNING THE SECOND LANGUAGE. For the individual, motivation for learning the second language may be

influenced by a wide variety of factors, including the relative social status of speakers of L2, the perceived utility or instrumental value of learning L2, and various educational, political, and economic pressures. Despite these individual variations, it may also be assumed that the general level of motivation for learning specific L2s varies over countries and regions. The survey should attempt to sample as wide a variety of regional variations in this respect as possible; in addition, it should study the effects of individual variation in motivation.

5 OPPORTUNITY TO LEARN THE LANGUAGE IN SCHOOL. Under this heading the survey should concern the age or grade at which the second language is introduced, whether the second language is made the language of instruction for other subjects, whether the second language becomes the medium of communication among children in school because, for example, of the heterogeneity of the children's language backgrounds, and whether the teacher is competent in the second language and skilled in teaching it.

Because these various factors interact in many ways, it may be impracticable for survey studies to investigate their functioning in any systematic manner except perhaps by elaborate statistical designs. The research strategy that may be proposed, however, entails the thorough investigation of a number of common types of language learning situations, each type representing a particular combination of key variables. Three rather common types of situations are the following:

Situation I. Children are taught a second language (a language completely different from L1) chiefly because of its presumed cultural and literary educational benefits; the second language is the language of a population residing at a long distance from the child and is practically never heard outside of school classes; intrinsic motivation is generally neutral or even negative for the child, but extrinsic motivation tends to be positive because teachers and parents reward the child for his efforts; the second language is introduced typically around the third or fourth grade, but only as a subject taught for a few minutes a day, never as a medium of instruction in other subjects. Either the teacher is a competent speaker of the second language, or audio-visual aids (tapes, TV) are used to present the instruction. An example of this situation would be American children learning French in an American public school, or French children learning German in a French elementary school in a region far from German-speaking territory.

Situation II. Children of homogeneous language backgrounds are taught a second language which is of a high status and which is clearly needed by the children, both in education and in out-of-school contexts; the second language is the language used in commerce and government in the immediate geographical environment of the children, and it is frequently heard or seen (in written form) by the children; it is the medium of instruction in the upper grades of school. The teacher is only a moderately competent speaker of the variety of the second language customarily employed by educated people of his own ethnic origin in the region or country. An example of this situation would be Nigerian children learning English in almost any primary school in Nigeria, or Congolese children learning French in a primary school in the Republic of the Congo.

Situation III. Children of homogeneous language backgrounds are taught a second language which is of high status and which is clearly needed by the children both in education and in many out-of-school contexts, but (in contrast to Situation II) the usual language of commerce and government is the child's native language or a 'standard language' variant thereof; the second language is used as a secondary language in business and government, however, and frequently as a medium of instruction in higher education. The teacher is a moderately competent speaker of the variety of the second language customarily employed by educated people of his own ethnic origin in the region or country. This is an extremely common type of situation; examples (exhibiting certain subtle variations) are: Singhalese-speaking children learning English in Ceylon, Marathi-speaking children learning Hindi in India; Spanish-speaking children learning English in Puerto Rico; Haitian children learning Standard French in Haiti.

5 Organization of the investigation

It is envisaged that Unesco or a similar agency would establish, at some appropriate location, a central office or directorate that would further plan and coordinate the types of studies described in this

Guide. It would also be the function of the central office to collate and analyse the information collected, whether by statistical or by other means, and to prepare reports and recommendations on the findings. The central office would contain appropriate staff to perform these functions.

It is also envisaged that the sponsoring agency would appoint an international committee of experts both in foreign language teaching and in educational research, to advise the staff of the central office, either by correspondence or by means of periodic meetings.

Each participating country would appoint one or more representatives to coordinate studies within that country and to function as liaison with the central office and the international committee.

In the preliminary stages of the study, plans and procedures would be carefully coordinated with the representatives of the several participating countries to insure that they are appropriate and acceptable in each country and that the highest possible degree of uniformity in the procedures is obtained.

Reports and recommendations emanating from the analyses to be conducted in the central office would also be submitted to country representatives before publication, for their comments and suggestions.

6 The collection of information at the country or regional level

A questionnaire schedule is provided herewith (Appendix A) whereby the respective countries, or regions within those countries, can supply systematic information concerning the linguistic situation, the requirements for foreign language learning, the number of schools and pupils involved in such instruction, the languages being taught, and other general information that is relevant to this inquiry.

The principle to be followed in deciding whether a country should submit one questionnaire covering the whole of that country or should submit separate questionnaires pertaining to the several regions of the country is that *any questionnaire should cover only a region in which the linguistic situation, conditions of foreign language learning, etc., are relatively homogeneous.* For example, the United States might decide to submit separate questionnaires for the North-east section of the country, the Midwest, the South-east, the Far West, the Hawaiian Islands, Puerto Rico, and Alaska, on the assumption that conditions are sufficiently different from one of these regions to another, yet fairly uniform within any one region. A country like Denmark, on the other hand, might elect to submit only one questionnaire, if its representative felt that the facts pertaining to teaching at primary level (FLES) are fairly uniform throughout the country. Difficult decisions would be faced by some countries, particularly those countries in which there are many vernaculars yet in which there is only one main second language and a relatively uniform policy concerning second language instruction, e.g. Senegal. The decision would rest on whether it is considered that variations in the local vernaculars would differentially affect the learning of the second language.

The timing of the submission of country or regional questionnaires should be coordinated by the central office of the investigation in such a way that it would as closely as possible coincide with information collected from schools (see section 7). In some cases, the central office might request country representatives to submit questionnaires on two or more separate occasions in order to reflect any changes in conditions that might have occurred in those countries.

It is assumed that the country representatives would gather the information for these questionnaires themselves or arrange to have it collected by those best in a position to do so.

Although the questionnaire set forth in Appendix A is couched in English (or French), it is permissible, if necessary, to translate this and submit it in the national language of the country involved. In this case, the central office will arrange for the translation of the the information into English and/or French for the common use of the International Committee.

7 The collection of information from local schools or local school authorities

The information to be collected from local schools or local school authorities is of several kinds:

1 Detailed information as to the nature of the second language instructional programme (Questionnaire Schedule, Appendix B).

One such questionnaire should be submitted for each school or group of schools for which the second language programme is relatively uniform.

2 Data on progress in acquiring the second language, mainly in the form of performances on a series of second language proficiency tests to be administered to children at the several grade levels in which a second language is taught. The tests would be administered near the end of the school year to children:

(a) At the end of the first year of instruction (Form A of each test)[1]

(b) at the end of the second year of instruction (Form B of each test)

(c) at the end of the fourth year of instruction (Form A of each test).

The tests would be supplied to the schools by country representatives; the schools would return the completed tests to the country representatives, who would in turn either score them themselves or send them to the central office for marking (scoring). In any case, the test materials should be returned to the central office for further analysis.

The tests will have been constructed by international committees in cooperation with country representatives. Suggestions concerning the construction of these tests appear in section 9, addressed to the committees that will be charged with test construction. The tests will cover proficiency in the more commonly taught second languages, such as English, French, Russian, Spanish, and Hindi. Except for the instructions and practice exercises, an effort will be made to avoid the use of L1s in these tests so that the results may be more comparable across nations.[2]

[1] For discussion of the two forms of each test, see section 9.
[2] The series of tests presently proposed does not include a foreign language aptitude test, because of several difficulties: (a) research has not yet clearly indicated how foreign language aptitude can effectively be measured in young children especially when it is necessary, as in the present study, to develop measures that would be equally applicable to children in different countries with different L1s; (b) measures that have been thus far developed are quite sensitive to the age and intellectual maturity of the child; (c) aptitude tests should be given before foreign language instruction is begun, rather than concurrently with the administration of proficiency tests, as would be most practical in the present study.

3 From the same children who are administered these tests, questionnaires (according to the schedule in Appendix C) will be collected. The questionnaires, like the tests, will have been provided by country representatives; they will be couched in whatever language is most familiar to the children to be tested. Where the child cannot read or write in the language of the questionnaire, the questionnaire will be filled out by the teachers, who will fill out the questionnaire for the child through personal interview. (Where the teacher marks the questionnaire for the child, that fact will be noted in the box provided at the beginning of the questionnaire.)

4 Schools should also supply rosters of all children tested, showing name, sex, birth-date, and school grade, together with any additional information that may be pertinent, such as IQ (and date of IQ testing, test used), occupation of parent(s), socio-economic level, etc.

The schools that would participate in this study in any given country or region would be selected by country representatives in consultation with the central office. The number and variety of schools to be selected will depend partly on local resources and the willingness of the respective schools to cooperate. It would be desirable, however, to have at least 5 to 10 schools from each region (as defined above) participate in the study. The following suggestions are made in this regard:

(a) Each school should have had a programme in the teaching of one or more second languages to young children in operation for at least five years prior to the time at which the study is to be made. (In this way, there is assurance that the programme is well established, and that there will be students in the more advanced phases of study available.)

(b) The schools should be selected to be representative of somewhat different types of situations, e.g. some urban, some suburban and/or rural; some catering to upper and middle classes, others to lower socio-economic levels; some large schools, some medium-sized schools, some small schools; some 'progressively minded', some more 'traditionally oriented' in general outlook and methods of foreign language instruction.

(c) In each school, there should be *for each language* at least ten (10) students in the first year of instruction and another ten (10) in the second year of instruction. (The number of students at the fourth year of instruction will not be prescribed.)

(d) The headmaster of each school would act as coordinator for all communications pertaining to the study, or would delegate this authority.

As in any case in which external testing is involved, there will be an inevitable temptation for teachers to try to 'teach for the test', in order that their classes or schools may show up well in the study. This temptation should be resisted as strongly as possible, for in the present case the object is not to evaluate the schools or the students but to accumulate basic scientific information on questions concerning the teaching of foreign languages to young children. If possible, the exact contents of the tests should not be seen by teachers until the time of the testing itself.

It is true that in certain instances the tests to be developed may not fairly test the linguistic content (grammar, vocabulary) that has been emphasized in a particular school or curriculum, although the testing committees will certainly attempt to avoid any such mismatching of test and curriculum. In view of the large number of schools at which the tests would be applied, however, such mismatchings will in all probability balance out on a statistical basis. It is better to give a group of children a test on material they have not covered, and to learn through the test that they have indeed not covered this material, than unknowingly to obtain from them test responses which yield spuriously high scores because they have been specially coached for the test.

8 Analysis of survey data

Persons collecting questionnaire and/or test data, whether at the national, regional, or local level will forward these data to the central office of the investigation, where they will be collated, transferred to punched cards, and analysed statistically. In this process, the identity of specific countries, regions, or local schools will be suppressed; statistical reports will concern general matters such as the average age of starting foreign language study, the amount of improvement noted at the different age levels, the attitudes of children towards foreign language study, etc. Data specifically labelled by countries will be forwarded only to the countries concerned in order to preserve the anonymity of the countries or regions supplying data.

The central office will prepare both general and special reports of the findings of the survey.

The central office will make its consultative and statistical services available to individuals and organizations that may wish to conduct educational experiments along the lines suggested in section 10. It will also serve as a clearing-house for reports on the findings of such educational experiments, arranging for the wide publication of those reports that are deemed of special interest throughout the cooperating countries.

9 The construction of tests of foreign language proficiency for young children

This section is addressed to committees of experts who may volunteer to construct tests of the proficiency attained by young children in learning foreign or second languages at various stages of their study. These committees should include both foreign language teaching specialists and experts in test construction and analysis, and should call on child development specialists for advice on the appropriateness of the tests for young children.

The practicability of formal tests of foreign language proficiency for young children has been demonstrated many times. To cite only recent examples, Johnson *et al.* (1963) produced a complete series of tests for assessing speaking, listening, reading, and writing skills of sixth-grade children in their third year of Spanish instruction. Andrade *et al.* (1963) developed formal measures of Spanish speaking and listening skills which were used to evaluate a city-wide experiment in the teaching of Spanish through television. Burstall supervised the development of a series of oral tests in French to evaluate a primary school foreign language teaching experiment in England.[1]

McArthur (1965) showed how item-analysis techniques could be used to refine measures of foreign language proficiency for children. The California Test Bureau has published a series of *Common Concepts Foreign Language Tests* for use in testing listening comprehension skills of children in a number of foreign languages; these tests have been described by Banathy *et al.* (1962).

[1] See chapter 16 above.

In the present context, however, there are several serious problems to be faced:

1 Curricula in foreign languages for young children are by no means standard throughout the cooperating countries. Syllabi differ in the extent to which various skills are emphasized, and the vocabularies taught to children do not have as large a common core as might be imagined. Yet, it would be desirable to construct a series of tests that are as fair as possible to all.

2 In an international study, there may be a tendency to devote more effort to the construction of tests in commonly taught second languages such as English and French than to the construction of tests in the less commonly taught languages such as Arabic and Hindi. If prototype tests are constructed in English and French and then translated or adapted to the less commonly taught languages, something may be lost in this process.

3 For the purpose of making international evaluations that will be fair to all, the tests must make only minimal use of the student's native language. Any use of vernaculars in the test format (e.g. for presenting general instructions) must have as little connection as possible with those parts of the test which are critical for the testing of foreign language proficiency.

4 Similarly, the tests must be as neutral as possible with respect to the cultural differences that inevitably exist from one country to another.

5 Since the early teaching of foreign languages often stresses oral language skills and sometimes delays the introduction of the written language for several years after the start of the instruction, the tests of oral skills must avoid the use of the written language. By the same token, in order to be fair to those programmes that introduce the written language before oral skills are firmly established, tests of written language skills should not be dependent upon the use of the spoken language.

RATIONALE FOR A BATTERY OF TESTS

Above all, the tests should be clearly designed for young children. The instructions for the tests should be simple, the structure of the tasks demanded of the children should be simple, and the content should be interesting and yet challenging to children.

In planning any set of proficiency tests in a foreign language, one must hold in mind that there are at least four kinds of skills to be considered—listening, speaking, reading and writing—and at least four kinds of content to be covered—phonology (in the case of listening and speaking), orthography (in the case of reading and writing), vocabulary, and grammatical structure. The interaction between skills and contents can be displayed in a table, as follows:

Content: Skill:	Phonology and orthography	Vocabulary	Grammatical structure
Listening	Sound discrimination	Passive vocabulary (spoken)	Recognition and understanding of grammar structures (spoken)
Speaking	Sound production	Active vocabulary (spoken)	Production of grammar structures (spoken)
Reading	Recognition of written symbols	Passive vocabulary (written)	Recognition and understanding of grammar structures (written)
Writing	Production of written symbols; spelling	Active vocabulary (written)	Production of grammar structures (written)

(Some authorities mention a fifth skill—that of translation to and from a foreign language, but this skill is so much dependent upon the basic knowledge of the language as represented in the above table that it may be safely ignored for the present purposes. Furthermore, the testing of translation skills would entail the use of native languages; this would be impractical in an international project involving many different native languages.)

In principle, a complete assessment of an individual's proficiency in a foreign language should include tests of each of the twelve skill-content combinations in the above table. Nevertheless, not all these skill-content combinations are really independent; with minor exceptions, the grammatical structures of the spoken language are the same as those of the written language, and the vocabulary of the spoken language is the same as the vocabulary of the written language. Tests of recognition of spoken vocabulary should correlate highly with tests of recognition of written vocabulary for children who have received instruction in both spoken and written language. Furthermore it is difficult to test recognition or production of grammar structures without at the same time testing knowledge of vocabulary. And finally, it is generally found that active skills are correlated with passive skills at least in the sense that those students with the best active skills are also those with the best passive skills, and students with the poorest passive skills are surely those with the poorest active skills. All these facts lead to the conclusion that it is not feasible or necessary to have separate tests for all the possible skill-content combinations in the above table.

In a far-reaching international study such as the present one, there are also important considerations of practicality. Active skills of speaking and writing are difficult to test on a uniform basis in large groups of students without becoming involved in two very elaborate, expensive, and time-consuming procedures: (a) the obtaining of tape recordings of speech, and (b) the establishment of panels of judges to rate and grade samples of speech or writing. The writer believes that neither of these procedures is practical for the present study, for obvious reasons. In any case, experience with batteries of foreign language proficiency tests prepared for use with secondary school students suggests that scores on speaking and writing tests are so highly correlated with scores on listening and reading tests that the former add little to the information obtainable from the latter. (Perhaps some small-scale studies could be done to extend and confirm this generalization for the case of tests for young children.) Therefore, his recommendation is that there be no tests of speaking or writing skills in the batteries of proficiency tests planned for uniform administration in the participating countries for the present investigation.

Nevertheless, the test battery must be planned to afford some discrimination among the skill-content areas displayed in the table above. In the first place, it is possible to construct listening tests that sample the individual's abilities in the separate areas of phonology, vocabulary, and grammar. For example, items can be constructed that test the ability to discriminate particular sound contrasts (i.e. phonemic contrasts); other items can be constructed to test the child's range of vocabulary; and still other items can be constructed that focus on the child's knowledge of particular grammatical structures. Similarly, reading comprehension tests can be built to sample abilities in the separate areas of word recognition, written vocabulary, and recognition of grammatical structures. Any lack of correlation between listening and reading tests would presumably reflect the degree to which instruction has emphasized one set of skills to the exclusion of the other.

Because of the importance of grammatical competence in language, it is also advisable to include objective (multiple-choice) tests that approach the measurement of active skills in grammar; these are tests that present several possible phrases or sentences and require the student to select the phrase or sentence that is the 'correct' or 'normal' one. It can be argued that the student who is thus able to select the correct or normal, 'well-formed' structure is the one who is more likely to be able to compose that structure in spontaneous speech or free written composition.

It may be highly desirable, nevertheless, to include 'open-ended' or 'constructed-response' tests of writing in some of the batteries to be prepared. These are tests where, for example, the student has to fill in a blank by writing the correct grammatical form, phrase, or sentence structure. Often such tests can be prepared in such a way that the answers can be 'post-coded' by a clerk who indicates which of a number of possible alternatives the student has written; after such post-coding the test answer sheets can be mechanically scored if desired.

Because the standards of teacher competence in pronunciation of the spoken language are likely to vary so widely, it is believed highly desirable to test listening skills *both* with a test that presents a high standard of educated speech by a tape recording *and* with a test that is to be read aloud by a teacher or other local test administrator. In this way, the effect of variation in standards of speech used by teachers can be assessed.

OTHER CONSIDERATIONS IN PLANNING THE TESTS

1 To meet the challenge of wide variations in foreign language curricula, the content of the tests must be selected from language elements (vocabulary items and grammatical structures) that are in wide use throughout all speech communities using the language. Such elements are those that universally exhibit substantial frequencies in samples of texts or discourse taken throughout all dialect regions of a language. Items tending to show local variation must be avoided. A 'common core' of test materials acceptable to the various countries involved must be selected and identified by appropriate analysis of the curricula and programmes utilized in these countries. Individual countries, however, may wish to supplement the 'common core' of test items with materials in which they have a special interest.

2 So far as possible, for any given language skill, there should be a single test that will span the range of levels of ability that are likely to manifest themselves after one year of instruction, two years of instruction, and four years of instruction. This would be done to insure that comparisons across years of instruction could be made on a single numerical scale of measurement. For example, if the test should happen to contain a total of 50 points, it should be possible to show that the average score after one year of instruction is, say, 15, the average score after two years of instruction is, say, 27, and the average score after four years of instruction is, say, 42. A test with such a characteristic is a 'wide-range' test. The items are sometimes arranged in order of difficulty, but they need not be.[1] A possible disadvantage of wide-range tests is that for students in early stages of instruction, some of the items are discouragingly difficult. It is believed, however, that this disadvantage can be circumvented by using instructions that explain this feature to the students— telling them that they are not necessarily expected to know how to answer the more difficult items, but that they should do as many as they can.

3 The tests must not be excessively long. Each subtest must be capable of being administered within an ordinary class period—not over 35 minutes, and the overall total should not exceed about 150 minutes. Administration of the tests cannot avoid some inter- ference with the school schedule, but most school administrators and teachers will be willing to give two or three hours of the school time to an important international project such as this, particularly if the tests can also be used as learning experiences. (Arrangements can be made to have scores furnished to teachers and possibly also to students, and teachers should be encouraged to discuss the test materials with their students after the tests have been administered.)

4 The tests should not be too much speeded, i.e. they should not have time-limits such as to penalize the student who has a certain degree of mastery of the second language but is not able to perform the test as rapidly as classmates with equal competence. (This does not preclude, however, the inclusion of certain tests with self-timing

---

[1] Experience has shown that for many types of tests to be administered to young children, particularly tests administered orally, it is advantageous to arrange the items randomly with respect to difficulty. In this way even the child who is not able to do many of the items may continue to find at least some items that he can do scattered throughout the test; thus, his motivation and interest will be main- tained despite his finding many items that he cannot do.

features, e.g. listening comprehension tests whose speed is held at a constant value by virtue of the fact that the stimuli are recorded and played from magnetic tape.)

5 The same tests must be prepared for all children to be tested in any one language. Only the general directions to be given in L1 might vary from one group of children to another.

6 Above all, the tests must pass through a rigorous process of pre-testing and subsequent revision in the light of try-out results. This process could take as long as one or two years before a final set of tests would become available for use in international studies. The pre-testing must be done on samples of school children in all the countries that are probably to be involved in such studies.

A PROPOSED SCHEDULE OF TESTS

The foregoing considerations lead to the pattern of a battery of tests described in this section. By 'pattern' is meant a general format that is to be followed in constructing the batteries for each of the languages that may be involved in the study. Wherever possible, the batteries would have identical or common features across languages, e.g. identical sets of pictorial materials.

For certain purposes, especially for experimentation that involves pre-tests and post-tests, or for studies tracing growth in language mastery over several years, it would be desirable to have at least two 'equivalent forms' of each test, i.e. tests with different content but constructed so that the contents of one form parallel the contents of the other form in difficulty, nature of task, etc.[1] In the list below, forms are denoted by A and B following the symbolic abbreviation for the test.

In outline form, the schedule of tests (and the order in which they are to be administered) is as follows:

1 Tests LTA and LTB: Each form is a wide-range *listening* test to be administered by the *teacher's voice*, with 50 items requiring approximately 35 minutes.

2 Tests LSA and LSB: Each form is a wide-range *listening* test to be administered by *sound-recording*, with 50 items requiring approximately 35 minutes.

---

[1] As noted in section 7, in the general survey investigation it is proposed that Form A of each test is to be given children at the end of the first year of instruction and at the end of the fourth year of instruction; Form B is to be given to children at the end of the second year of instruction.

(Note: Tests LTA, LTB, LSA and LSB are *four* equivalent tests, equivalence having been established in pilot studies using exclusively sound recordings of standard-dialect voices.)

3 Tests GTA and GTB: Each form is a spoken-language *grammar* test to be administered by the teacher, with 40 items requiring approximately 25 minutes.

4 Tests RCA and RCB: Each form is a wide-range reading comprehension test, an exclusively paper-and-pencil test, to be administered only to children who have been exposed to at least one year's instruction in reading, with 40 items requiring approximately 30 minutes.

5 Tests GWA and GWB: Each form is a written-language grammar test, an exclusively paper-and-pencil test to be administered only to children who have been exposed to at least one year's instruction in reading, with 40 items requiring approximately 25 minutes.

DETAILED DESCRIPTIONS OF TESTS

1 *Tests LTA and LTB, wide-range listening tests administered by the teacher's voice.* These tests use a series of picture-choice items. For each item, the child listens to a foreign-language stimulus that may be of any length from a single word to a complete sentence or short dialogue; while listening to this stimulus and immediately afterwards, he inspects a set of three or four pictures and chooses the one picture that is indicated or suggested by the foreign language stimulus. This type of test has been found to be exceedingly versatile; items can be constructed to test simple sound discriminations, knowledge of vocabulary, or comprehension of grammatical structures. Items are to be arranged in random order of difficulty (difficulty being indicated by the percentages of representative groups of children failing to answer the item correctly), to maintain interest for the less able students. The difficulty of items can be regulated not only by the actual content but also by the rate at which each oral stimulus is spoken, or by whether it is spoken once or twice. Since this test is to be administered by the teacher, instructions concerning the rate of speech and the pacing of the items must be as explicit as possible. (Rates of speech and item pacing should parallel those in Tests LSA and LSB as much as possible.)

Here are two items illustrating this type of test:

A. Stimulus read aloud by teacher: 'bread' . . . 'Find the picture of bread'. Picture stimuli in the child's test booklet:

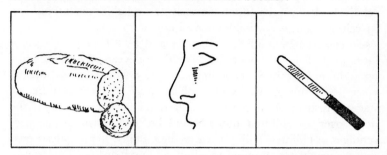

B. Stimulus read aloud by teacher: 'writing . . .' 'Find the picture that shows writing'. Picture stimuli in the child's test booklet:

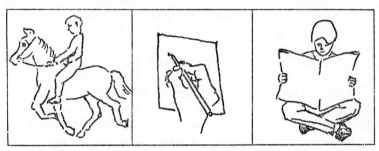

(Items much more difficult than this can be developed, either by making the language content more difficult or by requiring finer discrimination of pictorial content.)

2 *Tests LSA and LSB, wide-range listening tests administered by sound recordings.* These tests would be identical in type to Tests LTA and LTB. The only difference would be that they would be administered by sound recording; in this way it would be possible not only to control exactly the rate at which the stimuli are spoken and paced, but also to present stimuli spoken by persons with native competence in a 'standard' 'educated' dialect, e.g. English as used by the British Broadcasting Corporation or a type of 'General American' as used in American radio broadcasts, standard Parisian French, the form of Arabic used in Egyptian radio broadcasts, etc. Generally, male speakers would be used, chosen for naturalness of speech, clarity of pronunciation, and ability to vary rate of speech in a controlled manner. In the case of English it might be desirable to use both British and American English, say five items in British

English alternating with five items spoken in American English. The rate of speech would be carefully controlled, varying from relatively slow speech (approximately 140 syllables per minute) to speech at about 240 syllables per minute.

To construct tests LSA, LSB, LTA and LTB for equivalence, a large pool of items (about 250) would be developed and administered in one or more experimental forms with standard-dialect voices, to representative groups of language learners at different stages of instruction (about 500 children in all). The difficulty of the items over all children tested would be determined as the percentages of children failing each of these items; item-analysis procedures would also be used to eliminate any items not functioning satisfactorily to discriminate between high-scoring and low-scoring groups. The items would then be distributed among the four forms in such a way that each form would have a comparable distribution of item-difficulties.

3 *Tests GTA and GTB, spoken language grammar tests administered by the teacher.* This test is to be administered by the teacher or other appropriate person from the locality of the school since it is considered important for the child to hear the language spoken in dialect to which he is accustomed and since dialect in which the language is spoken for this test is regarded as immaterial as far as the mastery of grammatical patterns is concerned. In each item, three sentences would be read, and the child would be asked to indicate, on his answer sheet, which one of these (the first, second or third) is more 'correct' from a grammatical standpoint. The order of the correct answers would be randomized.

For example (to be read by the teacher):

'1 John gave a book to the teacher.
 2 John to the teacher gave a book.
 3 John gave the teacher to a book.
Which one is more correct?'

On child's answer sheet: (X) [ ] [ ]
                           1   2   3

The grammar structures to be tested would be chosen to represent various degrees of difficulty for learners of the language. Care would be taken not to emphasize structures of particular difficulty for learners of a particular language background; if such structures are included, they should be counterbalanced by the inclusion of items that represent points of particular difficulty for *other* groups of language learners, i.e. from other native language groups.

The two forms of the test would be constructed to be equivalent by a procedure analogous to that suggested previously; in this case the experimental item pool would be about 100, given to about 300 children. The items would be presented in random order of difficulty.

4 *Tests RCA and RCB, wide-range reading comprehension tests.* In the early portion of this test, the items would be simple four-choice items testing the ability to read the items and their options. A sample item might be as follows:

We travel on

1	clocks	3	needles
2	papers	4	trains

The test would become progressively more difficult, however, the leads and the options becoming longer and more complex in grammar and vocabulary. The last ten or so items would be three groups of multiple-choice items, each group based on a paragraph to be read and understood before the items are to be answered. The items must be constructed so that it is unlikely that a child could answer them correctly (beyond chance) without reading and understanding the paragraph, and the items associated with any given paragraph should be as independent as possible from each other.

5 *Tests GWA and GWB, written-language grammar tests.* These tests would be analogous to the spoken-language grammar tests GSA and GSB, except that the items could each have three or four options to make for greater reliability and precision of measurement. Also, some of the items could be 'open-ended', i.e. requiring the student to supply appropriate grammatical forms, phrases, or sentence structures.

OTHER REMARKS ON TEST CONSTRUCTION

The testing committee for a given language would have to draw on whatever syllabi, word-frequency lists, lists of grammar points, etc., may be available for that language. Since such sources are more plentiful for English and French, it may be wise to make prototype tests in those languages and then translate or adapt them into the other test languages, on the assumption that the lexical and grammatical content found appropriate for the English and French prototype tests would correspond approximately to appropriate content for tests in the other languages.

Each test would be accompanied by full instructions to the teacher or other administrator of the test. These instructions would be couched in the language to be tested, on the assumption that the teacher of such a language would understand such instructions. Consideration should be given, however, to supplying instructions for administration not only in that language but also in the national language of the country in which the test is to be given, e.g. Arabic for an English language test to be given in an Arabic-speaking country.

The tests would be scored centrally in order to avoid error. For tests in which it is the case that nearly all children give an answer for all or nearly all items, the scoring formula can be 'number right'. For tests in which this is not the case, a 'correction for guessing' formula is advisable; that is, the score is computed as equal to $[R-W/(a-1)]$, where R = number right, W = number wrong, and a = the number of alternatives in the multiple-choice items. Thus, the scoring formula for a test in which all items have four alternatives is $R - \dfrac{W}{3}$.

It will be advisable for the central office of the investigation to supply rosters to the cooperating schools showing the test scores of the children tested.

10 The conduct of educational experiments in the teaching of foreign or second languages to young children

TO WHOM THIS SECTION IS ADDRESSED

This section is addressed to persons who would be in a position to conduct educational experiments in the teaching of foreign or second languages to young children. It is expected that such persons might differ very widely in their degree of sophistication and training in the conduct of educational experiments. This section constitutes only a very brief manual on educational experimentation, only enough to get the novice started on his way. If it seems too technical and difficult to some readers, perhaps it may have the desirable effect of alerting them to the complexities of educational research and prompting them to seek competent professional help should they wish to pursue educational experiments. In fact, it is

a matter of prime importance that any serious efforts along these
lines should be preceded by thorough consultation with experts in
the design of educational experiments and the statistical analysis of
test data. For more details on the design and conduct of educational
experiments, the reader is referred to the following:

Rummel, J. Francis. *An introduction to research procedures in education.*
2nd edition. New York: Harper & Bros., 1964.

Travers, Robert M. W. *An introduction to educational research.* 2nd
edition. New York and London: Macmillan, 1964.

For help in the computation of statistics, the following is only one
of many such textbooks that could be recommended:

McNemar, Quinn, *Psychological Statistics.* 3rd edition. New York and
London: John Wiley & Sons Inc., 1962.

THE GENERAL NATURE OF EDUCATIONAL EXPERIMENTS

As noted briefly in section 1, the essence of a controlled experiment
in education is to determine the effect of specified procedures of
training, teaching, or selection upon learning or some other aspect
of behaviour.

When an experiment is called 'controlled', the implication is
that the experiment has been designed in such a way that any
results of the experiment (positive or negative) can with high
probability be traced back or ascribed to the specific influences of
one or more factors (or their interactions) that have been built
into the design. Sometimes teachers 'try out' a new method or
procedure of teaching and call this 'an experiment'. But when they
do this without controls, it cannot be called a true experiment
because the effects of the try-out cannot be traced necessarily to
the influence of the new procedure; they may equally well be the
effects of uncontrolled factors such as the ability of the students, the
increased effort put into the teaching, or even the time of day when
the classes are held.

From these considerations, the necessity for the careful design
and control of educational experiments becomes clear. All too often
one hears of an educational innovation that is reputed to make
teaching or learning remarkably easier or more effective than
before, but that on examination turns out not to have been adequately tested in properly controlled experiments. Sometimes the
very enthusiasm of a teacher or a sponsoring group for the merits of
an innovation inspires teachers and students to unusual effort,

with the result that whatever is accomplished is due not to the merits of the innovation but to the greater energy and effort that is put into teaching or learning. This is sometimes called the 'Hawthorne' effect, after a town in which a famous experiment in industrial psychology was carried out.

In a true experiment, it is useful to distinguish three types of variables that are involved:[1]

1 The *independent* variables are the variables whose effects are being investigated. For example, we might want to investigate the effect of a larger-than-normal type-size in a reader, in which case the size of the type would be an independent variable. Or we might want to study the effect of introducing moving pictures into instruction, in which case the use vs. non-use of moving pictures is an independent variable.

Independent variables may be either *treatment* variables or *selection* variables. A *treatment* variable has to do with variation in treatment of the subjects, such as the difference between a new method of teaching and a more conventional method, the difference between teaching in the morning and teaching in the afternoon, the difference between one order of presentation of material and another, etc. In every case treatment variables have to do with actions the experimenter can arrange to have taken to treat various groups of subjects differently; thus, we speak of *manipulating* a treatment variable. The various degrees or forms of a treatment variable may be called 'levels' of treatment. For example, if we are concerned with variations in methods of teaching, a certain new method, A, might be one 'level' of this treatment variable, another new method, B, is another 'level', and conventional instruction is still a third 'level' of this variable. One of the difficulties in educational research, incidentally, is that often the treatment levels 'leak' from one group to another; e.g. the teachers and/or children in the control group learn about the method being used in the experimental group and adopt it without telling the experimenter. Measures

---

[1] Terminological usage varies. Here we distinguish three major types of variables: independent, dependent, and control. But some authorities consider only two types of variables: independent and dependent, regarding control variables as a special class of independent variables. The confusion arises partly out of a variation in the sense of the term 'control': here, 'to control' is used to mean 'to hold constant (either by manipulation or by statistical means) so as to allow the effects of independent variables to be observed without interference from these control variables.'

must be taken to minimize such 'leakage', e.g. by conducting the different treatments in completely separate schools.

A *selection* variable has to do with the variation in the groups of students or learners selected for the experiment, such as the difference between high ability students and low ability students, or the difference between older students and younger students. The 'levels' of a selection variable are the different groups into which the students are classified for the design of an experiment.

Sometimes a particular variable can appear, in an experimental design, either as a treatment variable or as a selection variable. For example, when motivation is used as a treatment variable, one manipulates the incentives that are set for different groups—one group, say, being offered a reward for high achievement, and another group being offered no such reward. When motivation is used as a selection variable, however, one simply selects two or more groups with different degrees of measured motivation or interest with respect to something deemed relevant to the experiment, e.g. interest in learning foreign languages.

A single experiment may have one or more independent variables, of either the treatment or the selection type. One of the most common types of experiment is that which uses two levels of a treatment variable, one being called the 'experimental group', the other level being called the 'control group', when a particular treatment is present in the former group and absent in the latter.

2 The *dependent* variables are measures of the effects being investigated. For example, in an experiment on the effects of two methods of teaching (an independent variable), a dependent variable would probably be some measure of learning, such as performance on a test of foreign language listening comprehension. Or the dependent variable might be a measure of the amount of gain from one stage of learning to a later stage of learning, such as the difference between a student's score on a certain test given at the earlier stage of learning and his score on that same test (or a parallel form of the test) given at the later stage. A given experiment may involve one or more dependent variables; usually there are only a small number—say, two or three, and the effects are studied separately. For example, an experiment in foreign language teaching could utilize as dependent variables (a) a test of listening ability, and (b) a test of reading ability, in order to see whether the variation in teaching method affects listening ability more than reading ability.

3 *Control* variables are variables whose effects are not being

directly investigated and which are therefore 'controlled' either in advance of the experiment, by selecting groups that are uniform with respect to these variables, or after the experiment, by using certain statistical procedures. In other words, the effects of the control variables are held 'constant' or equal, *on the average*, across the levels of the independent variables. For example, in an experiment comparing two methods of teaching, we might want to 'control' the effects of 'intelligence' or scholastic aptitude; thus, we would want to make sure that the average intelligence of the children being taught under one method is equal to the average intelligence of the children being taught under the other method. This could be done either by selecting groups of equal intelligence, or by estimating by statistical means what the results would be if the groups were of equal intelligence.

In theory, *all possible* variables that might conceivably have effects upon the dependent variable(s), other than the independent variables themselves, should be controlled or held constant across levels of the independent variables. Variables that can often be reasonably expected to have such effects are intellectual ability, age, and prior training of learners. One procedure for controlling such variables is to attempt to 'match' experimental groups with respect to them; for example, in setting up two or more experimental groups, one assigns pupils to them so that in each group there is a pupil of a given degree (at least within a very small range) of intellectual ability, age, and prior training. Matching has its limitations, however, for one is never sure that one has matched on all the relevant variables; the children assigned to one group by a matching procedure might actually be superior in some critical way to the children assigned to another group. A much easier procedure, and one that is generally more defensible from the point of view of the statistical assumptions that are entailed, is simply to assign pupils to different experimental groups according to a completely random process, e.g. by throwing coins or dice or by using a table of random numbers. This can be assumed to have the effect of controlling *all* conceivable relevant variables other than the independent variables themselves.

Unfortunately it is often impossible to assign pupils to experimental groups randomly. This would be the case when one must conduct experiments with already 'intact' groups that have been selected or set up by somebody other than the investigator. (The problem arises only when a particular experimental treatment *must* be applied uniformly to all members of an intact group; it does not arise when the investigator can single out members of an intact group and apply different experimental treatments to them at will, in which case random assignment procedures can be used.) In this case measures of relevant control variables must be applied to all members of the experimental groups (i.e. both experimental and control groups, if they are designated in this way) so that statistical procedures can be used to control these variables. If the control variable is a measure of level of learning that can be applied also as dependent variable *after* the experimental treatment, the easiest method of statistical control is to redefine the dependent variable as a measure of 'gain'. That is, the measure of level of learning is first applied as a 'pre-test' to all experimental groups prior to the experimental treatment, and then it (or an 'equivalent' measure) is applied to all experimental groups as a 'post-test' *after* the experimental treatment; the dependent variable is then re-defined as the post-test score *minus* the pre-test score, i.e. the algebraic difference between them; a negative gain is possible, in effect a loss.[1]

If this cannot be done, the control variable must be used as a 'covariate' in a special statistical treatment known as the analysis of covariance (McNemar, *op. cit.*, chapter 18, or as discussed in many other textbooks of statistical methods).

Since the effects in educational experiments are rarely so large that they will appear strongly in every individual to whom they may be applied, it is always advisable to use a substantial number of persons in each of the experimental groups of an experiment. Just how many can be considered a 'substantial number' will depend on many factors, but as a rule of thumb for the present discussion let us say that there should be *at least* 10 persons in each experimental group. In certain complex designs in which a number of independent variables are studied simultaneously, smaller numbers than 10 may be permitted in each 'cell' of the cross-classification, but for the simple designs to be discussed here, 10 is a minimum number, and 20 or even more would be preferable. In this way, even though the effects may be small in magnitude, on the average the random effects will cancel out and the average amount of the experimental effect will have a chance to appear 'statistically' or even practically significant.

For various reasons, both statistical and practical, it is advisable

[1] Of course, there could be a certain amount of 'normal gain' in all groups, but the statistical procedure would examine whether some groups gain more than others.

to have the numbers in each experimental group equal. In order to make groups equal, cases can be eliminated from the analysis by a process of random de-selection. For example, if one group contains 22 children and another contains 19, three cases should be eliminated from the first group *in the statistical analysis* (not necessarily from the group itself) at random.

Campbell and Stanley, pp. 171–246 in Gage (1963), have classified possible experimental designs. One of the simplest of their 'true experimental designs' is the 'pre-test-post-test control group design', that can be diagrammed as follows:

	Experimental group	Pre-test	Experimental treatment	Post-test
Individuals assigned randomly to these groups	Control group	Pre-test	No experimental treatment (control treatment)	Post-test

Time ⟶

This design could be illustrated by an experiment in which 20 children are assigned randomly so that 10 are in the 'experimental group' and 10 are in the control group. As noted earlier, this random assignment controls any possible differences in the two groups existing prior to the experiment. Implicitly, all variables other than the independent and dependent variables are 'controlled'. The independent variable is represented by the fact that a certain treatment, e.g. use of films in the language laboratory, is applied for the experimental group and not for the control group. The dependent variable is the amount of gain for each individual as shown by the difference between his post-test score and his pre-test score (on a listening comprehension test, say).

To evaluate the results of such an experiment, some simple statistical methods must be employed. Suppose the actual results in this experiment are as shown in the table (p. 237). The table also shows the computed amount of gain for each individual, and the average gain for each of the groups, as well as certain other statistics that will be explained shortly. It will be noted that the average gain for the experimental group is greater than for the control group. The question is, is this gain 'statistically significant', or is it just an amount of gain that might occur 'by chance'?

To answer this question we have to compute a value called 't' and see whether it is large enough in absolute magnitude to indicate statistical significance according to a standard table that takes account of the number of cases in the experiment. When there are two groups of equal size, as here, call $N = N_1 = N_2$ the number of cases in each group and compute 't' by the formula:

$$t = \frac{\bar{G}_1 - \bar{G}_2}{\sqrt{\dfrac{\left[\dfrac{\Sigma G_1^2}{N_1} - \bar{G}_1^2\right] + \left[\dfrac{\Sigma G_2^2}{N_2} - \bar{G}_2^2\right]}{N - 1}}}$$

Results of an experiment

		Pre-test score	Post-test score	Gain (=G)
	Child # 10	20	23	3
	14	13	22	9
	3	8	16	8
	13	17	23	6
Experimental	1	4	26	22
Group	17	4	28	24
($N_1 = 10$)	5	7	19	12
	2	3	10	7
	12	15	31	16
	6	12	32	20

$$\Sigma G_1 = 127$$

$$\frac{\Sigma G_1}{N_1} = \text{Mean} = \bar{G}_1 = 12 \cdot 7$$

$$\Sigma G_1^2 = 2099$$

Child #			
20	12	10	—2
16	15	14	—1
7	9	19	10
15	1	8	7
9	8	18	10
4	13	27	14
8	7	11	4
19	4	6	2
11	0	12	12
18	19	25	6

Control Group ($N_2 = 10$)

$$\Sigma G_2 = 62$$

$$\frac{\Sigma G_2}{N_2} = \text{Mean} = \bar{G}_2 = 6\cdot2$$

$$\Sigma G_2^2 = 650$$

The expression ΣG means 'the sum of the G's' and the expression ΣG^2 means 'the sum of the squared G's'. The mean $\bar{G}_1 = \dfrac{\Sigma G_1}{N_1}$ and similarly $\bar{G}_2 = \dfrac{\Sigma G_2}{N_2}$. Working from the values computed in the tables, we find in the present case that

$$t = \frac{12\cdot7 - 6\cdot2}{\sqrt{\dfrac{\left[\dfrac{2099}{10} - (12\cdot7)^2\right] + \left[\dfrac{650}{10} - (6\cdot2)^2\right]}{9}}} = 2\cdot25$$

We then must look up 't' in the table of t's with the number of 'degrees of freedom' in the experiment. When $N_1 = N_2$, as here, the number of degrees of freedom is $2(N_1-1)$. In this case the number of degrees of freedom is 18. In the table of 't' opposite $df = 18$ we find that t must be equal to or greater than $2\cdot101$ to be significant at the $\cdot05$ level, or equal or greater than $2\cdot878$ to be significant at the $\cdot01$ level. In other words, with 18 degrees of freedom, a t-value of $2\cdot101$ will occur *by chance* 5 times out of 100 even when there is no 'true' difference, and a t-value of $2\cdot878$ will occur *by chance* 1 in 100 times even when there is no 'true' difference. By convention, statisticians agree to call a difference 'probably significant' (or 'significant at the 5 per cent level') when t exceeds the value that would occur 5 times out of 100 by chance, and they call a difference 'clearly significant' when t exceeds the value that would occur 1 in 100 times by chance.[1]

For the data we have supposed, we computed $t = 2\cdot25$. This value does not exceed the value that would occur by chance 1 out of 100 times; however, it does exceed the value that would occur by chance 5 times out of 100. Therefore, we can conclude that the difference in gains between the experimental and the control groups is statistically significant at the 5 per cent level. Another way of putting this conclusion is to say 'P $< \cdot05$' that is, the probability of obtaining a t-value of this size is less than $\cdot05$. If t had been, say, only $0\cdot76$, we would have concluded that the difference was not statistically significant, that is, that P $> \cdot05$, for the probability of obtaining by chance a t-value of this magnitude is greater than 5 in 100—an occurrence that would be too common and frequent to attach statistical significance to it. Finally, if t had been, say, $-2\cdot25$ rather than $+2\cdot25$, that is, if the average gain in the control group had been greater than that in the experimental group, we would have concluded that the control group gain was significantly greater than the experimental group gain at the 5 per cent level.

The formula for t given here would be useful only when mean scores (or mean gain scores) of two equally-sized groups are to be compared. Formulas for the case of unequally-sized groups may be found in statistics texts.

When results from more than two experimental groups are to be compared, the usual statistical procedure is called *analysis of variance*; it results in a so-called F-ratio which, if it is significant at the $\cdot05$ or $\cdot01$ level, can be interpreted as showing that the groups as a whole manifest at least some difference amongst each other such that they cannot be regarded as having been drawn from one uniform population.

Analysis of variance is also used to evaluate differences in a dependent variable that show up when two or more independent variables are used, e.g. one treatment variable and one selection variable. In this case, one is interested not only in the 'main effects', that is, the effects attributable to each of the independent variables, but also in the 'interaction' effect, that is, differential effects of combinations of the levels of the independent variables. Suppose, for example,

[1] This statement is somewhat oversimplified, but it is accurate enough for practical purposes. For more precise and full explanations of the principle of statistical inference, see textbooks of statistics, such as the book by McNemar previously cited.

A brief table of t

No. of degrees of freedom (f)	$P = \cdot 05$	$P = \cdot 01$
1	12·706	63·657
2	4·303	9·925
3	3·182	5·841
4	2·776	4·604
5	2·571	4·032
6	2·447	3·707
7	2·365	3·499
8	2·306	3·355
9	2·262	3·250
10	2·228	3·169
12	2·179	3·055
14	2·145	2·977
16	2·120	2·921
18	2·101	2·878
20	2·086	2·845
22	2·074	2·819
24	2·064	2·797
26	2·056	2·779
28	2·048	2·763
30	2·042	2·750
40	2·021	2·704
60	2·000	2·660
120	1·980	2·617
∞ (infinity)	1·960	2·576

This table is abridged from Table III of Fisher and Yates (1948) by permission of the authors and publishers.

that in an experiment on foreign language teaching the treatment variable is a contrast in teaching procedures (say, use of a phonetic transcription vs. use of standard orthography), and the selection variable is foreign language aptitude. This would involve a two-way design in which, say, 10 children are studied in each 'cell' of the following table:

	Phonetic transcription used	Standard orthography used
High aptitude children	10 children	10 children
Low aptitude children	10 children	10 children

Suppose further that average gain in each cell from pre-test to post-test is as given here:

	Phonetic transcription used	Standard orthography used	
High aptitude children	Mean gain = 6·00	Mean gain = 2·00	(For all high aptitude children, mean gain = 4·00)
Low aptitude children	Mean gain = 0·00	Mean gain = 4·00	(For all low aptitude children, mean gain = 2·00)
Mean gain for all children using each method	3·00	3·00	

Note, first, that for all children using each method, the mean gain is the same for each level of treatment; the 'main effect' of the treatment variable would be zero. The mean gain for high aptitude children is higher than for low aptitude children; thus, the 'main effect' of the selection variable would be appreciable (and depending upon the amount of variation within these groups, it might be found to be statistically significant).

Note, however, that the mean gain varies very markedly over different *combinations* of the treatment and selection variables; according to these purely hypothetical results, use of the phonetic transcription produces a large mean gain for high aptitude children, and no gain for low aptitude children. In contrast, use of the standard orthography produces only a small gain for high aptitude children, but an appreciable gain for low aptitude children. This would represent what is called an *interaction* effect; its statistical significance could be tested in the same way as the main effects. Interaction effects found to be significant could be very important for prescribing different kinds of educational treatments and procedures for different groups of children, and more educational experiments should be designed so as to identify such effects.

This illustration is presented merely to give an impression of the kinds of questions that might be studied by means of some of the more complex experimental designs. For details on these and other designs, the reader is referred to the following:

9

Edwards, Allen L. *Experimental design in psychological research* (Revised edition). New York: Holt, Rinehart & Winston, 1960. (This is a fairly simple and readable text for a person who has already had an introductory course in statistics.)

Winer, B. J. *Statistical principles in experimental design.* New York: McGraw-Hill Book Co., 1962. (This is an advanced treatment suitable only for persons thoroughly versed in statistical methods.)

QUESTIONS TO WHICH ANSWERS CAN BE SOUGHT BY EXPERIMENTAL STUDIES

In section 3, a series of questions were presented that could be attacked by means of broad survey studies. Nearly all of these, for example those numbered [4], [5], [6], [12], [20], [21], [24], [25], [26], [27], and [29],[1] could also be studied by experimental methods, although in many cases experimental studies would be difficult to arrange simply because it is inherently difficult to manipulate the school curriculum beyond a certain point. For example, suppose experimental methods were proposed as a way of studying problem [5], 'Are better results obtained when two L2s are introduced simultaneously, or are they better when the two L2s are introduced successively?' The time-table of the school might not permit one to introduce two foreign languages simultaneously, or if it did, one might find that parents either objected to such a procedure or (in other circumstances) objected to the *withholding* of the second foreign language for their children when other children were getting its presumed benefits!

It was suggested earlier that experimental methods would be more appropriate for the study of detailed variations in teaching materials and procedures. Among some of the questions that might be particularly amenable to such approaches are the following (again, the previous keying system will be used):

[8] What are the comparative roles of *imitation* and of *creative usage* in language learning? What are the comparative roles of 'drill' and 'conceptual learning' in formal instruction?[2]

[1] It will be recalled that the numbers in [ ] are keyed to the numbers used by the writer in Stern, *op. cit.*, pp. 103–9 in the English version and pp. 134–40 in the French version.

[2] Recent experimental studies pertinent to this issue are: Torrey, Jane W. *The learning of grammar: an experimental study of two methods* (New London, Conn.: Dept. of Psychology, Connecticut College, 1965) and McKinnon, Kenneth R. *An experimental study of the learning of syntax in second language learning.* (Unpublished Ed.D. Dissertation, Harvard University, 1965.) McKinnon's study, it should be noted, was conducted with Grade III children.

[15] To what degree can contrastive linguistic analyses predict learning difficulties, and to what extent, if any, is a teaching method based on contrastive linguistic analysis superior to one not so based?

[18] Assessments are needed, through empirical research or by other means, of the value and effectiveness of different techniques of teaching, for example, 'quick-response oral translation', dictation, pattern practice, etc.

[19] Is it better to plan the material of instruction very carefully and give it to students in controlled amounts, or is it better to use a 'language bath' approach in which the student is exposed to as much language—with as wide variety—as possible, or as a third alternative, is some compromise between these two methods superior to each of them?

[23] Does frequent testing have a beneficial effect on foreign language learning, as it usually is found to do in other subjects?

The reader may be referred to the following for still other ideas concerning research in foreign language teaching:

Carroll, John B. 'Research on teaching foreign languages.' Pp. 1060–1100 in Gage, N. L. (Ed.) *Handbook of research on teaching.* Chicago: Rand McNally, 1963.

Carroll, John B. 'Research in foreign language teaching: the last five years' in *Language Teaching: Broader Contexts. Reports of the Working Committees. Northeast Conference on the Teaching of Foreign Languages.* New York: MLA Materials Center, 1966, pp. 12–42.

COORDINATION OF RESEARCH EFFORTS

Successful prosecution of research depends on carefully laid out *written* plans that exhibit the problem or problems that are to be attacked, the hypotheses and assumptions posed, the details of the experimental design and procedures, the plans for statistical and other types of analysis, and the expected results. This statement should not be taken to exclude the possibility, indeed the probability that plans may change as a project proceeds and as new elements in the situation become disclosed. Still, the nature of changes in plans and the reasons therefore should be carefully documented.

The central directorate for this investigation should provide consultative services to persons wishing advice on research plans. It should also attempt to coordinate the efforts of research workers in the various participating countries so that they will complement rather than duplicate each other.

The central directorate will also take steps to assist in the publication and dissemination of results of experimental studies.

APPENDIX A

Questionnaire Schedule A, for countries or regions, concerning
policies and procedures for teaching foreign or second
languages to young children

COUNTRY OR REGION covered in this schedule	DATE
THIS QUESTIONNAIRE COMPLETED BY (Name and Title)	
ORGANIZATION	
ADDRESS	

GENERAL INFORMATION ON LANGUAGE SPOKEN IN THE COUNTRY OR REGION

Instructions: Please list below all languages that are either (1) native languages of substantial sectors of the population, or (2) languages that are commonly taught as second or foreign languages in schools. Also check boxes to indicate additional information as called for.

(1) NATIVE LANGUAGES. List one or more of the principal languages (if the region contains a great variety of native languages, list only the three most widely spoken, according to language statistics, and check the box below the last line of this sub-section); if, on the other hand, there is only one principal native language, fill in only the first line.

	Language	Approximate percentage of population who are native speakers	Indicate according to code on next page			
			Column 1	Column 2	Column 3	Column 4
1-1	....	......	....	....	....	....
1-2	....	......	....	....	....	....
1-3	....	......	....	....	....	....
1-4	☐	Mark this box if there are other native languages spoken by substantial sectors of the population, but do not specify.				

Code for section 1

Column 1   Indicate the official status of the language (whether used in government) by the following code:

> R—*Required* as the one official language of the country or region.
>
> P—*Permitted* as one of several official languages of the country or region.
>
> N—Not an official language.

Column 2   Indicate whether this language is taught as a native language in school (i.e. children taught to read and write the language).

> A—Regularly taught as a native language to children speaking the language natively.
>
> B—Taught as a native language only to special groups, for example, to certain ethnic religious groups or social groups.
>
> C—Seldom or never taught as a native language.

Column 3   Indicate whether this language is used as a medium of instruction in school (i.e. for subjects other than the language itself).

> A—Regularly used as the medium of instruction throughout all levels of schooling, primary to university.
>
> B—Regularly used as the medium of instruction only at the primary school level, seldom used at higher levels.
>
> D—Seldom or never used as the medium of instruction.

Column 4   Indicate to what extent this language is taught as a *second* language to children and others who do not speak it natively.

> A—It is mandatory to teach this language as a second language to those sectors of the population who do not speak it natively.
>
> B—Optionally taught as a second language to students electing it.
>
> C—Seldom or never taught as a second language.

(2) COMMONLY TAUGHT SECOND LANGUAGES—List only modern languages that are commonly taught as second or foreign languages in the primary and secondary schools of the country; do not include languages already listed above under 'native languages'; do not include classical languages; list languages in approximate order of size of enrolments. Also give additional information for each language as indicated by the code on the next page.

	Language (name)	Additional Information (See codes below and on next page)				
		Column 1	Column 2	Column 3	Column 4	Column 5
2–1	....	....	....	....	....	....
2–2	....	....	....	....	....	....
2–3	....	....	....	....	....	....
2–4	....	....	....	....	....	....
2–5	....	....	....	....	....	....

Codes for 'Additional Information'

Column 1　Indicate the official status of the language by the following code:
R—Required as the one official language of the country or region.
P—Permitted as one of several official languages.
N—Not an official language.

Column 2　Indicate whether this language is used as a medium of instruction in school (i.e. for subjects other than the language itself).
A—Regularly used as the medium of instruction throughout all levels of schooling, primary to university.
B—Regularly used as the medium of instruction only at the primary school level, seldom at higher levels.
C—Regularly used as the medium of instruction as soon as this is considered practical, and increasingly through secondary and university levels.
D—Seldom or never used as the medium of instruction.

Column 3　Is this language taught at primary school level?
A—Mandatory at all levels of primary school.
B—Optionally at early primary level, mandatory at later levels.
C—Only taught optionally at primary level.
D—Seldom or never taught at primary school level.

Column 4　Is this language taught at secondary school level?
A—Mandatory at all levels of secondary school.
B —Optionally at early secondary level, mandatory at upper levels.
C—Only taught optionally at secondary level.
D—Seldom or never taught at secondary level.

Column 5　List the letters corresponding to the principal reasons for teaching this language as a second or foreign language.
A—It is an official language of the country or region.
B—It is used as a medium of instruction in education.

C—It is a language that is frequently needed for intercommunication between different sectors of the population of the country or region.

Choose one

D—It is a language useful in international or inter-regional communication and *indispensable* or *highly desirable* because of the scientific and technical literature available in that language (and not available in the student's native language).

E—It is a language useful in international and inter-regional communication, or for general cultural and educational purposes, but it is *not* indispensable since a wide selection of scientific and technical literature is available in other languages likely to be known to the student (his native language, or other second languages).

(Do not use both D and E for one language.)

(3) INCIDENCE OF PRE-SCHOOL BILINGUALISM. Please estimate the percentage of children who acquire fluency in two languages before arriving at primary school; indicate the pairs of languages involved in each case:

Language pair	Approximate percentage of all children
.... and	....
.... and	....
.... and	....

(4) PROBLEMS OF BILINGUALISM. In the space below, please describe briefly any particular problems of bilingualism encountered in this country or region, especially educational and/or political controversies in these matters.

(5) TRENDS AND PROSPECTS OF CHANGES. In the space below, please describe briefly any trends in second language teaching that are taking place, or changes in educational policies in second language teaching that are contemplated, particularly as they may affect the teaching of second languages at the primary school level.

APPENDIX B

Questionnaire Schedule B, for schools, concerning the teaching
of second or foreign languages to young children

1. COUNTRY OR REGION IN WHICH SCHOOL IS LOCATED

2. NAME OF SCHOOL

3. MAILING ADDRESS

4. THIS QUESTIONNAIRE COMPLETED BY (NAME)	5. DATE

6. POSITION (Headmaster, Head of Foreign Language Department, etc.)

7. Please circle the numbers indicating the grades or levels included in this school. (Count the first primary school grade as *one*; consider the following numbers as consecutive grades regardless of how they are labelled in your particular case.)

N[1]   K[1]   1   2   3   4   5   6   7   8   9   10   11   12

8. What is the average age at which children enter grade *1* (either in this school, or in a school that 'feeds' children into this school)?

9. What are the principal native languages of the children in this school? (List one, two or more, depending on the local situation in order of frequency.)

	Native language	Approximate percentage of children
9–1	....	....
9–2	....	....
9–3	....	....

10. What language is used as the medium of instruction in the first grade of this school (or the school(s) that 'feed' children into this school), that is, what language does the teacher speak to the children in, in the first grade?

Name of language ....

10a. If the teacher uses more than one language as a medium of instruction in the first grade, explain here:

[1] N = Nursery; K = Kindergarten.

11. In what language are the children first taught to read and write?
    Name of language ....

    11a. If some children are taught first to read and write in one language,
    and other children in another language, explain here:

12. For each language that is taught as a second or foreign language, fill
    out the blanks below. (Include here any language taught as a second
    or foreign language to at least some of the children; do *not* include
    classical languages like Latin):

Language	Grade at which spoken language is introduced	Grade at which reading and writing are introduced	Grade at which first used as medium of instruction (if applicable)
12–1	......	......	......
12–2	......	......	......
12–3	......	......	......
12–4	......	......	......

13. If foreign languages are taught to some but not all children, describe
    how children are selected for foreign language study:

Other details concerning the school

14. Is this a day-school or a residential school? (check one)
    ...... Day-school only (children come to school from home each day).
    ...... Residential school (children live at school during school sessions).
    ...... Partly day-school, partly residential.

15. Describe the location of the school:
    ...... In an urban area.
    ...... In suburban area.
    ...... In a rural area.

16. Approximate enrolment of school by grades:

Nursery School	....	Grade Three	....
Kindergarten	....	Grade Four	....
Grade One	....	Grade Five	....
Grade Two	....	Grade Six	....
	Total		

17. Month in which the school year normally starts ....

18. Month in which the school year normally ends ....

19. Are any foreign languages taught to children outside of school, for example after school hours or on weekends on a voluntary basis? If so, indicate languages taught, grade level of children at the start of instruction, number of hours of instruction per week, qualifications of teachers, etc.

27. It will help me to know and appreciate the way of life of the people who speak the second language.

.... Yes .... No .... I'm not sure.

28. One needs a knowledge of at least one foreign language in order to be considered well educated.

.... Yes .... No .... I'm not sure.

29. I have to study it because it is part of the school curriculum.

.... Yes .... No .... I'm not sure.

30. I have to study it because it is used in school in the higher grades.

.... Yes .... No .... I'm not sure.

31. It will allow me to meet and talk with more interesting and different people.

.... Yes .... No .... I'm not sure.

32. I need it in order to be admitted to the next school I will attend.

.... Yes .... No .... I'm not sure.

33. I like to learn a foreign language because it is fun.

.... Yes .... No .... I'm not sure.

34. I need it in order to read books, magazines, or newspapers that I want to read.

.... Yes .... No .... I'm not sure.

In this part of the questionnaire you are asked to show how you feel about people who speak the second language you are studying. First fill in the following blank with the name of the second language you are studying: (if you are studying more than one other language, choose the one second language that you are spending most time on now).

35. Name of language...............................

Now, you are being asked to show how you feel about people who speak that language as their native tongue.

For example, do you think that these people are generally fair, or generally unfair, or somewhat between? You can show how you feel by placing a mark in one of the five places on this scale:

Fair .... : .... : .... : .... : .... Unfair

For instance, if you think they are generally very fair you can mark the scale by placing an X close to *fair*, as shown here:

Fair .X. : .... : .... : .... : .... Unfair

Or if you think they are sometimes fair and sometimes unfair, you could mark the scale by placing an X in the middle space, thus:

Fair .... : .... : .X. : .... : .... Unfair

Now go ahead with the other scales. Consider each one separately.

Remember you are showing your feelings or opinions about

PEOPLE WHO SPEAK .... AS THEIR NATIVE LANGUAGE

(fill in) name of second language

36.   interesting: .... : .... : .... : .... : ....: uninteresting
37.   prejudiced: .... : .... : .... : .... : ....: unprejudiced
38.   brave: .... : .... : .... : .... : ....: cowardly
39.   ugly: .... : .... : .... : .... : ....: handsome
40.   colourful: .... : .... : .... : .... : ....: colourless
41.   friendly: .... : .... : .... : .... : ....: unfriendly
42.   honest: .... : .... : .... : .... : ....: dishonest
43.   smart: .... : .... : .... : .... : ....: stupid
44.   cruel: .... : .... : .... : .... : ....: kind
45.   pleasant: .... : .... : .... : .... : ....: unpleasant
46.   polite: .... : .... : .... : .... : ....: impolite
47.   sincere: .... : .... : .... : .... : ....: insincere
48.   successful: .... : .... : .... : .... : ....: unsuccessful
49.   dependable: .... : .... : .... : .... : ....: undependable
50.   leader: .... : .... : .... : .... : ....: follower
51.   mature: .... : .... : .... : .... : ....: immature
52.   stable: .... : .... : .... : .... : ....: unstable
53.   sad: .... : .... : .... : .... : ....: happy
54.   popular: .... : .... : .... : .... : ....: unpopular
55.   lazy: .... : .... : .... : .... : ....: hard working
56.   ambitious: .... : .... : .... : .... : ....: not ambitious

Now please do the same thing, but it will be about people who speak *your own* native language as their native language. Go ahead and mark the scales, but first fill in the name of your native language just below:

57. PEOPLE WHO SPEAK .... AS THEIR NATIVE LANGUAGE
(fill in name of your own native language)

58.   interesting: .... : .... : .... : .... : ....: uninteresting
59.   prejudiced: .... : .... : .... : .... : ....: unprejudiced
60.   brave: .... : .... : .... : .... : ....: cowardly
61.   ugly: .... : .... : .... : .... : ....: handsome
62.   colourful: .... : .... : .... : .... : ....: colourless
63.   friendly: .... : .... : .... : .... : ....: unfriendly
64.   honest: .... : .... : .... : .... : ....: dishonest
65.   smart: .... : .... : .... : .... : ....: stupid
66.   cruel: .... : .... : .... : .... : ....: kind
67.   pleasant: .... : .... : .... : .... : ....: unpleasant
68.   polite: .... : .... : .... : .... : ....: impolite
69.   sincere: .... : .... : .... : .... : ....: insincere
70.   successful: .... : .... : .... : .... : ....: unsuccessful
71.   dependable: .... : .... : .... : .... : ....: undependable
72.   leader: .... : .... : .... : .... : ....: follower
73.   mature: .... : .... : .... : .... : ....: immature

74.   stable: .... : .... : .... : .... : .... : ....: unstable
75.   sad: .... : .... : .... : .... : .... : ....: happy
76.   popular: .... : .... : .... : .... : .... : ....: unpopular
77.   lazy: .... : .... : .... : .... : .... : ....: hard working
78.   ambitious: .... : .... : .... : .... : .... : ....: not ambitious

APPENDIX D

Questionnaire Schedule D

For teachers of foreign languages to young children

---

1. Name   2. Date

3. School address

---

4. How many years of regular schooling did you complete?..........

5. How many years of teacher preparation (beyond regular schooling) did you complete?............

6. How many years of teaching experience have you had (at any level)? ....

7. Are you a regular classroom teacher or a specialist foreign language teacher? (Check *one*.)

   .... Regular classroom teacher, teaching all or most subjects, including foreign language classes.

   .... Specialist foreign language teacher who teaches mainly foreign language classes.

   .... A combination of a regular classroom teacher and a specialist foreign language teacher.

8. IF YOU ARE A REGULAR CLASSROOM TEACHER, answer these questions: (otherwise skip to question 9)

   a. At what grade level(s) do you teach?....................
      How many children are in your class?..........

   b. What second language do you teach?......................

   c. To what extent do you use this second language as a medium of instruction in other subjects?

      .... I do not use it as a medium of instruction.

      .... I use it as a medium of instruction in some other subjects.

      .... I use it as a medium of instruction in all other subjects.

   d. At what grade level are your children first introduced to this second language?..............

   e. How many class periods a week do you teach this second language, or teach *in* this second language (if it is a medium of instruction)?

      .... Total number of hours per week ....

      Usual length of class periods ...... minutes.

9. IF YOU ARE A SPECIALIST FOREIGN-LANGUAGE TEACHER, answer these
   questions (otherwise skip to question 10):
9–1. At what grade levels do you teach?..........................
   Show the foreign languages you teach, number of different class groups,[1]
   average size of classes, length of class periods, total number of class
   periods, and total number of hours, for all classes.

Language	Grade levels	No. of class groups	Average no. in class	Total no. of class periods per week	Total no. of hours per week
9–2...............	......	......	......	......	......
(fill in)					
9–3...............	......	......	......	......	......

ALL TEACHERS SHOULD ANSWER THE FOLLOWING QUESTIONS

10. Indicate what languages you know (including your native language
    and all languages you teach) and the degree of your competence in
    various aspects of them (using the key below).

Language	How well do you *understand* it when you hear the language spoken	How fluent are you in *speaking*	How good is your *pronunciation*	How well can you *read* the language	How well can you *write* the language
10–1..........	$5(^2)$	$5(^2)$	$5(^2)$	......	......
(native language)					
10–2..........	......	......	......	......	......
10–3..........	......	......	......	......	......

   Key: 5 = competence equal to that of a native speaker of the
        language.
        4 = competence somewhat inferior to that of a native speaker
        of the language, but still quite adequate for most purposes.
        3 = competence *considerably inferior* to that of a native speaker.
        2 = competence is *quite rudimentary*.
        1 = competence is *very rudimentary*.
        0 = no competence at all in this aspect of the language.
11. How many years experience have you had in second language teaching?
   ....

[1] By this is meant the number of different groups of children you teach
(regardless of how often).
[2] It is assumed that in your native language your competence is equal
to that of any other native speaker.

12. In teaching a second language, what relative emphasis do you put on each of the four skills? In the list below, place a '1' next to the skill you emphasize most, a '2' next to the skill you emphasize next after that, and so forth, down to a '5' for the skill you emphasize least:

12–1. . . . . . . Listening comprehension.

12–2. . . . . . . Speaking fluency.

12–3. . . . . . . Correct pronunciation.

12–4. . . . . . . Reading comprehension.

12–5. . . . . . . Ability to write.

13. To what extent, if any, do you use the children's first language in teaching them a second language? (Check the *one* answer that applies.)

. . . . . . Never.

. . . . . . Seldom, only to explain word-meanings and grammar.

. . . . . . Often.

. . . . . . Most of the time.

14. In what order do you introduce the spoken and written forms of the second language? (Check the statement that *best* applies.)

. . . . . . The spoken form of the second language is learned before the written forms (reading and writing) are presented.

. . . . . . Spoken forms are presented generally before the corresponding written forms are presented, but the spoken and written forms of the language are learned together.

. . . . . . Written forms are presented generally before the corresponding spoken forms are presented, but the spoken and written forms of the language are learned together.

. . . . . . Reading and writing are learned before speaking and understanding are learned.

15. How do you teach grammar? (Check the one statement that *best* describes your method.)

. . . . . . The children learn rules of grammar formally and then apply them by translating sentences from one language to the other.

. . . . . . The children learn to speak and understand by imitating the teacher; from this, they learn to speak grammatically, just as they learn their native language.

. . . . . . I use a combination of inductive and deductive methods; the second language is learned by imitation and practice, after which grammar rules are explained to help in forming correct speech.

16. How do you teach your students the correct pronunciation of the second language sounds?

. . . . . . By making the children listen carefully and imitate.

. . . . . . By giving practice in imitation, supplemented with explanations about how the sounds are made.

. . . . . . I do not give any attention to correct pronunciation.

17. How often do you use each of the following aids in teaching (make a check in each row):

	Never	Sometimes	Often	Most of the time
17–1. The blackboard	......	......	......	......
17–2. Pictures	......	......	......	......
17–3. 'Props' (various real objects)	......	......	......	......
17–4. Film strips	......	......	......	......
17–5. Sound movies (cinema)	......	......	......	......
17–6. Phonograph records	......	......	......	......
17–7. Tape recorder (for whole class)	......	......	......	......
17–8. Language laboratory (individualized tape recorders)	......	......	......	......

REFERENCES[1]

ANDERSSON, T. (1966) (c.p.). 'A resolution concerning the education of bilingual children.' El Paso, Texas.

ANDERSSON, T. (1966). 'Foreign languages in the elementary school: a struggle against mediocrity.' Mimeographed.

ANDRADE, M., HAYMAN, J. L. JR., and JOHNSON, J. T. JR. (1963). 'Measurement of listening comprehension in elementary-school Spanish instruction.' *Elementary School Journal* 64, 84–93.

ANDRADE, M., HAYMAN, J. L. JR., and JOHNSON, J. T. JR. (1963). *Measurement of Speaking Skills in Elementary Level Spanish Instruction.* Institute for Communication Research, Stanford University, California.

ANTROBUS, A. L. (1966). *16 mm. Films for Foreign Language Teaching.* Nuffield Foundation Foreign Languages Teaching Materials Project, Occasional Paper No. 17.

BANATHY, B., POPHAM, W., and ROSENOFF, W. (1962). 'The common concepts foreign language test.' *Modern Language Journal* 46, 363–5.

BARKER-LUNN, J. C. (1967). 'The effects of streaming and other forms of grouping in junior schools.' *New Research in Education* 1, 4–45, 46–75.

BEL (c.p.). 'Le B.E.L. et l'enseignement des langues à l'école primaire.'

BERNSTEIN, B. (1965). 'A socio-linguistic approach to social learning' in GOULD, J. (ed.). *Penguin Survey of the Social Sciences 1965.* Harmondsworth: Penguin Books.

BRITISH BILINGUAL ASSOCIATION (1962). *A Manual of Suggestions for the Oral Teaching of the French Language to Children from the Ages of 7 and 8 Years.* Compiled by members of the Educational Advisory Committee of the British Bilingual Association and published by the Association.

CAMPBELL, D. T., and STANLEY, J. C. (1963). 'Experimental and quasi-experimental designs for research on teaching' in GAGE, N. L. (ed.). *Handbook of Research on Teaching*, ch. 5, 171–246. Chicago: Rand McNally.

CARROLL, J. B. (1953). *The Study of Language. A Survey of Linguistics and other Related Disciplines in America.* Cambridge: Harvard University Press, and London: Oxford University Press.

CARROLL, J. B. (1963). 'Research problems concerning the teaching of foreign or second languages to younger children.' Chapter 19 (chapter 20 of 1963 edition) of the 1962 Hamburg Report (Stern 1967).

CARROLL, J. B. (1963a). 'Research on teaching foreign languages' in GAGE, N. L. (ed.). *Handbook of Research on Teaching*, ch. 21, 1060–1100. Chicago: Rand McNally.

[1] As mentioned on page 7, c.p. (=conference papers) refers to papers and communications submitted to the 1966 Hamburg meeting.

CARROLL, J. B. (1966). 'Research in foreign language teaching: the last five years' in MEAD, R. G. (ed.). *Language Teaching: Broader Contexts. Reports of the Working Committees. Northeast Conference on the Teaching of Foreign Languages*, 12–42. New York: MLA Materials Center.

CREDIF, (Centre de Recherche et d'Étude pour la Diffusion du Français à l'École Normale Supérieure de St Cloud) (1965). *Enquête sur le langage de l'enfant français. Document no. 1 : Transcriptions de conversations d'enfants de 9 ans.* See also Nuffield Foundation Foreign Languages Teaching Materials Project (1966).

CSER, M. (c.p.). 'Rapport sur les expériences faites en Hongrie dans l'enseignement d'une seconde langue à de jeunes enfants.'

DODSON, C. J. (1966). *Foreign and Second Language Learning in the Primary School.* Aberystwyth: Education Faculty, University College of Wales.

DONNEN, Y. (c.p.). 'Rapport sur les expériences faites à l'école européenne de Bruxelles dans l'enseignement d'une seconde langue à de jeunes enfants.'

DOYÉ, P. (1966). *Frühbeginn des Englischunterrichts. Ein Berliner Schulversuch in der 3. Klasse.* Berlin: Cornelsen Verlag.

DUNKEL, H. B., and PILLET, R. A. (1962). *French in the Elementary School: Five Years' Experience.* Chicago: University of Chicago Press.

EDWARDS, A. L. (1960). *Experimental Design in Psychological Research* (Revised edition). New York: Holt, Rinehart and Winston.

EKSTRAND, L. H. (1964). *Språkfärdighet och Språkmetodik.* Stockholm: Kungl. Skolöverstyrelsen.

En Avant, the Nuffield Introductory French Course. (See Nuffield.)

ENKVIST, N-E., SPENCER, J., and GREGORY, M. (1964). *Linguistics and Style.* London: Oxford University Press.

EVRARD, H. (c.p.). 'L'enseignement des langues vivantes dans les écoles primaires de France en 1965–66.'

FÉRAUD, P. (c.p.). 'Mise à jour de la section du rapport de H. H. Stern se rapportant à l'enseignement des langues vivantes dans les écoles primaires en France.'

FISHER, R. A., and YATES, F. (1948). *Statistical Tables for Biological, Agricultural and Medical Research.* Edinburgh: Oliver & Boyd.

FISHMAN, J. A. (1966). 'The implications of bilingualism for language teaching and language learning' in VALDMAN, A. (ed.). *Trends in Language Teaching*, ch. 8, 121–32. New York: McGraw-Hill Book Company.

FOSHAY, A. W., THORNDIKE, R. L., HOTYAT, F., PIDGEON, D. A., and WALKER, A. (1962). *Educational Achievement of Thirteen-year-olds in Twelve Countries.* Hamburg: UNESCO Institute for Education.

FRAISSE, P., NOISET, G., and FLAMENT, C. (1963). 'Fréquence et familiarité du vocabulaire', 157–67, in *Problèmes de psycho-linguistique*, symposium de l'Association de psychologie scientifique de langue française. Paris: Presses universitaires de France.

GAARDER, A. B. (1965). 'The challenge of bilingualism' in BISHOP, G. R. JR. (ed.). *Foreign Language Teaching: Challenges to the Profession* 54–101. Reports of the Working Committees, Northeast Conference on the Teaching of Foreign Languages, 1965. Princeton, N.J.: Princeton University Press.

GAGE, N. L. (ed.) (1963). *Handbook of Research on Teaching*. Chicago: Rand McNally.

GARRY, R., and MAURIELLO, E. (1961). *Summary of Research on 'Parlons Français', Year Two*. Boston, Mass.: Mass. Council for Public Schools, Inc.

GILES, H. (c.p.). 'Reading at the Toronto French school.'

GINESTE, R. (c.p.). 'Facteurs linguistiques, pédagogiques et économiques.'

GREAT BRITAIN (1962). *The Teaching of Russian* (the Annan Report). Report of the Committee appointed by the Minister of Education and the Secretary of State for Scotland in September 1960. London: Her Majesty's Stationery Office.

GREAT BRITAIN (1963). *Half Our Future* (the Newsom Report). London: Her Majesty's Stationery Office.

HALSALL, E. (1963–4). 'A comparative study of attainments in French.' *International Review of Education* 9, 1, 41–59.

HANDSCOMBE, R. J. (1965). *Topics of Conversation and Centres of Interest in the Speech of Eleven- and Twelve-year-old Children*—A Child Language Survey publication. Nuffield Foundation Foreign Languages Teaching Materials Project, Occasional Paper No. 8.

HANDSCOMBE, R. J. (1966). *The First 1,000 Clauses: A Preliminary Analysis*. Nuffield Foundation Foreign Languages Teaching Materials Project, Occasional Paper No. 11.

HANDSCOMBE, R. J. (1967). *The Written Language of Nine- and Ten-year-old Children*. Nuffield Foundation Foreign Languages Teaching Materials Project, Occasional Paper No. 24.

HANDSCOMBE, R. J. (1967a). *The Written Language of Eleven- and-Twelve-year-old Children*. Nuffield Foundation Foreign Languages Teaching Materials Project, Occasional Paper No. 25.

HASAN, R. (1964). *Grammatical Analysis Code*. Nuffield Foundation Foreign Languages Teaching Materials Project, Occasional Paper No. 6.

HASAN, R. (1965). *The Language of Eight-year-old Children*—Transcript No. 1 of the Child Language Survey, recorded by R. Hasan. Two volumes. Nuffield Foundation Foreign Languages Teaching Materials Project, Occasional Paper No. 5.

HASAN, R., and HANDSCOMBE, R. J. (1965–6). *The Language of Nine-year-old Children*—Transcripts No. 2A, 2B, 2C, 2D, 2E of the Child Language Survey. Nuffield Foundation Foreign Languages Teaching Materials Project, Occasional Papers No. 7, 9, 10, 13, 14.

HASAN, R., and HANDSCOMBE, R. J., (1965–6). *The Language of Ten-year-old Children*—Transcripts No. 3A, 3B, 3C, 3D, 3E of the Child Language Survey. Nuffield Foundation Foreign Languages Teaching Materials Project, Occasional Papers No. 15, 18, 19, 21, 22.

HAUGEN, E. (1956). *Bilingualism in the Americas: A Bibliography and Research Guide.* University of Alabama Press. (Publications of the American Dialect Society, No. 26.)

HAYMAN, J. L. JR., and JOHNSON, J. T. JR. (1963). *Audio-Lingual Results in the Second Year of Research—1961–62.* Institute for Communication and Research, Stanford University, California.

HIRSCHBOLD, K. (c.p.). 'Preparatory English teaching in primary schools in Vienna.'

HIRSCHBOLD, K. (1956). *Der aktive englische Wortschatz der Wiener Hauptschüler am Ende des vierten Lehrjahres.* Vienna: Verlag für Jugend und Volk.

HORNBY, A. S. (1959). *The Teaching of Structural Words and Sentence Patterns.* London: Oxford University Press.

HUTASOIT, M., and PRATOR, C. H. (1965). *A Study of the 'New Primary Approach' in the Schools of Kenya.* Kenya: Ford Foundation/Ministry of Education.

HUTCHINSON, J. C. (1966). 'The language laboratory: equipment and utilization' in VALDMAN, A. (ed.). *Trends in Language Teaching,* ch. 12, 215–33. New York: McGraw-Hill Book Company.

JOHNSON, C. E., FLORES, J. S., ELLISON, F. P., and RIESTRA, M. A. (1963). *The Development and Evaluation of Methods and Materials to Facilitate Foreign Language Instruction in Elementary Schools.* Urbana, Illinois: Foreign Language Instruction Project (805W Pennsylvania Ave.).

JUNKER, G. (c.p.). 'L'enseignement du français deuxième langue dans le cycle primaire de l'école européenne de Mol.'

KELLERMANN, M. (1964). *Two Experiments on Language Teaching in Primary Schools in Leeds.* London: Nuffield Foundation.

KIESTRA, L. (c.p.). 'Projet relatif à une expérience en matière d'enseignement de langues étrangères à l'école primaire.' (See also van Willigen, c.p.)

KIRCH, M. S. (1956). 'At what age elementary school language teaching?' *Modern Language Journal* 40, 399–400.

LAHLOU, A. (c.p.). 'La seconde langue dans les communautés bilingues ou multilingues.'

LAMBERT, W. E. (1965). 'Social and psychological aspects of bilingualism.' GREAT BRITAIN, DEPARTMENT OF EDUCATION AND SCIENCE, *Report on an International Seminar on Bilingualism in Education, Aberystwyth, Wales.* London: Her Majesty's Stationery Office.

LAZARO, C. M. (1963). *Report on Foreign Language Teaching in British Primary Schools*. Nuffield Foundation Foreign Languages Teaching Materials Project, Occasional Paper No. 1.

LECLERCQ, J. (1966). *Enquête sur le langage de l'enfant français*. Nuffield Foundation Foreign Languages Teaching Materials Project, Occasional Paper No. 20. (See also CREDIF and Nuffield Foundation Foreign Languages Teaching Materials Project 1966.)

LEWIS, E. GLYN (1965). 'Report of the Seminar' in GREAT BRITAIN, DEPARTMENT OF EDUCATION AND SCIENCE. *Report on an International Seminar on Bilingualism in Education, Aberystwyth, Wales*. London: Her Majesty's Stationery Office.

LINDQUIST, E. F. (Ed.) (1963). *Educational Measurement*. Washington, D.C.: American Council on Education.

McARTHUR, J. (1965). 'Measurement, interpretation, and evaluation—TV FLES: Item analysis in test instruments', *Modern Language Journal*, 49, 4, 217–19.

MACKEY, W. F. (1965), (1967). *Language Teaching Analysis*. London: Longmans, Green & Co. Ltd. Bloomington: Indiana University Press.

MACKEY, W. F. (1965a). *Method Analysis*. Georgetown University Monographs on Languages and Linguistics, No. 18.

MACKEY, W. F. (1966). *Mechanolinguistic Method Analysis*. Ottawa: Royal Commission on Bilingualism and Biculturalism (with M. Mepham).

MACKEY, W. F. (1967). *Bilingualism as a World Problem*. Montreal: Harvest House.

MACKEY, W. F. (1967a). 'Tirocinio didattico: modelli e moduli'. *Homo Loquens*, 3, 25–34.

MACKEY, W. F., and NOONAN, J. H. (1952). 'An experiment in bilingual education', *English Language Teaching* 6, 125–32.

MACKEY, W. F., and SAVARD, J.-G. (1967). 'The Indices of Coverage: a new dimension in lexicometrics,' *IRAL*, 5/2–3, 71-121.

MACKEY, W. F., SAVARD, J.-G., and ARDOUIN, P. (forthcoming). *Le vocabulaire disponible du français: France et Acadie*, 2 vols. Paris: Didier.

McKINNON, K. R. (1965). *An Experimental Study of the Learning of Syntax in Second Language Learning*. Unpublished Ed.D. Dissertation, Harvard University, Cambridge, Mass.

McNEMAR, Q. (1962). *Psychological Statistics*. New York and London: J. Wiley & Sons.

MANUEL, A. (c.p.). 'L'école active bilingue: plan d'organisation des cours de langues étrangères.'

MINISTRY OF EDUCATION (Great Britain) (1959). *Primary Education*. London: Her Majesty's Stationery Office.

MOORE, S., and ANTROBUS, A. L. (1964). *Introduction to the Language Laboratory*. Nuffield Foundation Foreign Languages Teaching Materials Project, Occasional Paper No. 2.

MÜLLER, G. (c.p.). 'Report on the development of the John F. Kennedy School (German-American Community School), Berlin-Zehlendorf.'

NAYLOR, J. W. (1966). *French Readers for Primary Schools—An Annotated Bibliography.* Nuffield Foundation Foreign Languages Teaching Materials Project, Occasional Paper No. 12.

NUFFIELD FOREIGN LANGUAGES TEACHING MATERIALS PROJECT (1966, etc.). *En Avant,* The Nuffield Introductory French Course.

Stages 1A and 1B 1966.

Stage 2 1967.

Leeds: E. J. Arnold & Son.

NUFFIELD FOUNDATION FOREIGN LANGUAGES TEACHING MATERIALS PROJECT (1965). *Audio-Visual French Courses for Primary Schools: An Annotated Bibliography,* Occasional Paper No. 3. Leeds: E. J. Arnold & Son.

NUFFIELD FOUNDATION FOREIGN LANGUAGES TEACHING MATERIALS PROJECT (1966). *Enquête sur le langage de l'enfant français.* Transcriptions de conversations d'enfants de neuf ans, by J. Leclerq, Occasional Paper No. 20. See also CREDIF (1965).

OTTER, H. S. (1965). 'An oral proficiency assessment chart', *Modern Languages,* 46, 155-9.

PALMER, B. G. (Ed.) (1966). *Modern Languages in Colleges of Education.* Report of a conference organized jointly by the Department of Education and Science and the Modern Languages Section of the ATCDE. Harrogate, 8-11 October 1965. Modern Languages Section of the Association of Teachers in Colleges and Departments of Education, 151 Gower Street, London, W.C.1.

PERREN, G. E. (Ed.) (1968). *Teachers of English as a Second Language: their Training and Preparation.* Cambridge: University Press.

PERREN, G. E., and HOLLOWAY, M. F. (1965). *Language and Communication in the Commonwealth.* Published by the Commonwealth Education Liaison Committee. London: Her Majesty's Stationery Office.

PIMSLEUR, P. (1961). 'A French speaking proficiency test', *The French Review,* 34/5, 470-9.

POSTLETHWAITE, N. (1966). 'International project for the evaluation of educational achievement (I.E.A.)', *International Review of Education,* 12/3, 356-69.

REVZIN, I. I. (1966). *Models of Language.* Translated from the Russian by N. F. C. OWEN and A. S. C. ROSS. London: Methuen & Co.

RIDDY, D. C. (1965). 'The present position of modern language teaching in England and Wales' in PALMER, B. G. (Ed.), *Modern Languages in Colleges of Education,* 5-12. London: Modern Languages Section of the Association of Teachers in Colleges and Departments of Education.

RIESTRA, M. A., and JOHNSON, C. E. (1962). 'Changes in attitudes of elementary school pupils towards foreign speaking peoples resulting from the study of a foreign language'. University of Puerto Rico: Unpublished paper.

Rojo, A. J. (1964). 'État des recherches en cours pour l'établissement d'un "Español fundamental" et la réalisation d'une méthode audio-visuelle d'Espagnol.' (Paper presented at the Madrid Conference of the Council of Europe.)

Rowlands, D. (1965). *A Puppet Theatre for Language Teaching*. Nuffield Foundation Foreign Languages Teaching Materials Project, Occasional Paper No. 4.

Rummel, J. F. (1964). *An Introduction to Research Procedures in Education*. 2nd edition. New York: Harper & Bros.

Schonell, F. J. *et al.* (1956). *A Study of the Oral Vocabulary of Adults*. London and Brisbane: University of London Press and University of Queensland Press.

Schools Council (Great Britain) (1966). *French in the Primary School*, Working Paper No. 8. London: Her Majesty's Stationery Office.

Schools Council (Great Britain) (1966a). *Field Report No. 2: French in the Primary School*. London: Schools Council.

Schütt, H. (c.p.). 'Schulversuche mit Englischunterricht an Primary Schools in der Bundesrepublik Deutschland.'

Sirevåg, T. (c.p.). 'The place of foreign languages in Norwegian primary education.'

Sollohub, N. S. (1967). *A Survey of Russian Teaching in British Secondary Schools*. Nuffield Foreign Languages Teaching Materials Project. Occasional paper No. 23.

Spangenberg, K., and Müller, G. (1966). Written communication in a paper on the international schools.

Spencer, J. W. (Ed.) (1963). *Language in Africa*, Papers of the Leverhulme Conference on Universities and the Language Problems of Tropical Africa, held at University College, Ibadan. Cambridge: Cambridge University Press.

Stern, H. H. (1963). *Foreign Languages in Primary Education: the Teaching of Foreign or Second Languages to Younger Children; Report of an International Meeting of Experts, 9–14 April 1962*. Hamburg: Unesco Institute for Education.

Stern, H. H. (1965). *Les Langues Étrangères dans l'Enseignement Primaire: L'Enseignement d'une Seconde Langue ou d'une Langue Étrangère à de Jeunes Enfants; Rapport d'une Conférence Internationale d'Experts, 9 au 14 Avril 1962*. Hamburg: Institut de l'Unesco pour l'Éducation.

Stern, H. H. (1966). 'FLES: achievement and problems' in Valdman, A. (Ed.) *Trends in Language Teaching*, ch. 14, 253–83. New York, etc.: McGraw-Hill Book Company.

Stern, H. H. (1967). *Foreign Languages in Primary Education*. Second revised edition. London: Oxford University Press.

Titone, R. (1964). *Studies in the Psychology of Second Language Learning*. Zürich: Pas-Verlag

REFERENCES 267

TITONE, R. (c.p.). 'The spreading of the FLES movement and second language teaching experiments in primary schools in Italy.'

TORREY, J. W. (1965). *The Learning of Grammar: an Experimental Study of Two Methods*. New London, Conn.: Dept. of Psychology, Connecticut College.

TRAVERS, R. M. W. (1964). *An Introduction to Educational Research*. New York and London: Macmillan. (2nd edition).

VAN WILLIGEN, M. (c.p.). 'Recent development in the teaching of foreign languages in the primary school in The Netherlands.'

WEST, M. (Ed.) (1953). *A General Service List of English Words: with Semantic Frequencies and a Supplementary Word-List for the Writing of Popular Science and Technology*. London: Longmans, Green & Co. Ltd.

WEST, M. (1960). *Teaching English in Difficult Circumstances*. London: Longmans, Green and Co. Ltd.

WILLIAMS, J. (c.p.). '1962–66 developments in Wales: Supplement to Chapter 9 of 1962 Report.'

WINER, B. J. (1962). *Statistical Principles in Experimental Design*. New York: McGraw-Hill Book Co.

WOŹNICKI, T. (c.p.). 'L'enseignement des langues vivantes en Pologne.'

WOŹNICKI, T. (1965). 'Fazy Procesu Uczenia Się Języka Oncego', *Języki Obce w Szkole*, 1 and 2 (13–16, 101–6). (Stages in the foreign language learning process.)

WOŹNICKI, T. (1965a). 'Język Francuski w Liczbach' *Języki obce w Szkole*, 5, 268–73. (The French language in numbers.)

LIST OF PARTICIPANTS

at the

'International Meeting of Representatives of Institutions and Experimental Schools concerned with Second Language Teaching in Primary Education—Research and Development' held at the Unesco Institute for Education, Hamburg 13, Feldbrunnenstrasse 70, from 9 to 14 May 1966.

Miss Inger Axelsen Denmark	Dronningens Traergade 32, København
Mr Silvio Baridon Italy	Professor, Scuola Interpreti, Milano
Mrs Clare Burstall United Kingdom	Officer in charge of French Project, National Foundation for Educational Research in England and Wales, London
Prof. J. B. Carroll USA	Professor of Educational Psychology, Graduate School of Education, Harvard University, Cambridge
Miss Ahalya Chari India	Principal, Regional College of Education, Mysore
Mr L. Costers Netherlands	Chief-Inspector of Education, Apeldoorn
Mrs Martha Cser Hungary	Ministry of Education, Budapest
Prof. E. F. O'Doherty Ireland	Professor, Department of Psychology, University College, Dublin
Mr Peter Doyé West Berlin	Dozent, Pädagogische Hochschule, Berlin
M. Henri Évrard France	Inspecteur général de l'Instruction publique, Paris
Mr R. Gefen Israel	Senior Inspector of English in Elementary Schools, Jerusalem
Mr L. Grandía Mateu Spain	Professor, Instituto de Enseñanza Media Feminina, Granada
Mr Karl Hirschbold Austria	Fachreferent für Englisch, Wien
Prof A. Lahlou Morocco	Bureau International du Travail, Genève
Prof. W. F. Mackey Canada	Professeur, Département de linguistique, Faculté des Lettres, Université Laval, Québec

Mrs E. Pavluchenko USSR	Teacher, Srednei Shkoly, Kiev
Dr D. C. Riddy United Kingdom	Staff Inspector of Modern Languages, H.M. Inspectorate, Department of Education and Science, London
Miss Erika Sipmann West Berlin	Teacher, Björksonstr. 29, Berlin 41
Mr Tønnes Sirevåg Norway	Director General in charge of general and teacher education in the Royal Norwegian Ministry of Education, Oslo
Mr A. Spicer United Kingdom	Organizer, Nuffield Foundation Foreign Languages Teaching Materials Project, York
Dr H. H. Stern United Kingdom	Reader, Language Centre, University of Essex, Colchester
Mrs Irina Vereschagina USSR	The State Pedagogical Institute, Moscow
Dr Tadeusz Woźnicki Poland	Professeur-adjoint à l'Institut de Pédagogie de Varsovie

Representatives of UNESCO Department of School and Higher Education, Paris, and of the Department of Education of the Council of Europe, Strasbourg

M. Albert Legrand	Programme Specialist. Teaching of Modern Languages
Mr Sven Nord	Programme Specialist. Section of Modern Languages

Observers

Mlle C. Goldet France	Professeur, chargée de recherches au CREDIF, St. Cloud
Mr L. Kiestra Netherlands	Programme Specialist, Internationale Unie van Gezinsorganisaties, Bruxelles
Dr W. Koelle Federal Republic of Germany	Leiter, Beratungsstelle für den neusprach- lichen Unterricht, Institut für Lehrerfort- bildung, Hamburg
Mme A. Manuel France	Professeur à l'Ecole Active Bilingue, Paris
Mr G. Müller West Berlin	Wissenschaftlicher Mitarbeiter, Pädagogi- sches Zentrum, Berlin
Mr G. E. Perren United Kingdom	Director, English Teaching Information Centre, British Council, London
Mr H. Reiss Federal Republic of Germany	Wissenschaftlicher Leiter, Wanne-Schule, Universität Tübingen

Mrs E. Steel	Professeur chargée de la coordination des
France	cours d'anglais, Ecole Active Bilingue, Paris
M. André Didier	Librairie Marcel Didier, Paris and Associa-
France	tion Internationale d'Editeurs de Linguis-tique Appliquée (AIDELA), Strasbourg

Unesco Institute for Education

Dr Gustaf Ögren	Director, 1964–7
Mr J. O. J. Vanden Bossche	Senior Programme Officer
Mr T. N. Postlethwaite	IEA Coordinator
Miss G. Ulrich	Programme Officer
Miss A. Schurek	Librarian
Mrs E. Schöttler	Administrator